{ David and Renée Sanford }

how to
READ YOUR BIBLE

HOW TO READ YOUR BIBLE

Generous quantity discounts are available. Please contact the authors directly at dsanford@corban.edu or sanforddr@gmail.com. You also can reach the authors at 503-375-7173 and 503-890-0456.

To our children and grandchildren,
with much love and gratitude to the Lord—
Elizabeth and Billy Honeycutt and children
John, Havilah, David and Nathan
Shawna and Jordan Goertz and children
Elijah, Juliet, and Andrew
Jonathan and Chelsea Sanford and children
Abigail, Noah and Levi
Benjamin Sanford
Annalise Sanford

For you have been born again.
Your new life did not come from your earthly parents,
because the life they gave you will end in death.
But this new life will last forever, because it comes
from the eternal, living Word of God.

As the prophet says,
"People are like grass that dies away;
their beauty fades as quickly as the beauty of wildflowers.
The grass withers, and the flowers fall away.
But the word of the Lord will last forever."
(1 Peter 1:24–25 NLT)

{ contents }

contents

I was lost. Not turned around for a minute lost. Send out a search party lost.

When the day began, my plan seemed clear. I would leave my parked truck to follow a long ridge to its end. Just down from the ridge tip I would join my friends and begin a great camping trip. Though the territory was new to me, the path was simple. A beautiful hike through the mountains capped by dinner over an open fire with friends. Could not beat it.

Hours later, I homed in on my destination. Then I saw a strange and beautiful sight. As the sun set, I broke out of a thick stand of pines to a stunning network of valleys and snow-capped peaks awash in evening hues. Absolutely beautiful. But strange. Strange because I was nowhere near our camp. I was lost.

Often one's journey through the Scriptures begins with noble and simple plans. We'll read the Word and find the Lord's truth at the end. However, for some, the territory is new and foreign. We are not accustomed to some of the terms, people, or customs. For others, we have only read the Word in bits. Our minds have snapshots of isolated peaks and valleys in the lives of God's people, but they are disconnected from a grander view.

Like me on my hike, we need a guide, a map to help us see the whole picture. This book is your guide on an amazing journey through the Scriptures to a deeper understanding of the Lord.

How to Read Your Bible is designed to orient you to the landscape of Scripture and to maximize your enjoyment of the Word. Fictional college students Daniel and Maria and their friends help answer our questions as they seek to answer theirs.

Part One begins by answering crucial questions about the Word itself. Some wonder what makes the Bible special. Its unique inspiration and stunning preservation alone set it apart from any other literature. Its depth of truth about life and God make it more important than any reading we could find. And the wealth of spiritual benefits available in the Word move us to seek its treasure.

Part Two serves as your map of the Bible's message and plan. Suggesting different reading paths for surveying the Bible, the book then overviews the broad message of the Bible and adds helpful summaries of each of its 66 books. Intertwined throughout these sections are insightful "snapshots" and recommended activities to strengthen your grasp of God's Word.

Part Three is the savvy guide that helps you see the important and interesting details along the path. You learn what to look for in your reading, asking the questions that uncover spiritual insights to deepen you relationship with the Lord. It also helps you make sense of all the details so that you can find meaning for your life.

This book concludes with several different reading plans, allowing you to choose the length and depth of the journey that best fits you.

Through the Bible, we enter an amazing world of spiritual truth. With this guide, that truth can come alive in *your* world as well!

Gregory V. Trull, Ph.D.
Dean, School of Ministry
Corban University
www.corban.edu

{ part one }

why should i
READ THE BIBLE?

The warm autumn sun spread a glow across the campus that lit up leaves of gold and green and filtered through the windows of the nearby café.

Students rushed out with their cardboard-cradled drinks to soak up the rays on the steps of the brick-lined fountain. A few dozed in the coffee shop in the comfort of the overstuffed brown leather chairs. Others, energized by the brightness of the Indian summer day, engaged in lively debate or good-natured joking. Those who weren't carrying on gossipy conversations chatted with cell phones to their ears.

Daniel stood at the counter, waiting to place his order, while he and Maria discussed their separate conversations with friends who were interested in reading the Bible.

"How did you connect with Kendall?" he asked Maria before ordering a blended iced mocha.

"We're in a corporate communications class together—and she saw my Bible when I was taking my books out for class. She's a transfer student and would like to have some kind of Christian connection on campus. I gave her the name of several student ministries, but I also suggested that she might like to meet to simply read the Bible together."

Maria ordered a chai latte, and the two moved aside as they waited for the tall, dark-haired young man behind the counter to make their drinks.

"We had this great conversation about what reading the Bible means to us. I guess she's been a Christian since she was a kid, but Bible reading has always been on the back burner for her."

Daniel smiled. "And what did you tell her?"

{ Today's First Question: }
Why Should I Read the Bible? What's in It for Me?

Maria laughed. "You know how I can be," she said with a smile. "I hope I didn't embarrass her with my Latino intensity, but I launched into the whole story of how I started reading God's Word a few years ago when I was tired of being told what to believe. I wanted to get to know for myself what God says about himself. Her eyes teared up when I told her I continue to read the Bible because it's God's love letter to me. She said, 'I could use a letter like that in my life.' I told her we all need a letter like that. How else will we know the God of the universe—much less know how much he loves us?"

Maria's own dark eyes welled up as she continued. "I tried to explain how the Bible is a powerful tool that God uses to change us from the inside out. But I guess a person would have to know the fearful, angry person I was before to see just what God has done in my heart."

Daniel shook his head as the barista slid their drinks toward them. "Even if a person knew you for only five minutes, Maria, they'd know that God must be working in your life in a pretty cool way."

She waved off his words as they stood talking, waiting for a table to become free.

"But what about Erik—what's his interest?"

Daniel launched into his story of getting to know the new student from Montana. "Erik came to Christ through a campus ministry at his high school, but here he's running into questions about his faith that he never even knew existed. I gave him the names of some good books, but I encouraged him to read the Bible for himself if he wants to know the real foundation of his faith."

Maria was ready to rush to the point. "So to make the best use of our time, and to let me take advantage of your longer years of Bible study, I'd love it if Kendall and I could join you and Erik in reading the Bible together. When works best for you?"

"Not Mondays . . ." Daniel began.

Maria asked the barista, "When does the rush die down so you can actually get a seat around here?"

"Around three or four o'clock most days."

"How about three o'clock beginning next Thursday?" she suggested to

Daniel. "I can leave from here and get to the women's shelter before the evening shift begins."

The two moved toward an open table and continued their plans, not noticing the quizzical look on the barista's face. His thoughtful expression didn't escape the notice of Krista, the other barista. "What are you so serious about, Hamid? You look like you got a drink order you couldn't understand."

Hamid returned to his good-natured self instantly. "You know I know every possible combination of coffee drinks there is, and I can make them blindfolded and hanging upside down!"

"Let's try that on this next customer!" Krista laughed.

A few orders later, Krista prodded him again. "So what were you thinking about a few minutes ago?"

{ Today's Second Question: }
Why Don't People Read the Bible? What Holds Them Back?

"Did you hear those two people talking about reading the Bible? In my country, it is the Koran that we read and discuss. From the time I was a small child, I have read and memorized its verses, but I never talked about it like those people talked about the Bible. I don't think about the Koran as God speaking to me personally or changing my life."

"You're right, Hamid; the Bible is different."

Hamid looked at Krista. "Do you read the Bible too?"

She smiled brightly and hoped her nervousness at being knee-deep in a religious conversation with her Muslim friend didn't show. "Every day—and twice on Sundays. . . . But what about you? Are Muslims allowed to read the Jewish and Christian Scriptures?"

"Sure we are here in the States, but not back home. We're taught to respect these Scriptures—but the words of Mohammed are God's final word to mankind."

Krista pressed a little further. "But have you read them—the Scriptures that are the Bible?"

Hamid answered her with a teasing grin, "Have you read the Koran?"

Krista knew she was in really deep now. "No, but I'd be willing to do it—if you'll read the Bible at the same time."

Another wave of students and professors crowded through the door.

Hamid replied, "Definitely. You get me a Bible, and I'll get you a Koran."

"In English, please!"

"If you insist—I can read your Bible in either language."

"Show-off!"

The first of the new batch of customers decided on her drink, and Krista and Hamid's dialogue was limited to calling orders back and forth. Krista's smile took on a gleam as their conversation simmered in the back of her mind.

Hamid is willing to read the Bible, she thought. *That means he will find out for himself that the Bible is not a book just for Christians, but God's unchanging Word for a needy world. He will come face-to-face with the living Word of God—Jesus Christ.*

{ A Second Look at . . . Today's First Question: }
Why Should I Read the Bible? What's in It for Me?

Scripture itself teaches that God prospers those who delight in his Word, take it to heart, and apply it in every area of life.

How do we know that? Here are eight reasons:

1. In Joshua 1:7–9, God promises "you will make your way prosperous" if we study his Word, meditate on it daily, and faithfully obey his commands. What more could we ask?

2. In Ezra 7:6–10, we read that Ezra was well-versed in the Scriptures and the king "granted him all his request, according to the hand of the LORD his God upon him." God's blessing was on him indeed! The same can be our experience today.

3. In Psalm 1:1–3, God promises that anyone who delights in obeying his Word and meditates on it daily will prosper in "whatever he does." Why would he repeat such an extravagant promise? Because God wants us to take him at his Word!

4. In Psalm 19:7–14, David says God's Word revives our souls, makes us wise, brings us joy, and gives us insight into life if we desire it, delight in it, listen to it, obey it, confess any known sins, and seek to please the Lord.

5. In Psalm 119:97–104, the psalmist says he loves God's Word, which makes him wiser than his enemies, his teachers, and his elders, for he desires Scripture, meditates on it "all the day," and always obeys it.

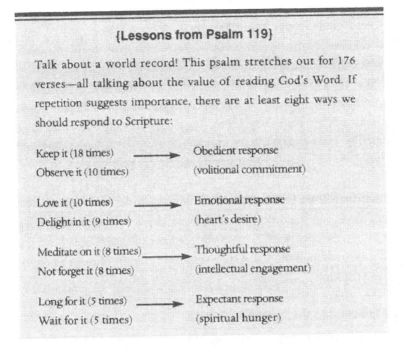

{Lessons from Psalm 119}

Talk about a world record! This psalm stretches out for 176 verses—all talking about the value of reading God's Word. If repetition suggests importance, there are at least eight ways we should respond to Scripture:

Keep it (18 times) ——→ Obedient response
Observe it (10 times)   (volitional commitment)

Love it (10 times) ——→ Emotional response
Delight in it (9 times)   (heart's desire)

Meditate on it (8 times) ——→ Thoughtful response
Not forget it (8 times)   (intellectual engagement)

Long for it (5 times) ——→ Expectant response
Wait for it (5 times)   (spiritual hunger)

6. In Jeremiah 15:16–17 and Ezekiel 3:1–11, the prophets describe God's Word as sweet as honey, despite the difficult mission God gave both of them. Scripture isn't just sweetness. It also contains the piercing light of God's holiness, righteousness, and purity—to keep us from sinning.

7. In John 13:17, Jesus says the path to God's blessing is knowing and doing what God says. All the blessings of the Beatitudes (Matt. 5:3–12; Luke 6:20–23) are ours, if only we will obey the Lord and heed his Word.

8. In James 1:16–25, James says the person who does what God's Word says "will be blessed in what he does." He accepts the Bible as God's inspired Word, repents of his sins, humbly accepts the Word, experiences salvation, and then intently and continually looks into Scripture and doesn't forget what he reads. Instead, he does what it says—and is blessed!

If reading the Bible offers so many benefits, why doesn't everyone read it?

{ A Second Look at . . . Today's Second Question: }
Why Don't People Read the Bible? What Holds Them Back?

What are some reasons people *outside* the church give for not reading the Bible?

No One I Know Reads the Bible

This was Hamid's reason earlier in this chapter. He grew up in a Muslim country where Bible reading was outlawed. It never crossed his mind to read the Old and New Testaments until he immigrated to the United States and met Krista.

According to pollsters like the Gallup organization, more than 10 percent of adults read the Bible daily. If you don't know anyone who reads the Bible, ask around. If they say no, ask if they would be interested in reading the Bible with you. Don't be surprised if several people say yes!

I Don't Have Time to Read the Bible

This is like saying you don't have time to eat, drink, or sleep. Instead of watching TV, listening to music, or surfing online, take that half hour to read Scripture. In six months you'll have read the entire Bible cover to cover! You do have the time.

It's Too Hard to Understand the Bible

Mark Twain once remarked that it wasn't the parts of Scripture he *didn't* understand that bothered him—it was the parts he *did* understand!

The reality is that the Bible isn't just written in Hebrew and Greek. It's also available in a number of wonderful, accurate, highly readable English translations. Even Jesus and the apostles read and quoted from the Greek translation of the Hebrew Scriptures, since Greek was the common language of their day. More than ever, the Scriptures are accessible to anyone and everyone.

The Bible Is Full of Errors

The fact is that this line of thinking is in error! We'll talk a lot more about this in chapter 4. For now, it's enough to say the Bible is completely accurate and wholly trustworthy.

❏ ❏

What are some reasons people *inside* the church have for not reading the Bible and taking it seriously?

It's Only for Seminary Graduates

If Moses were here, he would shake his head. "What?" he would say. "Are

God's blessings only for the elite?" Instead, in Deuteronomy 29:29, he says that what God has revealed in Scripture belongs to everyone, including our children. Granted, the Bible doesn't record everything God knows—not by a long shot! But Scripture is everything he's given us, it's eternal, and it's designed as a divine imperative to action ("do" is the operative word!).

A few paragraphs earlier, in Deuteronomy 29:9–15, Moses says that the person who knows, respects, preserves, and carefully follows God's Word will "prosper in all that [he does]."

You don't need a theological degree to read, understand, and apply the Bible to your life. Nothing we present in this book will be over your head. We've taught this material to adults, young adults, teenagers, and even sixth graders (who ate it up!).

With a little guidance, you can read your Bible with confidence!

It's Too Hard to Understand

Again, Moses would shake his head. In Deuteronomy 30:11–16, Moses says God's Word is clear enough for anyone to understand and obey—and reap God's blessings and prosperity in every area of life.

In John 3:1–16, Jesus explains the Old Testament concept of being "born again" to Nicodemus, who should have paid better attention in Sabbath school. Jesus chided the religious leader for not knowing the fundamentals of the faith. "Born again" describes a person who has repented of his or her sins, turned to God, and asked God to give a new heart that's attuned to his. This wasn't a new concept. It was clearly embedded in the Old Testament writings, especially those of the Major Prophets.

It Makes Me Feel Too Guilty

Now here's an honest excuse for not reading Scripture!

It's true—God's Word points out the errors in one's life. But it's important to note that God's purpose isn't to make us feel guilty. Instead, in Psalm 119:9–11, we read that Scripture keeps us pure. In John 15:3 and 17:17, Jesus reiterates the truth that God's Word makes us pure and holy.

Ultimately, there's no good excuse for not reading the Bible!

{ Today's Third Question: }
How Do I Get Serious About Reading the Bible?

It's easy to get started! Here are five steps:

1. Make a Goal. Make a personal goal to read the whole Bible cover to cover in 365 days or less. Start with Genesis 1. Select a personal reward for reading all the way through to Revelation 22 in a year. If you finish early, all the better!

2. Divide and Conquer. You can read the entire Bible fifteen minutes at a shot, about three chapters a day, in twelve months. Can't do it every day? Read twenty minutes (four chapters) five days a week. Too interested in today's passage? It's okay to read ahead a bit so you can take a break later on.

3. Read with Your Head and Heart. If you don't understand something, it's okay to ask questions. But as you read, focus on what is clear. Look for (a) examples to heed, (b) truths to believe, and (c) commands to obey.

4. Pick a Favorite Verse to Make Your Own. We chose Psalm 34:3 as a life verse for our marriage. A good friend of ours picked 1 Thessalonians 3:13 as a prayer focus for the year.

5. Talk to the Lord as You Read His Word. Literally say: "Yes, Lord, I want to live for you as Joseph and Mary and Peter and Paul did." "Yes, Lord, today and every day I choose to obey everything you have commanded." "Yes, Lord, I wholeheartedly believe what you have said in your Word."

We recently reviewed our answers in a Sunday school workbook we used thirty-five years ago. We've come a long way since then! How about you? You're not a kid anymore. Have you made the choice yet to say, "Yes, Lord"?

Why say, "Yes, Lord"?

Because of *who he is*.

Because of *what it means for eternity*.

Because of *God's desire to bless every sphere of your life here on earth . . . if you'll let him!* The key? Taking Scripture seriously. After all, it is God's Word!

is my bible
INSPIRED?

The coffee shop buzzed with intense conversation. Medical interns, sociology majors, business minors, aspiring musicians, and amateur philosophers were debating hot issues. Voices rose and fell, coffee was consumed, and occasionally people chopped the air with their hands for emphasis.

In the corner, Daniel and three fellow students came to a lull in their conversation on the advisability of using anything other than blue or black ink on Professor Marta's English exams. Colin took advantage of the pause. "So, Martin," he began, "how are you enjoying your Bible as Literature class?"

"Oh, okay," Martin mumbled as he shoved the last of his scone into his mouth.

"Why did you decide to take *that* elective, anyway? Isn't the subject matter a bit unrelated to your business major?"

Martin looked thoughtful. He wiped the crumbs from his mouth and leaned on the table, his arms folded in front of him. "Actually," he explained, "I took the class out of curiosity. I wanted to know why the Bible and those who hold to it are causing chaos in the media and the courts. It's only fair to understand where these people are coming from and what they're carrying on about."

"Well, have you found your answers?"

Martin shook his head. "All I can say is that this book has a lot of influence, but I have no clue why."

Colin smiled and looked over at Daniel, the only Christian in the group. "Daniel, what do you think about all this?"

{ **Today's First Question:** }
Is the Bible Inspired? If So, How?

Daniel returned Colin's smile. He knew how Colin loved a controversial topic. "Yeah, the Bible is certainly influential. That's because the Bible is God's Word to humanity. It isn't just a book of religious writings collected by religious people. It's God's message by which God himself communicates with us."

Andrea spoke up. "I think you're going a bit too far, Daniel. I can agree that the Bible is influential. But the Bible is no more inspired than any other great piece of literature."

View #1: Universal Inspiration

"Then why aren't we seeing people testify in court in the name of *Romeo and Juliet* or *The Lord of the Rings?*" Daniel countered.

"Come on, you know the effect religion has on some people," Andrea snapped back.

"What about you, Martin?" Daniel asked. "You know more on the subject than most people. What do you think?"

View #2: Partial Inspiration

Martin scratched the back of his head as he thought about his answer. "I respect the Bible as a great book, and I am impressed with its wisdom. I can accept certain passages as being the words of God, but I cannot accept the entire Bible as being inspired by God. The writers may have had some super-natural help in writing their works. Still, there seems to be a lot of added material."

"Not to mention myths and ancient folklore," Colin commented.

View #3: Dictational Inspiration

He turned to Daniel. "What about you? You're a Christian. You probably hold to the fundamentalist fantasy that the entire Bible was dictated by God, using humans to mechanically produce it."

View #4: Verbal Plenary Inspiration

Daniel slowly sipped his coffee before answering Colin's question. "Actually, Colin, most church leaders over the past four hundred years have not held that view. What I really believe is that the Holy Spirit guided the authors in the writing of all of Scripture but did it without stifling their personalities."

Daniel leaned back in his chair. Observing Colin's thick and frowning brows, Martin's attentive posture, and Andrea's look of defensiveness from behind her glasses, he was surprised at how calm he felt. This was an important issue. The basis of his whole life was at stake, Daniel realized. If the Bible was not God's Word (worse yet, if God had lied), he would be a fool!

Another thought came to Daniel, and he spoke. "Think about it, guys. The words and expressions must be given by God, because that is how thoughts are expressed—through language. But if you look at the Bible, it's obvious that the author of each part wrote from his own culture, style, vocabulary, and experiences.

"God's message was always communicated so people could understand it. And because the Bible is inspired by God, we can be sure he kept the authors from saying anything that was untrue."

"You sound like a theology book," Colin retorted, "but you still haven't proved anything—"

"If you've got a few free hours, I'd be glad to," Daniel interrupted with a grin.

Colin's deep voice rumbled. "I do have another question that you should think about. Maybe this Bible of yours is inspired like you're saying. Doesn't this pose a problem? You don't read Yiddish, do you?"

{ Today's Second Question: }
Are Contemporary Versions Inspired?

Andrea, the language major among them, laughed out loud. "The Bible was written in Hebrew, Aramaic, and Greek, not Yiddish," she teased.

"That's not the point," Colin replied sternly in an effort to cover his error. "The point is, if God spoke to Bible writers in their own languages, how can preachers today pound their English Bibles and say, 'Thus saith the Lord'?"

Martin spoke up. "Yeah, he has a good point. If the Bible is inspired, how can you be sure that what you read is what God meant to say?"

Andrea jumped in. "In other words, how can you be so sure that the book you carry around in your backpack is inspired just like Saint Peter's original scrolls?"

❑ ❐

Our university friends debate four main views regarding the inspiration of Scripture. *The Bible, its own best commentator, teaches verbal plenary inspiration.* In other words, God inspired the words of the Bible, but he allowed each author to write with his own individual style and vocabulary.

{ A Second Look At . . .Today's First Question: }
Is the Bible Inspired? If So, How?

How do we know that? Here are seven reasons:

1. Scripture Is Consistently Called "the Word of God." Psalm 119 best demonstrates this by using ten different terms for God's Word. What's more, the prophets indirectly identify their writings as God's Word by using introductory phrases such as "The Lord said to me" and "The Word of the Lord came to . . ." The authors knew they were speaking God's words (Deut. 18:15–22; Jer. 36:27).

2. Scripture States Directly That It Is Inspired by God. While only 2 Timothy 3:16 uses the word "inspiration" ("God-breathed"—NIV), other passages strongly support this truth. Second Peter 1:20–21 teaches that men "moved" ("carried along"— NIV) by the Holy Spirit wrote Scripture. In this way, Peter explains what inspiration is: God's choosing to communicate his message through men.

3. Scripture Is Spoken of as if It Were God. See Galatians 3:8 and Genesis 12:1–3. Conversely, God is spoken of as if he is Scripture (Heb. 3:7 with Ps. 95:7). This shows the close, intimate connection between God and his Word.

4. Old Testament Authors Recognized God as Their Source. Moses told the people of Israel that what he had commanded them was from the Lord God (Deut. 4:2). In 2 Samuel 23:2, King David on his deathbed stated that the Spirit of the Lord had spoken through him. God's Word had been on David's tongue.

5. Jesus Christ Fully Supported All of Scripture. See Matthew 5:17–19. He confirmed its historical accuracy, down to the tense of a verb (Mark 12:26). He declared that Scripture is permanent (Matt. 5:17–18), is inspired by the Holy Spirit (Mark 12:36), contains enough information to support our faith (Luke 16:29–31), is unbreakable (John 10:35), and agrees with his teachings (John 5:46–47; Luke 24:27, 44).

6. The New Testament Writers Viewed Both Testaments as the Word of God. Peter affirmed that the Holy Spirit inspired the Old Testament (Acts 4:25). He compared the commandments of Jesus Christ, which the apostles spoke, with the words the holy prophets spoke (2 Pet. 3:2). He declared that the gospel that was preached to them was the Word of the Lord (1 Pet. 1:23, 25). Peter also recognized Paul's writings as part of Scripture (2 Pet. 3:15–16).

The apostle Paul confirmed that the Old Testament is accurate in historical details (1 Cor. 10:1–11). Paul cited the Old Testament and Gospels as Scripture (1 Thess. 5:18). He went on to state forcefully that he preached God's Word, not his own message (1 Thess. 2:13). The New Testament authors knew they were entrusted with God's Word (1 Tim. 4:1–3; Titus 1:3; Rev. 1:1–3).

7. Scripture Claims Dual Authorship. That is, it is the message and words of *God* expressed through *men* without canceling out their personalities. Both Jesus Christ and Scripture itself confirm this (Mark 12:26; Acts 4:25; 2 Pet. 1:21).

{Insights on Inspiration}

The book of Jeremiah offers us nine insights.

1. Inspiration begins the moment God reveals any portion of his truth to his prophets for his people (Jer. 36:1). Text is not inspired when it's recognized as canonical (accepted by the church). It's not even inspired when it's written. Instead, it's inspired the second God communicates it. The prophet knew immediately that he had received a new revelation from God. He didn't have to think twice about it!

2. Inspiration often begins as an oral message that the prophet or apostle dictates or pens. It's inspired whether it's written down immediately or after an extended period of time (Jer. 36:1–2, 32). In this way, inspiration continues. It doesn't evaporate after God stops talking to a prophet or apostle.

3. **Inspired messages communicate God's words to human-ity in an exact form.** They become inspired Scriptures (writings) the moment they are penned. Their value as God's Word does *not* increase, but their effectiveness does. People can reconsider recorded messages and read them along with other messages from other times (Jer. 36:3).

4. **Inspiration is not dependent on the written Scriptures.** When we share portions of Scripture orally, we are transmitting God's Word to others (Jer. 36:9–16). In that way, we're becoming one of the links that helps God's Word become part of people's thoughts and actions.

5. **Verbal plenary inspiration does not depend on the actual existence of the originals today** (Jer. 36:32). Jeremiah dictated "all the former words that were in the first scroll" he wrote, a scroll of newly inspired Scripture that a wicked king had destroyed (36:22–23, 28).

6. **Inspiration is progressive.** Each book was inspired one thought at a time. Often long gaps separated sections (Jer. 36:2, 32).

7. **Inspiration is exclusively God's message to humanity, through human instruments and their secretaries** (Jer. 36:4; Rom. 16:22).

8. **Inspiration is always dependent on the Lord.** Even though Jeremiah was a prophet of the Lord, he couldn't prophesy whenever he felt like it. Sometimes the word of the Lord came to Jeremiah, compelling him to prophesy (Jer. 37:6). Sometimes the Lord gave Jeremiah a message as he spoke (37:17—this was essen-tially a message Jeremiah had delivered often before). Sometimes Jeremiah had to wait on the Lord until the Lord gave him a mes-sage (42:7).

9. **Inspiration applies to the very choice of words.** Jeremiah felt strongly that he had to deliver the whole message of the Lord, without omitting a word (Jer. 42:4; 43:1). Jeremiah also wrote down his own thoughts and the remarks of others, but the Holy Spirit directed every word he wrote.

"But is my English Bible the inspired Word of God, just like the original manuscripts?" many ask.

{ A Second Look At . . .Today's Second Question: }
Are Contemporary Versions Inspired?

In answering this question, it is helpful to understand the process by which God communicates his thoughts to us today. The following diagram illustrates how we receive God's message:

God's Heart

Inspiration *(God's Word)*

Transmission > Translation > Publication *(in my hands)*

Observation > Interpretation *(in my head)*

Principlization > Application *(in my heart)*

My Life

As the diagram shows, this issue goes beyond the question of *inspiration*, which we have already examined.

We must also examine *transmission* (copying Scripture) and *translation* (putting Scripture into a language that the audience can read) to determine whether our Bible is the real Word of God. Our efforts at *interpretation* (discovering what it means), *principalization* (personalizing it), and *application* (applying it to our lives) are useless unless our English Bibles are God's inspired message to humanity.

Let's take a look at the preservation of Scripture and textual criticism in deciding the reliability of Bible transmission.

The Preservation of Scripture
The first books of the Bible reveal the preservation of Scripture from generation to generation.

The Books of Moses. The first five books of the Bible weren't put away in some obscure place after Moses wrote them. God gave Moses and the Israelites careful instructions during the latter part of Moses's life for the care and regular reading of the Law before "all Israel" (Deut. 31:9–13, 24–29).

By the time Joshua found himself leading the Israelite nation, he recognized Genesis through Deuteronomy as written by Moses through God's direction (Josh. 1:8–9). Joshua probably had possession of the original writings.

Scribes made fastidious copies of the original autographs (with word-for-word precision), and God's people considered these equally authoritative (Josh. 8:32–35; Deut. 27:3, 8). Verbal transmission was also authoritative (Josh. 8:34–35).

The Book of Joshua. Joshua wrote his book soon after the events occurred. Records of what God told him suggest this. Specific historical references date the book to the time of Joshua, certainly much earlier than 1000 BC (see Josh. 15:63; 16:10).

Writers added other authoritative material to Joshua's records later. This includes material added soon after his death (Josh. 15:13–19; 24:29–33), when the records were being collected and probably copied in more permanent form.

At least two sections may have been added much later ("all the territory of the Philistines," 13:2, perhaps in 1200 BC, and 10:12–15 after 1000 BC). Or it is possible that the reference to the Book of Jasher (10:13) was added later, unless this book of songs was, like *Foxe's Book of Martyrs*, appended over the centuries, allowing King David to add a song (2 Sam. 1:18–27).

Most of the Old Testament. Most of the books of the Old Testament were miraculously preserved despite persecution and national apostasy.

Wicked King Manasseh reigned over Judah hundreds of years after Moses, David, and many of the other Old Testament writers. Manasseh considered nothing sacred. You can compare him to the wicked sorcerer in *Indiana Jones and the Temple of Doom*—but instead of sacrificing other people's children, he passed his own son through the fire (2 Kings 21:6)—as well as any copies of the Scriptures he could find, it seems.

A generation later, not even the high priest in Jerusalem had a copy of God's Word, until the day Hilkiah the high priest exclaimed, "I have found the Book of the Law" (2 Kings 22:8). This occurred just before the Babylonian captivity of the nation of Israel in 386 BC.

Fortunately, the Israelites took the then completed books of the Old Testament to Babylon and preserved them throughout their captivity. Hilkiah's family apparently retained the rediscovered Scriptures and passed them down from generation to generation.

Hilkiah's great-grandson Ezra had a copy of the Scriptures with him when he returned with the released captives to Jerusalem. He was known as a man of the Word (Ezra 7:10; Neh. 8:1–3).

The Completed Old Testament. Tradition suggests that Ezra wrote part of the Old Testament himself and helped confirm much of the Old Testament canon—the books the Jewish people believed God spoke through the prophets. This canon was started about 1400 BC (the books of Moses) and completed about 400 BC (Malachi).

According to Josephus, the Jewish people divided the Old Testament into the following sections:

- The Five Books of Moses: Genesis, Exodus, Leviticus, Numbers, Deuteronomy.
- The Thirteen Prophets: Joshua; Judges and Ruth (considered one book); Samuel; Kings; Isaiah; Jeremiah and Lamentations (one book); Ezekiel; the twelve Minor Prophets (one book); Daniel; Job; Esther; Ezra and Nehemiah (one book); and Chronicles.
- The Four Writings: Psalms, Proverbs, Song of Solomon, and Ecclesiastes. Sometimes Job, Ruth, Lamentations, Esther, Daniel, Ezra and Nehemiah, and Chronicles were added to this third section of writings.

The New Testament. Soon after the church began, the need for a second canon of accepted Scripture writings developed.

The New Testament canon formed much more quickly than that of the Old Testament because of the loss of the apostles and other witnesses, the expansion of Christianity beyond Palestine, the need to protect the message from false teachings, the persecution of believers (they needed to know which books they would die for), and the missionary enterprise (they needed to know which books to translate and use in preaching).

The early church went through several steps to finalize the New Testament canon. Most of the books were widely recognized as canonical in the second and third centuries. Some seriously questioned only a few of the latter books in the New Testament. By AD 397, two official church councils had confirmed the canonical nature of the twenty-seven books of the New Testament.

Members of these councils asked specific questions to determine which books were canonical: Is it written by or under the direction of an apostle? Is it inspired by the Holy Spirit? Is it circulated among the churches? Is it consistent with the rest of Scripture?

Some very reliable books were left out of the canon, including a Harmony of the Four Gospels. It was widely read among the churches, but it didn't measure up to the four rigid standards of canonicity.

Many other unreliable books were left out as well, including spurious "gospels" that borrowed the names of various apostles but were clearly written long after the first century.

Textual Criticism

Now let's take a look at the role textual criticism plays in determining the inspiration of Scripture. Textual criticism is a careful science that uses thousands of ancient manuscripts to determine the text that is most like the original copies. None of the manuscripts considered are originals (since they have long since been lost or destroyed), so the reliability of the copies must be proved. We can confirm the accuracy of the transmission of the original message to the copies in four ways.

First, after the Babylonian captivity, Ezra and other scribes carefully went to work to ensure that plenty of copies of God's Word would always exist. These scribes became known as "lawyers" because of their knowledge of the Old Testament law.

Second, the Talmudists (AD 100–450), the Massoretes (AD 450–900), and other such groups who copied under the strictest of rules reproduced the Old Testament. Their high standards reflect the accuracy of their copying. Here are some of the rules they followed:

- They could not copy from memory.
- They could not correct the original if they felt it was wrong (they could only add notations in the margins).
- On each line they copied, they counted the number of letters and words, compared middle words, checked the frequency of each letter, and the like.
- They used the space of a hair between each letter. (Talk about precise!)

- They reverently burned or buried old, worn copies of Scripture (to avoid profaning the Lord's name, should they become smudged or otherwise unreadable).

How accurate were these scribes? Bible scholars familiar with the work of these scribes confidently assert that the time gap doesn't mean the text has degenerated over the millennia. In his *Survey of the Bible*, William Hendriksen quotes one scholar, "If we had in our possession a first- or second-century manuscript, we would find it to have substantially the same text as those of much later date."

Only months after that statement was published, the Dead Sea Scrolls were discovered in a cave in Qumran. Among the findings were two copies of the book of Isaiah dating back to 150 BC. Hebrew scholars diligently compared the newly discovered manuscripts with much more recent manuscripts that had come from the Massoretic tradition and were dated from the medieval period. Their conclusion? Only a few insignificant changes (mostly spelling variations) had crept into the Isaiah text after more than a millennium!

Thanks to the careful work of Jewish scribes, we can rest assured that the Old Testament has been passed on to us with a very high degree of accuracy.

Third, there is an overwhelming amount of evidence for the New Testament. Men wrote its twenty-seven books between AD 40 and 100. The earliest known copy of part of the New Testament is dated only a few short decades after the completion of the original. Also, there are 5,400 ancient copies of the New Testament in Greek alone, 10,000 more in Latin, and 9,300 in other languages. From this wealth of sources, scholars and experts have made comparisons to accurately determine the original.

Sir Frederic George Kenyon, former director and principal librarian of the British Museum, said, "Thanks to these manuscripts, the ordinary reader of the Bible may feel comfortable about the soundness of the text. Apart from a few unimportant verbal alterations, natural in books transcribed by hand, the New Testament, we now feel assured, has come down intact" (see http://reformedlibrary.net).

In contrast, other classical writings are suspect at best. We have only seven copies of Plato's writings, dating 1,200 years after his death. We have only five copies of Aristotle's writings, dating 1,400 years after his death. We have 643 copies of Homer's writings, dating 1,800 years after his death, with errors prevalent in 5 percent of his 15,600 lines.

Even more recent classics are suspect. William Shakespeare is hailed as the greatest English playwright of all time. Since the 1600s, however, scholars have discovered an average of one hundred major errors in each of his plays. In some cases, even Shakespeare's name is spelled wrong. Now some scholars question whether Shakespeare even wrote the plays.

James Joyce's epic novel *Ulysses* transformed twentieth-century literature. Yet more than five thousand errors (many major) have been identified in the book since it first went to press in 1922. Whole sections of crucial dialogue have been restored to the text only in recent years. In contrast, the New Testament stands out as wholly trustworthy and reliable.

Fourth, almost the entire New Testament can be reproduced from the writings of the second- and third-century church fathers alone. All but eleven verses can be reconstructed from the verses they cited.

But even if we accept the ancient New Testament manuscripts as reliable, can we accept translations of these copies as reliable?

The Translation of Scripture

The apostle Paul gives us the biblical perspective we should have toward copies and translations. The Scripture that Paul referred to as "inspired by God" was not a collection of the original works. It was only one among thousands of copies of the Old Testament Scriptures. Additionally, these Scriptures were translated from Hebrew and Aramaic into Greek (a translation known as the Septuagint).

Without hesitation, Paul told Timothy that the sacred writings he had known from childhood were able to give him wisdom leading to salvation: "All Scripture is God-breathed and is useful for teaching, rebuking, correcting and training in righteousness, so that the man of God may be thoroughly equipped for every good work" (2 Tim. 3:16–17 NIV).

Because of this, we can see that copies and translated works are still inspired. They accurately reflect the original manuscripts and communicate God's intended meaning.

The verdict?

Our English Bibles truly *are* inspired. They are the Word of God communicated to us in a language we can read, understand, personalize, and apply to our lives.

{ God's Revelation to Humanity }

God has chosen to reveal himself in many ways. *General revelation* is God's self-disclosure through natural means to all of humanity. Examples:

- Creation (Ps. 19:1–6; Rom. 1:18–21). Why is there an ordered universe?
- Preservation (Col. 1:17). Why doesn't it all fall apart?
- Providence (Acts 14:17). Why do good things happen to bad people?
- Conscience (Rom. 2:15). Why do we have a sense of right and wrong?
- Reason (Acts 17:16–34). What is "obvious" about the unknown God?

Special revelation is God's self-disclosure of his message through supernatural means to some for all of humanity. Examples:

- Theophanies or special appearances by the Lord (Gen. 18:1–2; 19:1). The Lord revealed himself in the form of men and angels.
- Visions (1 Sam. 3:1–4; Acts 16:9). The Lord speaks in dreams and angelic appearances.
- Jesus Christ (John 1:1–18; Heb. 1:1–2). After speaking to the Old Testament saints in many ways, God spoke through his Son.
- Prophecies (1 Kings 17:1; Titus 1:1–3). The Lord spoke to the prophets, giving oral messages to Israel and the nations.
- Inspiration (2 Tim. 3:16–17; 2 Pet. 1:20–21). The Lord directed the prophets and apostles to write certain messages.

As we consider the various special revelations, we might long to have been one of those who saw Jesus Christ face-to-face. And we might envy those who received theophanies, visions, and prophecies from the Lord. Yet in a real way, we are more privileged than those of any other age, because we have free access to the inspired Word of God.

is my translation
TRUSTWORTHY?

Even after months at his internship, Daniel still found that the view from the fourteenth floor caught him by surprise.

His boss had just handed him a report from the company's Asian headquarters in Hong Kong, and he was looking over the professionally translated text on his way back to his desk. But out of the corner of his eye he caught the flight of a passing helicopter and paused to admire the billowing cloud formations.

A coworker's voice over the top of a nearby cubicle brought him back to his task.

"Hey, Daniel, can you spare a minute to go over that chart you put together for human resources? I think I need one or two more updates before I submit it."

It was Dean, an older man who had been with the Fortune 500 company for a long time and had gone out of his way to help Daniel get the most out of his internship. That was before Dean learned that they were fellow believers. Connecting with another Christian on the job had certainly been a plus for both of them.

Daniel nodded and headed toward Dean's desk. While Dean pulled up the charts on his computer and printed the appropriate file, Daniel continued to study the Asian division's report.

"Wow, Dean, whoever we're hiring to translate these reports really does a good job using appropriate terminology. He even seems to grasp the subtleties of the English language."

"That's probably because the translator is a native English speaker—at least that's my guess. I wonder how perfect it would be if the same translator did the report from English to Chinese."

"That would be interesting to find out. Speaking of translation, did I tell you about the conversation I had with some of my fellow students the other day? We got into this discussion about the Bible—about whether what we're reading today in English is as 'real' as what Peter and Paul wrote down twenty centuries ago."

{ Today's First Question: }
Is My English Bible Really Trustworthy?
If So, How Trustworthy?

Dean looked up. "You mean they wanted to know how trustworthy the English Bible is—and they're not even Christians? Do you think they're interested in reading it?"

Daniel sighed. "I don't think so at this point. One guy just wants to argue, so he assumes the original authors are untrustworthy—whether or not the translations are accurate doesn't even matter to him. The other guy, Martin, is taking a Bible as Literature class, so at least he's reading the Scriptures. But he's not looking to find God—just trying to figure out religion. From what I can tell, he's assuming that even if the Bible is inspired—and we talked about that too—the translated Bible is corrupted from its original meaning."

"So he's not really close to trusting the Bible either."

"I don't think so. But at least he's not trying to attack it."

Dean put down the folder and looked thoughtful. "You know, Daniel, I've been a Christian for a number of years, and I hate to admit it, but I don't understand all this inspiration stuff either. I read my Bible and I believe it, and I know God teaches me, but sometimes I still wonder how I can know for sure that I'm reading exactly what God wants me to read. What that guy's talking about reminds me of playing Telephone—maybe something got messed up in the message on the way down the line."

"That's one reason I'm glad God wrote it down and didn't just leave his message up to oral tradition."

"That's true—but it seems as if only the originals would be perfect and anything less couldn't be inspired. How does that work?" Dean asked.

"The problem with that assumption is that a person might think the Scriptures are not worth reading unless they're the original documents."

"I guess that would be impractical!" Dean chuckled. "I couldn't even learn Spanish—I don't think I'm up for Greek and Hebrew!"

Daniel reached for the charts and started marking them up as he talked. "You and me both. I tried my hand at Greek. That's a lot of work! Fortunately, there are a lot of experts who have done that work for us. It gets pretty technical, but the translation process for the Bible has always met rigorous standards—much more rigorous than this company ever would demand for its reports. I'll loan you one of my books sometime, Dean. The whole process is fascinating, and you come away even more convinced that our English Bibles are amazingly accurate."

"Well, you know I believe my Bible—but it's a little confusing when you're reading the weekly newsmagazines. Sometimes it seems as if the Jesus and the apostles they're writing about are completely different from the real people I know from reading the Bible. As if they were a bunch of guys trying to make up a religion and the Bible is just an incidental project on the side."

Daniel nodded his head. "I know what you mean. The idea that God's Word could actually mean what it says seems utterly foreign to some of these intellectual types. Funny how Jesus didn't have a problem accepting the Scriptures—even the ones that had been translated into Greek!"

Daniel handed Dean the charts, glanced at his watch, and stood to leave. "I'd better finish taking care of this report for Christina before I leave today. But I'll bring a book for you tomorrow. And maybe we can talk more at lunch. You've got the important thing right, Dean—trusting God's Word."

(A Second Look at . . . Today's First Question:)
Is My English Bible Really Trustworthy?
If So, How Trustworthy?

Throughout the ages, God's people have accepted, valued, created, and used Bible translations to reach the widest possible audiences.

How do we know that Bible translations are trustworthy? Here are eight reasons:

1. The apostle Paul affirmed the inspiration of Bible translations (2 Tim. 3:14–17). Paul spoke Hebrew fluently. Still, to effectively communicate to his listeners and readers, he often quoted from the Greek translation of the Old Testament (Acts 13:34; Rom. 9:12; 1 Cor. 2:9).

2. The apostle Peter affirmed the inspiration of Bible translations (2 Pet.

1:19–21). Peter probably spoke all three of the original languages of the Bible. Because the Greek translation of the Old Testament was popular in his day, he often quoted from it (Acts 2:17–21; 3:22).

3. Jesus himself affirmed the eternal nature of the Bible (Matt. 5:17–18), exemplified God's great love for the whole world (John 3:16; 17:20), and often quoted from the Greek translation of the Old Testament (Matt. 9:13; Mark 14:27; Luke 4:12; John 15:25).

4. The apostle John affirmed the eternal nature of the Bible (Rev. 22:18–19), proclaimed God's great love for the whole world (1 John 2:2; Rev. 4:9–10), and often quoted from the Greek translation of the Old Testament (John 12:38; 19:36–37).

5. The apostle Matthew is the only New Testament writer who apparently didn't quote from the Greek translation of the Old Testament because his original audience was predominately Jewish.

6. The early church produced a number of important translations of the Old and New Testaments into Old Latin, Latin, Syriac, Coptic, Armenian, Old Georgian, Ethiopic, and Gothic during the first four centuries after Jesus Christ's ascension. They used these translations to reach as many people as possible with God's Word. New Christians weren't forced to learn the original Bible languages.

7. To help fulfill Jesus Christ's Great Commission, the church has now translated the Bible or portions of the Bible into more than two thousand languages. Why? Because less than 0.00001 percent of the people alive today understand the three ancient biblical languages, and more than 80 percent don't understand English fluently. The Scriptures are best understood when translated into the reader's (or listener's) native language.

8. Every significant English Bible published within the past generation or two has been translated by an interdenominational team of scores of scholars working from the Hebrew, Aramaic, and Greek texts. They're aided by contemporary literary consultants and by a library of scholarship compiled over the past few centuries.

Most of the newer English Bibles include translation footnotes citing places where the scholars had to make an editorial decision. The footnotes never leave any biblical truth or command in question. They simply indicate alternate readings for specific words or phrases.

Want to know what the Scriptures originally said? Read two or three good

English Bibles and you'll have your answer. Read five or six and you'll discover relatively few places where scholars disagree on the content of any given biblical passage.

A good translation, then, is one that accurately expresses the true meaning in understandable language.

Over the years, some translators have sought to update the much-loved and cherished King James Version. The best example is the New King James Version, which offers a contemporary take on the old classic.

Other translators have sought to produce a more literal, word-for-word translation of Scripture. This approach to translation is sometimes called *formal equivalence*. Their efforts, including the highly respected New American Standard Bible, are great for scholarly Bible students. But these translations have not always used conventional English and sometimes have been difficult to memorize or read in public. The translators of the more recent English Standard Version and Holman Christian Standard Bible have sought to offer a balance between literal translation and readability.

To ensure accurate translation of the originally intended message, many translators use the principle of *dynamic equivalence*. Instead of finding an exact word-for-word equivalent (which can distort the true meaning or make it hard to understand), the translators for the New International Version, the New Living Translation, Today's English Version, the Contemporary English Version, and the New Century Version have sought to find an exact meaning-for-meaning equivalent for each statement.

While these translation approaches differ, the end result is still the same: an accurate, readable contemporary English translation of the Scriptures.

Why the need for newer translations? God's Word hasn't changed, but the English language changes dramatically from decade to decade! Putting Scripture into contemporary language enhances rather than obscures meaning.

{What It Cost to Have the Bible in English}

Often we take our English Bibles for granted. Little do we realize how much it cost the early translators to put the Scriptures into English.

Two years after Columbus "discovered" America, William Tyndale was born. Tyndale lived during a time when it was illegal to translate or even read an English version of the Bible unless one had official church approval. Obviously, the church had its problems.

When Tyndale was still in his twenties, he asked for church approval to translate the Bible. His request was denied.

So Tyndale went to Germany, where he started printing his revolutionary translation. But his printing operation was shut down, and Tyndale escaped to another German city. There he succeeded in publishing the first major translation of the Bible into English.

Needless to say, the English church authorities were furious that the common people were buying English Bibles in the streets of London. So they quickly went out and bought all the remaining Bibles still for sale.

Tyndale was hardly discouraged—his translation was a best seller! With his profits, he printed even more Bibles to smuggle back into England.

By 1536, ten years after the first English translation appeared for sale, Tyndale was condemned for heresy, and his strangled body was burned at the stake.

Just before Tyndale breathed his last, he said, "Lord, open the King of England's eyes." Within three years, his prayer was answered, and Bibles were sold freely throughout England—at the cost of Tyndale's life. His translation was so good that nine-tenths of the King James Version two generations later shows his influence.

Tyndale was willing to lay down his life to make the Bible available in English. How willing are you and I to read it?

The verdict?

As we saw in the last chapter, our English Bibles truly *are* inspired and trustworthy. They are the Word of God communicated to us in a language we can read, understand, personalize, and apply to our lives.

{ Today's Second Question: }
What About Questionable Translations?

We don't need to worry about questionable English Bible translations for several reasons.

First, they're often the product of an individual, small group, or cult.

Second, they're rarely available for sale in Christian bookstores.

Third, these questionable translations still contain God's Word. Except for verses in which the translators twisted Scripture (say, John 1:1 in the New World Translation), you and I could read these translations with benefit. We don't recommend that! But these translations are still well over 95 percent the inspired Word of God. However, this doesn't excuse the Scripture-twisting the translators did in a few places.

Fourth, these translations are often highly revered but little read. Many members of these religious communities memorize specific Scriptures and do their prescribed Bible studies each week, but they don't actually read the Bible like a book, cover to cover.

So the next time two cult members come knocking on your door, don't be afraid to discuss the Scriptures with them. Ask them to open up their Bibles right on the spot. Don't be afraid to read over their shoulders, so to speak. Their questionable Bible translation isn't going to hurt you!

Pray that God will reveal himself to these individuals through his Word, despite known translation errors.

{Principles for Quality Bible Translation}

Over the years, the Wycliffe Bible Translator organization has used the following rules for its translation work around the world. Each translation must be:

Based on the best Hebrew and Greek texts. English isn't good enough.

Other than word-for-word. Martin Luther put it this way: "What do the Germans say in such a situation?" In other words, how would the man on the street say it in plain German?

Fastidious in meaning or form. The Living Bible's (TLB) paraphrase of Revelation 18:22 says, "Never again will the sound of music be there—no more pianos, saxophones, and trumpets." Many translators would agree that this paraphrase is a bit too free since pianos and saxophones had not been invented at the time Revelation was written.

Structurally adapted to maintain accuracy. In the Philippines, for example, the phrase "verily, verily" or "truly, truly" is best translated as one word, not two.

Updated regularly as language changes. In the King James Version, 1 Thessalonians 4:15 uses an archaic form of the verb "prevent." Instead, modern translations use the current form of the verb "precede" to ensure readers know what the apostle Paul is really saying.

Free from any theological biases. The New World Translation twists John 1:1 to say—counter to all grammatical rules in Greek—that Jesus was merely "a god," not God himself. That's a blatant mistranslation of a key verse in Scripture. Thankfully, virtually all major English Bibles are free from such theological errors.

{ Today's Third Question: }
What About Bible Paraphrases?

What about Bible paraphrases? Are they helpful? Here are a few facts about paraphrases:

- Paraphrases typically are the work of an individual or small team.
- Some of the most popular paraphrases of the past generation include Eugene Peterson's *The Message*, Kenneth Taylor's *The Living Bible*, and J. B. Phillips's *The New Testament in Modern English*.
- These paraphrases are designed for devotional reading, not Bible study.
- They're best read by Christians who want a fresh way to look at familiar biblical passages.
- When reading paraphrases, you should always go back to solid translations as the basis for affirming the truths, obeying the commands, and heeding the examples of Scripture.

• Once you've absorbed a passage of Scripture in your heart and life, you can try your hand at writing a paraphrase yourself. This is a wonderful way to personalize Scripture and express the ways you want to apply the passage in your own life.

Here is a paraphrase I (David) wrote that freely interprets 1 Corinthians 13, the love chapter, with a twenty-first-century American evangelical twist:

Love

(A Paraphrase of 1 Corinthians 13:1–8)

If I talk about the hypostatic union of the second person of the trinitarian Godhead, and can exegetically analyze the word "propitiation" in the original Greek, but fail to ask about your needs and truly help you, I'm simply making a lot of empty religious noise.

If I graduate from a big-name theological seminary *summa cum laude* and know all the answers to questions you'll never even think of asking, and if I have all the degrees to prove it . . . and if I say I believe in God with all my heart, soul, and strength, and have incredible answers to my prayers to show it, but fail to take the time to find out where you're at and what makes you laugh and cry, I'm a big fat zero.

If I sell an extra car and some of my books to raise money for some poor, starving kids somewhere, and if I give my life for God's service and burn out after pouring everything I have into the work, but do it all without ever once thinking about the people, the real, hurting people—the moms and dads and sons and daughters and orphans and widows and the lonely and hurting—if I pour my life into the kingdom but forget to make it relevant to those here on earth, my energy is wasted, and so is my life.

Here is what love is like—genuine love . . . God's kind of love. It's patient. It can wait. It helps others, even if they never find out who did it. Love doesn't look for greener pastures or dream of how things could be better if the person just got rid of all his current commitments. Love doesn't boast. It doesn't try to build itself up to be something it isn't.

Love doesn't act in a loose, immoral way. It doesn't seek to take, but it willingly gives. Love doesn't lose its cool. It doesn't turn on and off. Love doesn't think about how bad the other person is, and certainly doesn't think of how it could get back at someone. Love is grieved deeply (as God is) over sin, but rejoices over truth. It gets excited when God's Word is read, and learned, and believed, and lived.

Love comes and sits with you when you're feeling down, and finds out what is wrong. It truly feels with you and believes in you. Love knows you'll come through just as God planned, and love sticks right beside you all the way.

Love doesn't give up, or quit, or diminish, or go home. Love keeps on keeping on, even when everything goes wrong and the feelings leave and the other person doesn't seem as special anymore. Love succeeds 100 percent of the time.

That, my friend, is what real love is!

Compare this paraphrase of 1 Corinthians 13:1–8 with your own Bible translation. If this paraphrase helps you see how to apply this chapter to your own life, great. That's the goal!

what about
APPARENT ERRORS?

Daniel pushed open the glass door and let the vibrant hues of the coffee shop push the grayness of the day back out behind him. He took a deep breath of the warm, espresso-scented air and searched the room for his friends. They had planned on meeting to study for an upcoming exam on *Hamlet*.

Andrea had already spotted Daniel and was waving from a table near the windows. She and Martin looked as if they were anxious to begin.

"Sorry about the delay," Daniel apologized as he slid into his chair. "I was doing some last-minute research for my paper on the historical inaccuracies within Shakespeare's work."

"Don't remind me," Andrea groaned. "I don't understand how that woman can expect us to finalize a full-length research paper the day after a major exam."

"How is your research going?" Martin asked Daniel.

"Pretty good. It's amazing how we assume that Shakespeare's plays were some sort of work of divine inspiration—perfect and pristine. Do you realize how many contradictions there are between various manuscripts—and how often Shakespeare, or the actors themselves, simply changed the text? Not too surprising, I guess, for a man who didn't always sign his name the same way! It's certainly made me appreciate the consistency and accuracy of the Bible." Daniel casually slipped in the last sentence to see how his friends would respond. Ever since their last conversation, he had been excited to realize they were willing to discuss the Bible with him instead of turning him off.

{ Today's First Question: }
Are There Errors in the Bible? If So, Why?

Andrea was quick to jump on Daniel's comment. "Come on, Daniel. Maybe the King James Version did come out in the time of Shakespeare, but I don't think you can be so arrogant as to suggest that the Bible's accuracy is that superior. Everyone knows the Bible is full of errors.

"The authors may have thought they were inspired by God, but their writings simply reflect a very time-bound, geographically limited, narrow religious world-view. At best, they had good motives. Worst case, they were deluded crackpots."

As always, Martin had a more thoughtful response. "I won't say the Bible is full of errors. Much of it seems genuine and authentic. Still, the writers were only human. Like Shakespeare, Mark Twain, and J. R. R. Tolkien, they made mistakes."

"And you know what Colin would say if he were here," Andrea started.

Daniel laughed and finished her sentence for her: "That I'm the sort of nutcase who believes that every Bible on the planet from the time of Adam to the present is perfect—without error."

Andrea relaxed a little. "He'd probably think that Adam wrote Genesis too."

"Seriously, Andrea, God inspired the original writings; they were perfect. Down through the ages, however, little mistakes have been made as the Scriptures were hand copied. Even after Gutenberg invented the printing press, errors occurred—but were corrected. It's not surprising—the Bible is a huge book. But those typographical errors haven't changed the Bible's message one iota.

"What's more amazing is that the fanatical commitment to accuracy of scribes and monks through the ages has given us a Bible that mirrors the early manuscripts. I know I can trust what the Bible *says* even if I don't always understand what it *means.*"

{ Today's Second Question: }
How Do You Explain Apparent Contradictions?

"That's great for you," said Martin. "You know I respect you, Daniel—and I'd certainly expect you to revere your Scriptures. But what *do* you do with the contradictions in the Bible? Just ignore them and have faith?"

"You can't blame every contradiction on a few typos, you know," Andrea interjected.

"Definitely not. I'm not into hiding from hard questions. I don't want someone just feeding me answers any more than you do. But because the Bible is so amazingly consistent, I'm more than willing to take the time to look for answers when it seems like it's not."

Martin noticed Andrea's tightened lips. "I think it's time to get back to Shakespeare. This is going to be a tough exam."

Daniel raised his cup of coffee. "Agreed."

{ A Second Look at . . . Today's First Question: }
Are There Errors in the Bible? If So, Why?

God has carefully protected the Bible. How do we know that? Here are eight reasons:

1. The psalmist affirms that Scripture is eternal (Ps. 119:89). Unlike the world's fads, which come and go, God's Word has endured the test of time.

2. The greatest prophet after Moses and a leading apostle of Jesus Christ both affirm that Scripture stands forever (Isa. 40:8; 1 Pet. 1:23–25).

3. Jesus himself promises that Scripture will remain until its purpose is achieved (Matt. 5:18). Nothing will be lost before the end of time.

4. The first prophet and the last apostle both issue harsh warnings to anyone who dares tamper with Scripture (Deut. 4:2; Rev. 22:18–19; see Prov. 30:6).

5. The discovery of the Dead Sea Scrolls confirms the remarkable accuracy of the transmission of the Old Testament over thousands of years.

6. The wealth of manuscripts dating back to the first century AD confirms the text of the New Testament beyond any shadow of a doubt.

7. Every critic's claim to have found a supposed "error" in Scripture has been discredited without exception for the past three centuries. That's a remarkable track record!

8. God himself promises that Scripture is completely true and trustworthy (Ps. 19:7; 33:4; 119:42). God wants us to take it seriously!

Still, if you carefully read parallel passages of Scripture in Kings and Chronicles, or in the Gospels, it's possible to find apparent contradictions. What do you do?

{ **A Second Look at . . . Today's Second Question:** }
How Do You Explain Apparent Contradictions?

When it comes to addressing apparent Bible contradictions, perhaps it would be best to start with the basic principles of journalism. These include seeking answers to six key questions: Who? What? When? Where? Why? How?

Any journalist worth his or her salt will compile far more facts than can be reported in an article, then use the principle of selectivity to report only the facts deemed most relevant to the intended readers.

As a result, a news story about an NBA game will sound far different in the guest team's hometown than in the home team's. Same game, same facts—but a different audience.

The same principle of selectivity applies to Scripture. Moses didn't write down everything that happened in Adam's life. Far from it. He recorded only what God said was relevant.

The same is true when John wrote his Gospel. He wasn't trying to write *The Exhaustive Life of Jesus Christ*. Instead, he admits, "And there are also many other things that Jesus did, which if they were written one by one, I suppose that even the world itself could not contain the books that would be written" (John 21:25). John selected only those events, miracles, interviews, teachings, prayers, persecutions, and sufferings that best communicated the gospel message to his intended audience.

Not surprisingly, the four Gospels differ widely in their introductions, scopes, messages, lengths, and conclusions.

{**Worksheet for Analyzing Problem Passages**}

When you're doing your daily Bible reading, an apparent "error" may trigger a red light in your thinking. Rather than ignoring it, use this form to help discover if there's really a problem.

1. Identify the Scripture passage(s): _____

_____

_____

2. Define the problem in the passage(s): _____

_____

_____

3. Classify the "error":

   ❏ contradiction in parallel accounts

   ❏ mistake in historical detail

   ❏ problem in scientific description

   ❏ inconsistency in moral teaching

4. Examine possible sources for the "error":

   ❏ faulty transmission (did a scribal error occur?)

   ❏ faulty translation (do contemporary versions differ?)

   ❏ faulty observation (have I carefully examined the text and context?)

   ❏ faulty interpretation (have I understood this passage correctly?)

5. Identify possible source of problem: _____

_____

6. Suggest tentative answer to the problem: _____

_____

_____

_____

_____

One of the few things all four Gospels record is Peter's three denials the night before Jesus's crucifixion. But to whom did Peter deny the Lord? Here is what the four Gospel writers tell us.

To Whom Did Peter Deny Jesus Christ?

Gospel	First Denial	Second Denial	Third Denial
Matthew	"a servant girl"	"another girl"	"those who stood by"
Mark	"one of the servant girls of the high priest"	"the servant girl . . . again"	"those who stood by . . . again"
Luke	"a certain servant girl"	"another" (a man)	"another"
John	"the servant girl"	"they"	"one of the servants of the high priest" (a relative of the man whose ear Peter cut off)

As the chart shows, the four Gospel writers give differing accounts of Peter's denials. Do their differences contradict each other?

Like a good journalist, each Gospel writer had a specific purpose for writing his account. He had a specific audience in mind. By definition, he had to leave out most of what he knew (otherwise, he never would have finished writing!). Leaving out secondary and tertiary details isn't wrong—it's what *every* good writer does.

Actually, their differences don't contradict—they *complement* each other. So to whom did Peter deny Jesus Christ? Any good journalist can harmonize the four Gospel accounts rather easily.

Harmony of the four Gospels:

- First denial: one maid who talked to a second maid about Peter
- Second denial: the two maids plus others who confronted Peter
- Third denial: a larger group of bystanders, including a servant who was upset with Peter

Over the years, critics have cited Peter's three denials as "proof" that the Bible contains errors. Their adamant remarks, however, haven't proven anything.

{Worksheet for Analyzing Problem Passages: Peter's Denials}

1. Identify the Scripture passage(s): *Matthew 26:69–75; Mark 14:66–71; Luke 22:55–62; John 18:16–27.*

2. Define the problem in the passage(s): *The Gospel writers seem to contradict each other regarding those to whom Peter denied Jesus Christ.*

3. Classify the "error":

   ☒ contradiction in parallel accounts

   ☐ mistake in historical detail

   ☐ problem in scientific description

   ☐ inconsistency in moral teaching

4. Examine possible sources for the "error":

   ☐ faulty transmission (did a scribal error occur?)

   ☐ faulty translation (do contemporary versions differ?)

   ☒ faulty observation (have I carefully examined the text and context?)

   ☐ faulty interpretation (have I understood this passage correctly?)

5. Identify possible source of problem: *I could be mistakenly assuming each Gospel writer is telling the whole story.*

6. Suggest tentative answer to the problem: *Actually, each Gospel writer selectively includes certain details in order to get the story across without elaborate explanations. The four Gospel writers complement (not contradict) each other.*

Critics haven't just had a heyday with apparent contradictions regarding Peter's three denials. They've also cited apparent contradictions in other parallel accounts, including

- who incited King David to number the people (2 Sam. 24:1 vs. 1 Chron. 21:1);
- who killed Goliath (1 Sam. 17:49–51; 21:9 vs. 2 Sam. 21:19);
- who owned the threshing floor (2 Sam. 6:6 vs. 1 Chron. 13:9);
- which city King David captured (2 Sam. 8:1 vs. 1 Chron. 18:1);
- how many enemies were killed (2 Sam. 23:8 vs. 1 Chron. 11:11); and

- how much King David paid (2 Sam. 24:24 vs. 1 Chron. 21:24–25).

Thankfully, all of these problems are easily resolved using the Worksheet for Analyzing Problem Passages.

In years gone by, critics also argued that the Bible contains historical errors. They claimed Scripture wrongly attributes the authorship of Genesis through Deuteronomy to Moses, "even though writing wasn't invented until after his death." Scholars, however, have long since proved the critics wrong. These scholars can point to at least six languages that extend back before the time of Moses.

Other historical "problems" include these two notorious claims:

1. Historians have no record of King Belshazzar. Until the past generation, the only record of this king appeared in Daniel 5. Then, in 1854, scholar Sir Henry Rawlinson discovered ancient Babylonian records reporting that Nabonidus, the last king of Babylon, entrusted the kingship to his son, Belsharusus, while he retired to Arabia.

2. Quirinius wasn't governor when Jesus was born. Many scholars now believe Quirinius held the office of governor of Syria for two three-year terms, first when Jesus was born, then again a decade later.

Even *Time* magazine conceded, thirty years ago, that "after more than two centuries of facing the heaviest . . . guns that could be brought to bear, the Bible has survived—and is perhaps the better for the siege. Even on the critics' own terms—historical fact—the Scriptures seem more acceptable now than they did when the rationalists began the attack" (see "The Bible: The Believers Gain," *Time*, December 30, 1974).

Examples of Historical Accuracy in the Bible

The biblical writers often took the time to describe the historical accuracy of their writings. Here are a few brief examples from the New Testament:

- Luke anchors the main narrative section of his Gospel on a solid group of authenticating historical reference points (Luke 3:1–2).
- John verifies the actual physical death of Jesus Christ by reminding his readers that he was an eyewitness of Jesus's final moments on the cross (John 19:34–35).
- John mentions that he had many more historical facts on hand that he had to leave out for the sake of brevity (John 21:25).
- Peter appealed to the knowledge of the crowd when he talked about

Jesus Christ on the day of Pentecost (Acts 2:22). If he had been fabricating a story, he would have received a far different response at the end of his sermon.

- Paul appealed to the knowledge of King Agrippa as he talked about Jesus Christ (Acts 26:26). Jesus Christ and his disciples hadn't performed miracles in some obscure corner—everyone knew about them.
- Paul said that to deny the possibility of someone's rising from the dead was to deny the obvious historical fact of Jesus Christ's resurrection (1 Cor. 15:1–8).
- Peter rightfully claimed to have been an eyewitness of one of Jesus Christ's most glorious miracles—the Transfiguration (2 Pet. 1:16–18).
- John reminded the early Christians toward the end of the first century that he had actually touched Jesus Christ (1 John 1:1–3).

Other critics have argued that the Bible has scientific errors. They claim Scripture incorrectly speaks of the sun "going down" (see Eph. 4:26). They gleefully point out that Galileo discredited this concept centuries ago. Despite the critics' claims, however, the idea of the sun "going down" is still part of the English language. Almost everyone loves to watch a spectacular sunrise or sunset. Every day newspapers across the country list the times for the sun to come up and go down.

Other scientific "problems" include these two false ideas:

1. The Bible can't be proven scientifically. The problem is a matter of confusion on the part of the critics. The scientific method is a very limited test. It can't prove historical facts (Abraham Lincoln was president of the United States), musical standards (Mozart was a brilliant composer), tenets of faith (Jesus Christ is the one and only Son of God), or matters of the heart (I love my children).

2. The uniformity of nature makes supernatural intervention (miracles) impossible. Of course, these critics are leaving God out of their picture! If God *is* God, he can do whatever he wants—even supersede the principles governing his creation. Besides, the scientific theory of the universe as an absolutely uniform system is a century out of date!

Scientific Accuracy of the Bible

Even though the Bible isn't a scientific textbook, its scientific descriptions contain no real problems. In fact, many of its statements, though contrary to scientific thought at the time, have long since been proven true. Here are four examples:

1. Many hundreds of years before the theory of the circulation of blood within the body was even proposed, the Bible declared, "Blood gives life" (Gen. 9:4 NCV).

2. Ancient civilizations commonly believed the earth was held in place by some support such as a large reptile's back or a set of pillars. But Job 26:7 declares, "He [God] stretches out the north over empty space; / He hangs the earth on nothing."

3. The Greek astronomer Hipparchus confidently stated, "There are only 1,056 stars in the heavens. I have counted them." Later, Ptolemy counted 1,056 and agreed that no others existed. Yet Jeremiah 33:22 insists, "The host [stars] of heaven cannot be numbered." Not until AD 1610 did Galileo look through a telescope and prove the Bible right. Estimate: some 100 billion stars in our galaxy alone.

4. On a clear night, many of the stars that appear in the sky look alike. Modern astronomers have photographed millions, however, and found no two alike. Paul talked about this nearly two thousand years ago: "One star differs from another star in glory" (1 Cor. 15:41).

Still other critics have argued that the Bible has moral errors. They claim that Jesus and his disciples violated one of the Ten Commandments by working on the Sabbath. Did they? In Matthew 12:1–2, the Pharisees emphatically said yes. According to their list of rules, someone was "working" if he walked through a field when the heads of grain were mature. Yet their rule went far beyond anything the Old Testament said. In fact, Deuteronomy 23:25 says someone could pick grain from someone else's field if he or she was hungry. Jesus said he came to fulfill the law (Matt. 5:16), but he had little patience for those who oppressed the multitudes with all their man-made regulations.

Other moral "problems" include these two dubious criticisms:

1. **The Bible is full of sex and violence.** It's true that the Bible doesn't gloss over the violent and sometimes lustful lives of the people it mentions. Yet the Bible's purpose isn't to provide crude entertainment but to provide clear examples of what honors God—and what doesn't.

2. **The Bible is often offensive.** It's true that the Bible speaks of God's ultimate judgment against wrongdoers and provides many examples of his

judgment here on earth. The real moral problem, however, resides not with the Lord or his Word but with those who would set themselves up as judges of either.

Presuppositions for Analyzing Problem Passages

Before tackling an apparent "error" in Scripture, it's important to think through one's basic assumptions about the reliability of the Bible. The following presuppositions should form the grid through which you and I study potential biblical mistakes.

1. The Bible is inerrant (without error) in the original manuscripts.

2. Some apparent errors were caused by faulty transmission or translation of Scripture.

3. Some apparent errors are caused by faulty observations or interpretations of Scripture.

4. Most apparent errors can be solved by discovering the source of the problem and examining it carefully and honestly.

5. Some apparent errors will be fully solved only when further information is available.

6. We must reserve judgment on apparent errors we can't solve because of our limited knowledge, recognizing that it is always wiser to depend on God's Word than to trust the words of men.

The verdict?

Our English Bibles are *very* accurate. God has carefully preserved the Scriptures down through the ages. We can read God's Word with the utmost confidence that it *is* still God's message for us today.

⟨ Today's Third Question: ⟩
What Do I Do When I Have Doubts About God's Word?

Even the godliest Christians struggle with doubts. Doubts are a natural by-product of taking God's Word seriously while living in a fallen world.

If left unaddressed, doubts will fester in our souls and can lead to a lack of faith or outright unbelief. So whatever we do, we can't ignore doubts!

Instead, here's how to handle them:

Revelation. We have to get back to the question, *how do we know what we believe?* The answer is that God has revealed his message in a book. It's called the Bible. In this book we find all the answers we need for life and godliness. We don't find answers to all of life's tough questions. But most of them are answered with far greater authority and clarity than a thousand years of philosophy has provided.

Authority. We have to address the question, *who decides what is true?* Ultimately, the answer is God. He has stated his position quite clearly in the Scriptures. God's Word is our absolute authority for faith and practice.

Orthodoxy. We have to answer the question, *where do we draw the lines?* The answer is in the classic, orthodox teachings of the church. Those teachings are based solidly on Scripture. Here is a survey to rate your belief in ten major areas of traditional Christian orthodoxy. Circle the number that best represents your belief about each one.

	Not Sure			Fully Believe	
Jesus made the heavens and the earth.	1	2	3	4	5
Jesus is the one and only Son of God.	1	2	3	4	5
Jesus became fully man two thousand years ago.	1	2	3	4	5
Jesus was born of the virgin Mary in Bethlehem of Judea.	1	2	3	4	5
Jesus performed many miracles not recorded in the Bible.	1	2	3	4	5
Jesus was alive on earth for less than forty years.	1	2	3	4	5
Jesus died on the cross for the sins of the whole world.	1	2	3	4	5
Jesus rose from the dead three days after he was buried.	1	2	3	4	5
Jesus is sitting in heaven at the right hand of God the Father.	1	2	3	4	5
Jesus is coming back to earth someday.	1	2	3	4	5

The Bible teaches that all ten statements are positively true. How close did your answers come to what the Bible teaches?

Inspiration. We have to tackle the question, *is every word in Scripture inspired by God?* Scripture itself says yes. The early church fathers agreed. Many reformers and other great Bible teachers down through the centuries concurred. Many believed that every sentence of Scripture is infallible (incapable of error) and every verse is inerrant (completely without error). They also believed that the Bible contains a unified message and story.

Doctrine. We have to wrestle with the question, *what do I believe?* The answer is in the teachings of your particular denomination or church. To the degree that they're based solidly on Scripture, you can bank on them. The answer is also found in your own beliefs and convictions—and questions and doubts.

Questions. We have to keep asking questions! Five fast facts about asking questions:

1. The world's smartest people ask lots of questions.

2. The person who doesn't ask questions doesn't care or is afraid.

3. The person who is afraid to ask questions doesn't know whom to ask, is worried about sounding dumb, or is afraid of the answer.

4. The person who is afraid of the answer wants to believe something is true no matter what—even if it's not true—or is more afraid of the answerer's rebuke than of the answer itself.

5. Fortunately, God doesn't rebuke us when we ask honest questions.

{A Quick Survey from Scripture}

1. Is it okay to ask questions when praying to God?

    yes   no   *See Habakkuk 1:12–13.*

2. Is it okay to ask God, "Why did you let this happen?"

    yes   no   *See Malachi 3:13–15.*

3. Is it okay to ask questions about God's Word?

    yes   no   *See Acts 8:30–35.*

4. Is it okay to ask questions in church?

    yes   no   *See Acts 15:6–11.*

Doubts. We need to bring our toughest questions to the Lord. Scripture makes it clear that Jesus can remove people's doubts (Matt. 14:25–31; Luke 24:36–45). Where do doubts come from? Here are some possibilities:

- Life has been very painful for you.
- You wonder if something Scripture says is too good to be true.
- You have an incorrect perception of God or Scripture.
- You have been introduced to false ideas.
- You are struggling with depression.

How do you get rid of doubts? Here are some possibilities:

- Tell God about what has happened.
- Ask God to search your heart.
- Read Scripture and study what it says.
- Affirm what you believe, obey, and heed.
- Ask the Lord to speak to your heart as you read and pray.
- Ask God to fill you with the Holy Spirit and teach you.
- Talk with someone you respect for his or her faith.

Again, it's not a sin to have doubts—everyone has them. Don't pretend you don't. And whatever you do, don't hide them.

Instead, deal with your doubts head-on. Address each one that comes up. In the end, your faith will be stronger!

{ part two }

where do i start
READING THE BIBLE?

True to Hamid's prediction, a comfortable calm simmered in the coffee shop on Thursday afternoon as Maria and Kendall settled into the leather chairs conveniently facing Daniel and Erik's.

"Wow," Maria remarked, "not only did we get the best seats in the house, but we can even hear the music this time of day!"

"Let's hope they keep it to something we like," Kendall said.

Daniel said, "Since we don't all know each other that well, let's share a little bit about ourselves. Maybe our favorite music and then our favorite passage of Scripture. Erik, why don't you go first?"

"Okay, now you're going to put me in a box. Yes, I like country music—I'm a country boy, but I also really like alternative. And my favorite passage of Scripture? I don't know that much yet, but I'd have to say books like Philippians and Ephesians that say straight and clear what my Christian life is supposed to be."

"Kendall, what about you?"

"I grew up with parents who are classical musicians, so I've got plenty of that in my taste repertoire, but I'd have to say that it's Christian rock that really speaks to me. As for Scripture, the Gospels because they're the most accessible to me."

"Maria?"

"Now if we're talking upbringing, you'll all expect me to say 'a mariachi band.' Not quite! Give me hard rock any day. As for Scripture, I could swim in the Prophets. The poetry and the passion just take my breath away. I'd like to know more about what they actually *mean*—but I get the idea that God feels pretty strongly about love and sin and obedience. What about you, Daniel?"

"I guess I should have thought about the answer to my own question. Right now I'm listening to worship CDs, but that could change next week. I have to admit I love history—so all the details of the historical books really fascinate me. But I know some people don't get quite as excited about them as I do.

"Hey, we've had separate conversations about this, but why do we want to actually *read* the Bible together instead of just answering questions out of a study book?" Daniel left his question open for response.

"I'll start," said Kendall. "I came to this university to get my education and my degree, and I'm working hard to accomplish that goal. I realized that I also want to stay a Christian while I'm doing it and that it might mean putting just as much educational effort into it as I do into the other goal. College is primarily about reading. They make you read so many books you'd never touch on your own. I know lots of Bible stories, but I've never read the whole thing cover to cover. I figure the least I can do in college is read the whole thing for myself."

"That's impressive, Kendall," Erik responded. "I'm still just learning the basics. I have a lot of catching up to do, and I'm realistic about the fact that I can't learn all the answers to people's challenges to my faith in one term. Like you, I figure actually reading the Bible for myself is a good place to begin."

"And you'll be ahead of most of your challengers just by doing that," Daniel commented.

Maria leaned forward. "This is so exciting to me, because I know that God is going to take you on a journey you can't even imagine as you read. You're not going to be reading just words—you're going to be encountering God in the stories and poems and lives of the people you read about. You're opening yourself up to the powerful Word of God. I've started to experience that in my life—I see the whole world differently than I used to. I want to keep meeting God this way. And I'm excited to do it with other people too."

Daniel nodded. "I still have a ways to go before I feel as deeply as Maria does—maybe I'll never get that good at my emotions—but I'm excited to meet together as a group to keep myself consistent in reading God's Word—and to share with you guys in the process of discovering the Bible. If I can be of any help when it comes to technical questions, that would be cool too."

"So when do we start?" Kendall was ready to get to practicalities.

"Well," Daniel responded, "we're going to start right away. But another question we have to ask is, where do we start reading the Bible?"

{ **Today's First Question:** }
Where Do I Start Reading the Bible? On Page 1?

Erik said, "They told me to start reading the Gospel of John and the New Testament when I first became a Christian, but I thought this whole thing was about starting at the beginning."

"Yes, exactly. I guess I should rephrase my question. We're going to start in Genesis, but if we read straight through, three to four chapters in about fifteen minutes a day, we could get through the whole thing in a year. Since we only have eight weeks left before Christmas and only seven months in the school year, maybe we should consider a different plan for getting through the Bible from start to finish."

"Like reading ten chapters a day?"

"Not exactly! We could read through the Bible biographically, reading the stories of significant people from Adam through Paul, and we could get through in about sixteen weeks. Or we could read through it survey-style—reading the most significant and famous passages from each book. We could easily do that in the two months before Christmas."

Maria was ready to begin. "We could do the survey plan in the fall and the biographical plan beginning in January."

Kendall agreed with Maria. "The survey idea sounds fine for this fall. It sounds like an easy victory for someone who hasn't even opened up certain books in her Bible in her whole life—that would be me. But I don't want to do the biographical plan right now. That's the whole problem with how I learned about the Bible growing up in Sunday school. I learned a bunch of stories about a bunch of people that never had any connection to the big picture. I already know stories—I want to read the Bible cover to cover and see how it all fits."

"That's a fair suggestion, Kendall," Daniel agreed. "If you're all willing, after Christmas we can start with a straight read-through of the whole Bible. We'll get through as much as we can before school is out. We'll be through the least familiar parts before then."

"Willing and agreed?" Maria asked. "Now for the good part: Daniel has some papers with the daily reading listed, right, Daniel? Here's what we'll do: Read the Scriptures with a pen in hand. Underline the passages that stand out to you or that speak to you in a special way. Write down in a notebook the questions you have or the convictions that the verses bring. When we come together, we'll discuss the questions and read the verses that mean the most to us."

"That's it?" Erik was a bit surprised. "No fill-in-the-blank or essay questions?"

"Just you and the Spirit of God this time through," Maria replied.

"Don't worry," Daniel assured him. "You can use the notes in your study Bible to answer the immediate questions as you go along. Just don't forget to read the text all at once and let it hit you in the gut."

"Okay, whatever you say, man. I guess this is going to be easier—and harder—than I thought."

{ A Second Look at . . . Today's First Question: }
Where Do I Start Reading the Bible? On Page 1?

The one way *not* to read the Bible is simply to open it randomly and start reading. That's a favorite of some people when they're suddenly faced with seemingly insurmountable problems. It's better than nothing—but surely we can do better than that!

You may want to alternate between three Bible reading plans: the survey plan, the biographical plan, and the one-year plan.

The Survey Plan

Want to read highlights from every book of the Bible? You can read important excerpts from Genesis to Revelation in a little more than two months. The advantages of this approach include simplicity, comprehensiveness, and brevity. You'll find this reading plan featured on pages 217–19. You're welcome to photocopy this plan to insert in your Bible and begin using. That's why we created it!

The Biographical Plan

Want to read highlights about every important person from Adam to Zechariah? You can do it in about four months. The advantages of this approach include enjoying the human-interest side of biblical accounts, ease in seeing the story of the Bible, and ease in becoming acquainted with the entire Who's Who of the Bible. You'll find this reading plan on pages 221–24. Again, feel free to photocopy this plan and begin using it!

The One-Year Plan

You can read the whole Bible cover to cover in 365 days or less. Here are four approaches:

1. **Genesis Through Revelation.** This is the one-year plan we recommend. The advantages of this approach include ease of use and ease of seeing the progressive nature of God's written revelation. You'll find two versions of this reading plan on pages 225–30 and 231–36. Make a copy and start your way through the entire Bible!

2. **Blended.** Some publishers offer one-year Bibles with daily readings from the Old and New Testaments, sometimes including extra selections from Psalms and / or Proverbs. This approach has been popular on and off for well over a century.

3. **Chronological.** Some publishers offer one-year Bibles arranged chronologically. After the story of David and Bathsheba in 2 Samuel 11, for instance, David's psalm of repentance (Ps. 51) appears.

4. **Canonical.** Some scholars suggest reading the Old Testament Scriptures in the order the books appear in the Hebrew Scriptures. Unless you're a seminary student, however, this probably isn't the best approach to use.

Because the books of the Bible are grouped logically, it makes the most sense to read them from Genesis to Revelation.

{ Today's Second Question: }
How Is the Bible Organized? Is There a Pattern?

Once you see the big picture, you'll always be able to see the Bible's design!

One Author, Forty Writers

Unlike other books, the Bible doesn't list any author on the cover or title page. Then again, the Bible isn't any book! God is the Author. He inspired a diverse group of forty individuals to write the Bible over the course of sixteen hundred years. The first writer was Moses, who penned the first five books. Other important writers include David, Solomon, Isaiah, Jeremiah, Ezekiel, Daniel,

Hosea, Matthew, Mark, Luke, Paul, James, and Peter. The last writer was John, who wrote the fourth Gospel, three letters, and the book of Revelation. The Holy Spirit guided all of these individuals to write what they did.

Sixty-Six Books, One Story

The Bible contains a total of sixty-six books (not chapters). Because God inspired all the writers, the Bible contains a unified message from beginning to end. In fact, the opening page talks about the beginning of time. The last page talks about the end of time as we know it. In between, the story of the Bible unfolds in all its drama, conflict, violence, irony, and glory.

The hero of the Bible is Jesus Christ. The enemies of Jesus Christ are Satan, evil people, and death. Everything and everybody in the first three-fourths of the Bible foreshadow the life, death, burial, and resurrection of Jesus Christ (or the ultimately futile opposition of his enemies).

One Work, Two Testaments

Like some books, the Bible is divided into two parts (called *testaments*, which is another word for covenants). The following lists clearly show how each testament is divided into four distinct, logical sections:

Old Testament
1. Pentateuch: Genesis–Deuteronomy (five books written by Moses)
2. History: Joshua–Esther (mostly anonymous authors)
3. Literature: Job–Song of Songs (primarily by David and Solomon)
4. Prophets: Isaiah–Malachi (by more than fifteen authors)

New Testament
1. Gospels: Matthew–John (by four Gospel writers)
2. Acts (by Luke)
3. Letters: Romans–Jude (by Paul, James, Peter, John, and Jude)
4. Revelation (by John)

{ **Today's Third Question:** }
What Should I Look for in the Bible?
What Kind of Books Does It Contain?

Let's look at each section of the Bible in more depth.

Part One: Old Testament

The first three-fourths of the Bible is called the Old Testament or the Hebrew Scriptures. The Old Testament contains thirty-nine books written by Moses and other Jewish prophets over the course of a thousand years. The Old Testament was finished four hundred years before the birth of Jesus Christ. Every section of the Old Testament looks forward to his coming.

Pentateuch. This section contains five books. Moses, one of the earliest and greatest prophets of God's people, wrote these. God clearly chose Moses, called him to service, and revealed to him what to write in each of these five foundational books of the Bible.

Moses wrote these books in a straightforward, selective narrative format. (This means that he provides only selected narratives, not all the stories that could possibly be told about Adam and Eve, Noah, Abraham, etc.) His narratives of creation are breathtaking. Moses goes on to record important epic stories of early human history. Then he records the stories of God at work to create a godly nation that would be his witness to the world. Sadly, this nation (Israel) often turns from God, with disastrous results.

In these five books, Moses also includes quite a bit of discourse (by God and Moses), several beautiful poetic sections (by God, Moses, and possibly his sister, Miriam), and a few important genealogical records (we'll see the value of those records later in Scripture).

Expectations of a coming Messiah (Jesus Christ) appear throughout the books of Moses, from Genesis (3:15) to Deuteronomy (18:15).

History. This section contains twelve books. Joshua, Ezra, and other anonymous biblical writers wrote these books.

These twelve books tell the story of God's people, the Israelite nation, for a thousand years from the death of Moses (c. 1400 BC) until the completion of the Old Testament (c. 400 BC).

Like Moses did, Joshua, Ezra, and the other authors wrote these books in a straightforward, selective narrative format. The narratives of Joshua's early exploits are riveting. Joshua then records how the Israelites divide up and settle the Promised Land. Sadly, the Israelites often rebel against the Lord, fight against each other, and—after a period of great prosperity—ultimately fight again and split into two kingdoms. The northern kingdom, Israel (ten Israelite tribes), never turns back to the Lord, and eventually the Assyrian Empire conquers it (722 BC). The southern kingdom, Judah (two tribes), turns back to the Lord on several occasions, but eventually the newly dominant Babylonian Empire conquers it (586 BC).

After the seventy years of Babylonian captivity, a remnant of the people from Judah (and Israel) returns to the former Promised Land, eventually rebuilds Jerusalem, and seeks to start over.

In these twelve books of history, you'll find not just narrative but also these things:

- discourse (especially see 2 Kings 17);
- some great poetry (especially see Judg. 5; 1 Sam. 2:1–10; 2 Sam. 22:1–23:7; 1 Chron. 16:7–36);
- a number of important prayers (especially see Josh. 10:12–14; 2 Sam. 7:18–29; 1 Kings 8:22–53; 18:36–39; 2 Kings 19:14–19; 1 Chron. 17:16–27; 29:10–20; 2 Chron. 6:12–42; 20:5–12; Ezra 9:5–15; Neh. 1:4–11; 9:5–38); and
- several genealogical records (especially see 1 Chron. 1–9).

The anticipation of the coming Messiah is evident in mostly subtle ways, from Joshua (his name is the Hebrew form of "Jesus") to Esther (where the Lord isn't mentioned, but his covenantal name—YHWH (pronounced YAH-way)—appears in acrostic form in the Hebrew text).

Literature. This section contains five books. David and Solomon wrote most of them, but they include writings by Moses and many other contributors.

These five books present the best of five kinds of Hebrew literature written between 1450 BC (Psalm 90 by Moses, probably before the Lord called him to deliver the Israelites from slavery in Egypt) and 450 BC (Psalm 137 by Jeremiah, according to ancient Jewish tradition). The types of literature include drama, worship lyrics, wise sayings, a sermon, and a love song.

The anticipation of the coming of Jesus Christ is especially evident in over a dozen psalms that include detailed messianic prophecies.

Prophets. This section contains seventeen books, written by Isaiah,

Jeremiah, Ezekiel, and Daniel (known as the *Major Prophets*) and twelve other prophets (known as the *Minor Prophets*—but "minor" only in the sense that they wrote shorter books).

Isaiah and the others wrote these books in the prophetic genre, largely in poetic form with some narrative interludes. These books contain a series of messages from God dating from 850 BC to 400 BC. Many of these prophetic messages call the Israelites to repent of their sins and turn back to the Lord. Other messages foretell future events, including God's coming judgment on the kingdoms of Israel and Judah and surrounding nations.

The expectation of the coming Messiah is strongly apparent throughout these prophetic writings, from Isaiah (especially see 52:13–53:12, which describes Jesus Christ's passion [suffering] in great detail nearly seven hundred years ahead of time) to Malachi (especially see 3:1, which speaks of John the Baptist and the beginning of Jesus's ministry four centuries beforehand).

{Getting the Whole Picture}

When the Old Testament prophets predicted the coming of the Messiah, Jesus Christ, they didn't have the whole picture. Collectively, they said the Messiah would come from least six different places:

1. Bethlehem (Mic. 5:2)
2. Egypt (Hosea 11:1)
3. Galilee (Isa. 9:1)
4. The Mount of Olives (Zech. 14:4)
5. Jerusalem (Zech. 9:9)
6. The temple (Mal. 3:1)

So who was right? They all were! It isn't until we read the four Gospels, however, that we can put this all together. Keep reading!

The Silent Years

After the close of the Old Testament, it appears that God was silent for more than four hundred years. Why did God wait so long before sending Jesus Christ to earth?

A prophecy in the book of Daniel holds part of the key to the answer. In

Daniel 9:24–27, the prophet foretells that more than four hundred years must pass from the return from captivity until the Messiah would come and be "cut off." That time was drawing near when Jesus began his public ministry among a people longing for and anticipating the Messiah's coming.

The cultural and political situation in Palestine during the first century AD also explains God's purpose in waiting so long. Three different peoples had a tremendous influence on the times of the life of Jesus Christ and his newborn church.

1. The Romans. Some sixty years before Jesus Christ was born, the Roman Empire (the last great world empire) formed. The Romans ruled all of the Mediterranean area and the rest of the known world at that time. The Caesars brought world peace under one government, which aided the early church as it began to spread from Palestine. Also, vastly improved transportation systems the Romans developed gave the first missionaries the opportunity to carry the gospel of Jesus Christ to new areas. It wasn't until after AD 60 that local persecution against Christians started engulfing the empire.

2. The Greeks. Earlier, the Greeks had ruled the world, and their culture influenced the Romans. The Greeks passed from the scene politically, but their language survived as the universal world language for many years. This was the language in which the New Testament was written. Greek culture, particularly philosophy, influenced much thinking in the first century AD.

3. The Jews. The Jewish people had lived in Palestine for nearly fourteen hundred years. Then they found themselves under the yoke of Rome, and most found it unpleasant. The Jewish people's hope was deliverance from Roman domination.

Sadly, Judaism had degenerated from a religion based on faith into a weighty compilation of human laws and traditions. The leadership and masses no longer worshiped God, and soon Jerusalem and Palestinian Judaism were destroyed (AD 70).

Into this world situation Jesus Christ came to redirect people (all people, Jewish and Gentile) back to God.

The Lord waited until the right time!

Part Two: New Testament

The last quarter of the Bible is called the *New Testament* or *new covenant*. The New Testament contains twenty-seven books that apostles and other church leaders wrote after Jesus Christ returned to heaven. The New Testament was finished before the twelve apostles had all died. The first half of the New Testament presents the life, ministry, teachings, and passion of Jesus Christ. The second half explains what it means to follow Jesus Christ.

Gospels. This section contains four books, written by Matthew, Mark, Luke, and John. These four men tell us about the significance of the divinity, birth, life, ministry, teachings, miracles, suffering, death, burial, resurrection, ascension, heavenly reign, and future return of Jesus Christ.

Matthew and the others wrote these books in the Gospel genre, mostly in narrative with a number of sections of discourse, some poetic passages and prayers, and two genealogies. The key period of time these Gospels cover stretches from about 6 BC to about AD 30, which represents the years Jesus lived here on earth.

The expectation of the coming Messiah is realized—and the Lord offers the good news (gospel) of salvation to everyone.

Acts. This section contains one book, written by Luke. It picks up the narrative at the end of Jesus's time here on earth, records the birth of the church, and shows how the church spread from Jerusalem and Judah to Samaria, and then to many regions throughout the Roman Empire, from about AD 30 to AD 61. The church's message is clear: believe in Jesus Christ, the Savior of the world. Some meet that good news with open arms—many others with much resistance.

The theme of Jesus Christ as the Messiah is strongly emphasized in this book.

Letters. This section contains twenty-one books, written by Paul, James, Peter, John, and Jude. These twenty-one books present what the life, ministry, and message of the church should (and shouldn't) look like. Most of the books address problems in the early churches. Many sections, however, provide positive explanations of Christian teachings and practices.

Paul and the other authors wrote these books in the epistle genre, mostly as discourse with some poetry and prayers. Most of these books were written between AD 45 and AD 70, but John may have written his several shorter letters after AD 85.

The theme of Jesus Christ as Messiah is clearly proclaimed throughout these letters.

Revelation. This section contains one book, written by the apostle John about AD 95. John wrote this book in an apocalyptic manner, enfolding poetry and discourse in a narrative framework. In many ways, this book echoes the passion and some of the themes of the Old Testament prophets: turn from your sins, turn back to God, and get ready for the Lord's pending judgments on the whole earth. Interestingly, the theme of Revelation isn't so much how the world ends but rather the question, *how will your life end—will you stay true to the Lord or not?*

The Lord Jesus Christ is clearly worshiped as God's Son, the Messiah, and the Savior of the world.

More Silent Years

After the close of the New Testament, it appears that God has been silent for almost two thousand years. In reality, God has been speaking powerfully through the Bible's sixty-six books, which easily fill a thousand pages in most Bibles.

During the past two millennia, God has been using Scripture to build his church around the world. Today more than 1.5 billion people call themselves Christians. Even in the remotest corners of the world, despite intense persecution, people of every nation, people, and tongue are starting to believe.

Part of the key to the expansion of the church has been the translation, publication, reading, and teaching of the Bible among thousands of groups. That expansion has accelerated at a phenomenal rate over the past two generations.

Bible reading isn't a luxury. It's the way the Christian faith takes root in our hearts and is shared with others.

Ready to begin?

how do i read the first half of
THE OLD TESTAMENT?

The next Thursday afternoon found the coffee shop a bit busier. The steady rain outside seemed to push more people inside, huddling over their coffee for a bit of extra warmth. Daniel quickly claimed a table vacated by two professors. Maria, Kendall, and Erik soon joined him.

"What, you're not having a drink?" Daniel teased Kendall, who was by far the most caffeine-committed among them.

"Of course I am—the guy said he'd bring it over so we could get started," she replied. "I thought it was kind of weird that he knew all about what we were doing, but I guess that's part of being clued into the customers. He already knows what my regular drink is, so I guess it's not that unusual for him to keep track of our movements!"

Maria laughed. "Actually, that guy is Hamid, and Krista told me that he overheard Daniel and me talking about this study. He was so interested in the concept of reading Scripture for meaning—not just to get points with God— that she suggested he read it for himself. The deal is, she's going to read the Koran at the same time. In fact, I suggested that she encourage Hamid to use the same survey reading plan that we're using. I need to give her a call soon and find out how it's going."

Daniel looked at her quizzically. "How do you always know so much about so many different people? I can't figure out how you can get all that information—much less keep track of it!"

"It's all about being interested in people, Daniel! Of course, my increased cranium capacity certainly helps!"

At that moment Hamid appeared with Kendall's drink. Maria smiled at him brightly. "Thanks so much, Hamid! Your suggestion for our meeting time certainly worked out well. Say, how is *your* Bible reading going so far?"

Hamid chuckled. "Yes, I am reading your Bible. Fascinating. I'm so

63

interested with the beginning of the world and with the stories of our prophet Ibrahim. Of course, some stories are new to me and some details seem to be wrong, but you cannot deny what a great man he was. Now, please pardon me, but I must be getting back to work."

"Of course, but feel free to join us anytime!"

After Hamid walked away, the others looked at Maria in surprise. "Do you really think a Muslim guy would fit in with us?"

"It doesn't hurt to ask."

(Today's First Question:)
What's So Important About the Book of Genesis?

Daniel spoke up. "Well, let's pray for Hamid—reading the truth is going to move his heart more powerfully than any discussions or debates we might have with him. But he brought up a good question—and, I think, part of the answer. That is, *what's so fascinating about the book of Genesis?*

"How about we just share what we've gotten out of reading Genesis this week? Then we'll get to the other passages later. Kendall, you want to go first? What seemed important to you in this first book?"

Kendall's Bible was already opened and her notes arranged neatly beside it. "Since I knew many of the stories, I tried extra hard not to just assume I knew what was going to happen next. I decided to try to look for the big picture.

"What really impressed me was the way God set up this whole world to have a relationship with these people—but they just walked away. Then the whole rest of the book, God is working to get people back into a relationship with him. But they seem so clueless sometimes! He really is starting from scratch—and it seems like he's willing to take his time and put up with a lot!

"I know God gets pretty judgmental at times—but it was weirder to me what he seems to let the good guys get away with. I had a real hard time with all that polygamy and servant girl stuff."

"Reminded me of a few country songs I've heard!" Erik grinned.

"Well, Kendall," Daniel said, "you really hit two main points we have to remember in reading the Old Testament. One, God's main mission is having his people in relationship with him. Second, it was a whole different world back then! If we get too freaked out by the cultural stuff, we can miss the whole point."

Maria commented, "Even if their circumstances are so different from mine, I love that the people are so very real. And God's willing to make all these incredible promises and bless them even in their worst moments."

Daniel continued, "And don't forget that even if the text doesn't give you God's commentary on their bad actions—doesn't tell you, 'This was a bad thing to do'—how the story turns out should give you a clue.

"Erik, what about you? Any questions come up or any verses stand out? Not just in Genesis, but in the whole first section?"

Erik leaned back in his chair and rearranged his long legs so that they stuck out from under the side of the table. "Like I said before, some of these stories are so bizarre they remind me of country music! But seriously, I get the idea that there's a lot to learn in all that history! I'm not sure what it is—it's going to take me awhile to get it."

"Not that memorizing all the details is the main point," Daniel assured him. "But it does take some time and effort to become familiar with what's happening. The main point is what God is doing in history—that he's writing *his* story. If we want to understand the whole rest of the Bible, it pays to understand the people and the plot from the very beginning."

{ A Second Look at . . . Today's First Question: }
What's So Important About the Book of Genesis?

Genesis is the book of beginnings. It shows how deeply God longs to bless those who know and love him.

The key chapters in Genesis are 1–3, 12, 15, and 22. These chapters tell the accounts of Creation and the Fall, then give us highlights from the life of Abraham. Additional key passages include 11:1–9 (the Tower of Babel) and 18:16–19:29 (Sodom and Gomorrah).

The key individuals we'll meet in this survey are Adam and Eve, whom God made to begin the human race. We'll meet Abraham, whom God called to be "the father of all those who believe" (Rom. 4:11). We'll also meet Abraham's wife, Sarah, and their son, Isaac.

Other key individuals we'll meet later when we read the Bible in its entirety are Adam and Eve's first two sons, Cain and Abel (4:1–16); Enoch, a godly man whom God took to heaven before he died (5:21–24); Noah, whom God called to build the ark before the great Flood (6:1–9:17); and Abraham's first son, Ishmael (16:1ff.), who was not the son God promised. We'll also meet

Abraham's daughter-in-law, Rebekah, who married Isaac (24:1ff.); their sons, Jacob and Esau (25:19ff.); and Jacob's wives and twelve sons (29:1ff.), including Joseph, whom God used to save and prosper his extended family (37:1ff.).

Once you read the key chapters of Genesis, you'll be tempted to go back and read the whole book. This is one of the most popular books in the Bible. Enjoy! You can read Genesis three chapters a day in two and a half weeks. You may prefer to read it like a novel, however, in two or three sittings.

Because this book doesn't gloss over sin, some parts probably would be rated PG-13 or R for violence, sexuality, and other mature themes.

{Snapshot}

Genesis records the *genesis* of the human race (chapters 1–11), focusing on four events—Creation, the Fall, the Flood, and the Tower of Babel. Genesis also records the beginnings of the Israelite nation (chapters 12–50), focusing on four individuals—Abraham, Isaac, Jacob, and Joseph. Through this line of people, God's Son, Jesus Christ, would one day be born.

Of course, Genesis is only the first of the five books Moses wrote.

Four hundred silent years elapse between Genesis and the next book. During that time, the Israelites grow from a small clan (around seventy-five) to a small nation (approximately two million strong).

During that same time, the Egyptian pharaohs enslave the Israelites, who help build some of Egypt's great cities and monuments. The Israelites cry out to God for deliverance. At the right time, the Lord prepares a great (but unlikely) deliverer—Moses.

The events in the next four books of the Bible all take place within a forty-year span.

{ Today's Second Question: }
What's So Important About the Other Books of Moses?

In answering this question, it is helpful to look at an overview of the first five books of the Bible. This table illustrates their similarities and differences.

Book	Period of History	Key Individuals	Primary Focus

History begins with the creation of the world and humanity.

Book	Period of History	Key Individuals	Primary Focus
Genesis	Beginning of world until tribe of Israel moves to Egypt (c. 1800 BC)	Adam, Noah, Abraham, Isaac, Jacob, Joseph	Beginning of the human race; beginning of the Israelite nation

The Israelites are enslaved by the Egyptian pharaohs.

Book	Period of History	Key Individuals	Primary Focus
Exodus	The Israelite nation escapes from Egypt; God gives them the Ten Commandments and other laws (c. 1445 BC).	Moses, Aaron, Pharaoh	The Israelite nation emerges two million strong; God offers them the Promised Land and much more; the Israelites repeatedly turn from God.
Leviticus	God gives more laws on offering sacrifices for the people's sins (c. 1445 BC).	Moses, Aaron	The offer of atonement and forgiveness dominates this book.
Numbers	The Israelites wander in the wilderness for forty years (c. 1145 to c. 1406 BC).	Moses, Aaron	The Israelite nation continues to rebel against God; God raises up a new generation to enter the Promised Land.
Deuteronomy	Moses challenges the new generation to follow the Lord wholeheartedly (c. 1406 BC).	Moses, Joshua	The Israelite nation receives a second opportunity to obey the Lord and receive all that he has promised.

Moses dies and Joshua becomes Israel's new leader.

This opening section of Scripture is sometimes called the *Five Books of Moses*. It's also sometimes referred to as the *Law* or *Law of Moses*.

We've already looked at Genesis, so let's now take a quick look at the rest of the story!

Exodus tells how Israel became a nation. It reveals the amazing lengths to which God will go to save his less-than-perfect people.

The key chapters in Exodus are 1–5, 12–14, and 20. These chapters introduce Moses and Aaron, tell how God instituted the Passover and brought the nation of Israel out of slavery in Egypt, and record how God gave the Ten Commandments to Moses. Additional key passages include 6:1–11:10 (God sends terrible plagues on Egypt), 32:1ff. (the people turn from God, worship a golden calf, and endure a great plague), and 33:13–34:7 (the Lord reveals part of his glory to Moses).

The key individuals we'll meet in this survey are Moses, Aaron, and Pharaoh. We'll also briefly meet Moses's parents and his sister (2:1–10).

Other key individuals we'll meet later when we read the whole book of Exodus include Moses's sister, Miriam (especially see 15:1–21); his father-in-law, Jethro (especially see 18:1–27); and the skilled craftsmen Bezalel and Aholiab (especially see 35:30–36:2), whom God called to supervise the construction of the tabernacle, which the Israelites used to worship God for four hundred years.

You can read Exodus three chapters a day in two weeks.

Some sections probably would be rated PG-13 or R for violence, sexuality, and other mature themes.

{Snapshot}

Exodus records the miraculous account of how the Israelite nation *exited* from Egypt (chapters 1–18), focusing on four events: (1) the call of Moses, (2) the plagues on Egypt, (3) the Passover, and (4) the dramatic *exodus* from Egypt. Exodus also records how the Israelite nation received God's laws (chapters 19–40), focusing on three types of laws: general laws, tabernacle laws, and priesthood laws.

Leviticus explains the Old Testament sacrificial system. It shows God's extravagant offer of atonement and forgiveness when the Israelites sinned against him.

The key chapters in Leviticus are 1, 10, 16, and 25. These chapters introduce God's laws regarding sacrificial offerings, his requirement of holiness for every priest, his instructions for the Day of Atonement, and his laws regarding Sabbath years and Years of Jubilee. Additional key passages include Moses's consecrating Aaron and his sons (8:1–9:24), "Be holy, because I am holy" (11:44–45 NIV; 19:2; 20:7, 26; 21:8), and "Love your neighbor as yourself" (19:18, 34).

Only a few sections of this book contain narrative stories, so we won't meet anyone besides Moses, Aaron, and Aaron's sons during this survey. Other individuals we'll meet later when we read the whole book of Leviticus include a man who blasphemes against the Lord and is judged (24:10–16).

You can read the book of Leviticus in nine days. You may want to read it more quickly in one or two sittings. Instead of getting enmeshed in all the details of the Old Testament sacrifices, you may want to focus on the recurring themes of atonement and forgiveness.

Some sections of this book probably would be rated PG-13 or R for violence, sexuality, and other mature themes.

{Snapshot}

Leviticus details the many *levitical* laws about how the Israelites could approach God's holiness (chapters 1–10), focusing on five kinds of sacrificial offerings (which picture Jesus Christ's passion) and the commissioning of different types of *levitical* priests. Leviticus also records how the Israelites could walk with God in holiness (chapters 11–27), focusing on personal cleansing, the Day of Atonement, standards for the people and priests, seven feasts, and seasonal regulations.

Numbers tells the story of forty wasted years. It warns against the tragic consequences of rebelling against the Lord.

The key chapters in Numbers are 3–4, 6, and 11–14. These chapters record the commissioning of the priests (Levites), the instructions for taking a Nazirite vow (which John the Baptist did), a number of the Israelites' rebellious actions, and God's decision that the older generation couldn't enter the Promised Land.

Additional key passages include the dedication of the Levites (8:5–22), the second
Passover (9:1–14), the Lord's leading by a cloud (9:15–23), the rebellion of Korah
and others (16:1–50), Moses's sin (20:2–13), God's offer of salvation if individuals
trusted God and looked at a bronze snake on a pole (21:4–9; see also John 3:14–16),
and Moses's commissioning Joshua to lead Israel after he died (27:12–23).

The key individuals we'll meet in this survey include Moses, Aaron,
Aaron's sons, the Levite clan leaders Eldad and Medad (two of seventy
Israelite leaders), and Miriam, as well as Joshua, Caleb, and ten other spies.

Other individuals we'll meet later when we read the whole book of
Numbers include Israelite tribal leaders, Phinehas (grandson of Aaron), the
daughters of Zelophehad (who requested inheritance rights for women), and
a series of bad guys: Korah and his fellow conspirators, the kings of Sihon and
Og, Balak, and Balaam (a renegade prophet).

You can read Numbers three chapters a day in less than two weeks.

Some sections of this book probably would be rated PG-13 for violence,
sexuality, and other mature themes.

{Snapshot}

Numbers lists the *census* of the generation that left Egypt and of the
next generation that entered the Promised Land. This book records
how the Israelites prepared to enter the Promised Land (chapters
1–12), focusing on preparations at Sinai and the march to Kadesh-
Barnea. Numbers also records how the Israelites rebelled against the
Lord and wandered for forty years (chapters 13–36), focusing on the
spies' rebellion, the eventual death of the old generation, and the
preparations of a new generation who could enter the Promised
Land.

Deuteronomy offers the Israelites a second chance. It contains the last
words of Moses in the form of a deeply compelling sermon. In this sermon,
Moses recalls what the Lord has said to the new generation of Israelites and
then urges them to diligently seek God's blessings. How? By obeying God's
commands faithfully—unlike the previous generation.

The key chapters in Deuteronomy are 5–8, 28–31, and 34. These chapters present the heart of Moses's sermon and his appeal to choose God's blessings. They also record the installation of Joshua as Israel's new leader and Moses's death. Additional key passages include the declaration that the Lord alone is God (4:32–40), the repetition of the Ten Commandments (5:6–21), the command to love the Lord wholeheartedly (6:4–9; 10:12–13), the warning against false prophets (13:1–5), and the prophecy of the Prophet to come (18:15–19, speaking of Jesus Christ).

The key individuals we'll meet in this survey are Moses and Joshua.

Other individuals we'll meet later when we read the whole book of Deuteronomy include Moses's retelling of stories about the twelve spies, the kings of Sihon and Og, and others who rebelled against the Lord.

You can read the book of Deuteronomy three chapters a day in a week and a half. This book all takes place on a single day. So if you have time, try reading it in a single sitting. It's a powerful book!

Some sections of this book probably would be rated PG-13 for violence, sexuality, and other mature themes.

{Snapshot}

Deuteronomy records the *second* giving of the *Law* of God to the new generation of Israelites (chapters 1–28), focusing on a historical review, sermon by Moses, repetition of the Law, and listing of curses and blessings. Deuteronomy also records the covenant of God with the new Israelites (chapters 29–33), focusing on the covenant terms, installation of Joshua, final sermon and song by Moses, and Moses's death (chapter 34).

You can read all five books—Genesis through Deuteronomy—three chapters a day in two months. Or you can quickly survey these first five books of the Bible in a week and a half.

Why not invite several friends to join you? Select a comfortable and convenient place, day, and time when you can meet. Offer coffee, tea, or other favorite beverages.

Let the adventure begin!

{ Today's Third Question: }
What's So Important About the Old Testament Books of History?

In answering this question, it is helpful to look at an overview of these twelve books of the Bible. The following table illustrates their similarities and differences.

Book	Period of History	Key Individuals	Primary Focus
Between Moses and the Kings			
Joshua	The generation after Moses	Joshua, Caleb	The Israelites conquer and settle the Promised Land.
Judges	The three centuries after Joshua	Ehud, Deborah, Barak, Gideon, Jephthah, Samson	The Israelites repeat cycle of rebellion, political oppression, national repentance, divine intervention, peace, and rebellion.
Ruth	During the middle of Judges	Ruth, Boaz, Naomi	The Lord brings a Moabite woman into the genealogy of King David (and Jesus Christ).
From the Kings to the Exile (Historical Perspective)			
1 Samuel	The last judge and the first two kings of Israel	Samuel, Saul, Jonathan, David, Goliath	The Israelites plead for a king (Saul), who turns and rebels against the Lord; God selects a new king (David), whom Saul tries to kill.

Book	Period of History	Key Individuals	Primary Focus
2 Samuel	The reign of King David, Israel's greatest king	David, Bathsheba, Nathan, Absalom	Israel flourishes under David's rule until he sins; even though David repents, his family and the nation suffer greatly.
1 Kings	The reign of kings for 120 years after David	Solomon, Rehoboam, Asa Elijah, Jehoshaphat	After a time of national glory, Solomon rebels, his son splits the nation into two kingdoms, and the people spiral away from God; Judah repents repeatedly.
2 Kings	The reign of kings until both kingdoms were exiled	Elisha, Joash, Uzziah, Hezekiah Manasseh, Josiah	After further spiraling, Assyria conquers the kingdom of Israel; later, Babylonia conquers Judah.

From the Kings to the Exile (Priestly Perspective)

Book	Period of History	Key Individuals	Primary Focus
1 Chronicles	Genealogies from Adam to David; David's reign	Saul, David, Solomon	Israel flourishes during David's reign; he makes elaborate preparations to build the temple.
2 Chronicles	The reign of kings for nearly four centuries after	Solomon, Rehoboam, Asa, Jehoshaphat,	Israel splits into two kingdoms; the kingdom of Judah

Book	Period of History	Key Individuals	Primary Focus
	David	Joash, Uzziah, Hezekiah, Josiah, Cyrus king of Persia	repents repeatedly but continues spiraling; Babylonia conquers Judah.

After the Babylonian exile

Book	Period of History	Key Individuals	Primary Focus
Ezra	The return of Israelites to Judah after the exile	Zerubbabel, Ezra	Nearly fifty thousand Israelites return to Judah and begin rebuilding but are stopped; two generations later, more Israelites return and their leader, Ezra, sparks a national religious revival.
Nehemiah	About a century after the Babylonian exile ended	Nehemiah, Ezra	The Israelites finally rebuild the wall of Jerusalem and experience a national religious revival.
Esther	About seventy years after the Babylonian captivity ended	King Xerxes, Esther, Mordecai, Haman	God works behind the scenes to save the Israelites from an evil plot to annihilate them.

Four Hundred Silent Years

Between Moses and the Kings

Joshua is a book filled with promise. It describes how the Israelite nation finally entered, conquered, and settled in the Promised Land.

The key chapters are 1–6 and 23–24. These chapters describe the epic stories of Joshua's leading the people into the Promised Land and conquering the massive city of Jericho. They also record Joshua's final exhortations to the Israelites before he died many years later. Additional key passages include the Gibeonites' deceiving Joshua (9:3–27), the sun's standing still during a battle (10:12–14), Caleb's receiving a special inheritance (14:6–15; 15:13–19), and the high priest Phinehas's averting civil war (22:13–34).

The key individuals we'll meet in this survey are Joshua, two spies, Rahab, and the "commander of the Lord's army."

Other individuals we'll meet later when we read the whole book of Joshua include Achan, the Gibeonites, various enemy kings, Caleb, and Phinehas.

You can read Joshua three chapters a day in eight days.

Some sections of this book probably would be rated PG-13 for violence and other mature themes.

{Snapshot}

Joshua records how—under the leadership of Moses's right-hand man, *Joshua*—the Israelite nation entered (chapters 1–5), conquered (chapters 6–12), and occupied (chapters 13–22) the Promised Land. This book also records *Joshua's* stirring challenge to the people before he died (chapters 23–24). Like Moses, *Joshua* was a godly, upright man who ruled the people well. This book is the first of three set before the reign of Israel's kings.

Judges is a book filled with cycles of remorse and tragedy. It records how the Israelite people failed to drive out their remaining enemies, who seduced them to worship foreign gods and rebel against the Lord. As a result, the Israelites were repeatedly attacked, oppressed, and driven to their knees in despair.

The key chapters in Judges are 1–4 and 13–16. These chapters explain Israel's tragic cycles, tell accounts of the first few judges, and record the epic stories of the most famous of all the judges, Samson. Additional key passages include the accounts of Gideon (chapters 6–8) and Jephthah (11:1–12:7), and the appendices of some of the horrible atrocities that occurred during the days of the judges (chapters 17–21).

The key individuals we'll meet in this survey are Joshua, Caleb, Othniel, Ehud, Samson, and Delilah.

Other individuals we'll meet later when we read the whole book of Judges include Deborah, Barak, Jael, Gideon, Abimelech, Jephthah, Jephthah's daughter, Micah, and an unnamed Levite.

You can read Judges three chapters a day in a week.

Some sections of this book probably would be rated R for violence, sexuality, and other mature themes.

{Snapshot}

Judges records the repeated cycles that the Israelites went through during the reign of *judges* during three hundred years between the death of Joshua and the reign of Israel's last judge. Judges explains the background of this period (1:1–3:7) and the history of this period (3:8–16:31) and includes several appendices (17:1–21:25). Each cycle revolved around periods of rest, rebellion, retribution, repentance, restoration, rest, rebellion, and—well, you guessed it—the cycle continues. The appendices are pretty disturbing—definitely rated R.

Ruth is a wonderful story of redemption. In contrast with the book of Judges, it presents a story that figures prominently into the genealogy of Israel's greatest king. After the main character, Ruth, affirms her trust in the Lord God of Israel, she providentially is asked to marry a respected elder in the city of Bethlehem, later known as *the City of David*. Boaz "redeems" Ruth by "purchasing" the right to marry her from the closest kinsman. His redemption of Ruth pictures Jesus's redemption of us.

The key chapters in Ruth are, well, all four chapters!

The key individuals we'll meet are Naomi, Ruth, Boaz, and David.

You can read Ruth in a day.

This book probably would be rated PG.

{Snapshot}

Ruth tells a beautiful love story set during the days of the judges. This story explains the lineage of Israel's greatest king, David, through his great-grandmother, *Ruth*. Through this same line the Savior would be born eleven hundred years later! The book of Ruth is the last of three set before the reign of Israel's kings.

From the Kings to the Exile (Historical Perspective)

First Samuel is filled with important transitions. It records the end of the period of the judges, the reign of Israel's first king, God's decision to start a new dynasty, and the resulting conflict between the first two kings.

The key chapters in 1 Samuel are 7–10, 12, 15–20, 28, and 31. These chapters introduce Samuel's deliverance of Israel from the Philistines, Samuel's appointment of Saul as king of Israel many years later, Samuel's farewell address to the nation, Saul's rebellion against the Lord, God's selection of David as Israel's new king, David's triumph over the giant Goliath, Saul's fanatical opposition against David, Saul's desperate meeting with a medium, and Saul's death. Additional key passages include the account of Samuel's birth and childhood (chapters 1–3), accounts of David's sparing Saul's life twice (chapters 24 and 26), and Samuel's death (25:1).

The key individuals we'll meet in this survey are Samuel, Saul, Jonathan, David, and the medium at Endor.

Other individuals we'll meet later when we read the whole book of 1 Samuel include Samuel's parents, Eli the priest, Michal, Ahimelech, Doeg the Edomite, Nabal, Abner, and Abigail.

You can read 1 Samuel three chapters a day in a week and a half. Some sections of this book probably would be rated PG-13 or R for violence, sexuality, and other mature themes.

{Snapshot}

First Samuel is the first in a series of four books telling about the reign of Israel's (and Judah's) kings in a straightforward historical manner. This book records the story of Israel's last judge, *Samuel*, and Israel's first king, Saul (the people's choice). At first Saul was halfhearted in his allegiance to God. Sadly, he began rebelling against the Lord, so God selected a new king, a young shepherd and musician named David.

Second Samuel is filled with contradictions. It presents the reign of King David at its best—and worst.

The key chapters in 2 Samuel are 5–8, 11–13, 15, and 18. These chapters present David's coronation as king of all twelve tribes of Israel, the establishment of Jerusalem as his capital and place of worship, the Lord's covenant with David, and David's military victories. They also recount David's sins against Uriah and Bathsheba; his repentance; the tragic rape of his daughter Tamar; and his son Absalom's vengeance, exile, usurping of the throne, military defeat, and death.

Additional key passages include David's lament over the deaths of Saul and Jonathan (1:17–27), David's kindness to Jonathan's son (9:1–13), the Israelites' battles against the Philistine giants (21:15–22), David's song of praise (22:1–51), David's last written words (23:1–7), David's "mighty men" (23:8–39), and David's census and the plague that followed (24:1–25), which the Lord used to identify the location of the temple that David's son Solomon would build.

The key individuals we'll meet in this survey are David, King Hiram, Uzzah, Obed-Edom, Michal, Nathan, Joab, Bathsheba, Uriah, Solomon, Absalom, Tamar, Amnon, Jonadab, Ahithophel, Ittai, Abiathar, Zadok, Hushai, Ahimaaz, and a man from Cush.

Other individuals we'll meet later when we read the whole book of 2 Samuel include Saul, Jonathan, an Amalekite, Ishosheth, Asahel, Abner, Abishai, Recab, Baanah, Mephibosheth, Ziba, Shimei, Shobi, Makir, Barzillai, Sheba, and Rizpah.

We'll also meet some of David's "mighty men," including Jashobeam, Eleazar, Shammah, and Benaiah, who won epic battles.

Finally, we'll meet Araunah the Jebusite, on whose threshing floor David offered sacrifices to stop a terrible plague.

You can read 2 Samuel three chapters a day in eight days.

Some sections of this book probably would be rated R for violence, sexuality, and other mature themes.

{Snapshot}

Second Samuel records the reign of David, God's choice for king. David was "a man after My [God's] own heart" (Acts 13:22). The Lord promised that one of his descendants would be the Savior of the world. Nevertheless, David later sinned terribly and seriously jeopardized the security of the nation. The consequences of David's failures would be felt for generations to come.

First Kings is filled with both greatness and tragedy. It records Israel's rise to its greatest glory, its rebellion against the Lord, its division into two kingdoms, and the growing paganism of both kingdoms. In fact, the northern kingdom, Israel (ten tribes), never experiences a spiritual revival. Only the southern kingdom, Judah (two tribes), shows any hope of fully returning to the Lord.

The key chapters in 1 Kings are 3, 6–12, 17–19, and 21. These chapters record the Lord's granting great wisdom to Solomon, Solomon's building the temple and his palace, Solomon's dedicating the temple, the Lord's speaking to Solomon again, Solomon's wealth and splendor, Solomon's many wives, Solomon's decision to turn away from the Lord and worship his wives' false gods, the division of the nation after Solomon's death, and the northern kingdom's development of its own pagan religion. These chapters also record the dramatic ministry of the prophet Elijah, who fearlessly confronted one of Israel's worst royal couples, King Ahab and Queen Jezebel.

Additional key passages include further descriptions of Solomon's prosperity and wisdom (4:20–34), the prophet Ahijah's condemnation of Israel's paganism (14:6–16), the southern kingdom's embrace of paganism (14:21–24), and King Asa's efforts to drive paganism out of Judah (15:9–15).

The key individuals we'll meet in this survey are Solomon, two prostitutes, Pharaoh's daughter, Huram, King Hiram, and the queen of Sheba. We'll also meet Solomon's enemies, including Hadad the Edomite, Pharaoh, Rezon, and Jeroboah. Later in the book, we'll meet Elijah, King Ahab, the widow at Zarephath, Obadiah, Queen Jezebel, Elisha, and Naboth (chapters 13–22).

Other individuals we'll meet later when we read the whole book of 1 Kings include King David, Abishag, Adonijah, Joab, Abiathar, Nathan, Bathsheba, Zadok, Benaiah, Barzillai, Shimei, Ahijah, Rehoboam, Abijam, Asa, Nadab, Baasha, Elah, Zimri, Omri, Ben-Hadad, Jehoshaphat, Micaiah, and Ahaziah.

You can read 1 Kings three chapters a day in a week.

Some sections of this book probably would be rated PG-13 for violence, sexuality, and other mature themes.

{Snapshot}

First Kings records the reign of Solomon, David's son, who took the nation to new heights, then rebelled against the Lord and sowed the seeds of the nation's destruction. After his reign, the nation split into two *kingdoms*. The two kingdoms often were at odds with each other. Only the southern kingdom of Judah had any good *kings*.

Second Kings ends with destruction. It tells the story of the increased paganism of Israel, which the Assyrian Empire destroyed in 722 BC, and the downward spiral of Judah, which the Babylonian Empire took into captivity in 586 BC.

The key chapters in 2 Kings are 1–2, 6–7, 11–12, and 17–23. These chapters tell about the final days of the prophet Elijah, the ministry of the prophet Elisha, the religious revival in Judah under an old high priest and boy king, and the destruction of the kingdom of Israel for its unrepentant paganism. These chapters also present accounts of the reigns of a series of very good and very bad kings of Judah.

Additional key passages include the account of Babylon's conquering and ruling over Judah (24:10–17) and Judah's rebelling against Babylon only to be destroyed (24:20–25:21).

The key individuals we'll meet in this survey are Elijah, Ahaziah, Elisha, Ben-Hadad, four lepers, Athaliah, Jehoiada, Joash, Hoshea, Hezekiah, Sennacherib, Isaiah, Manasseh, Amon, Josiah, Hilkiah, Jehoahaz, and Jehoiakim.

Other individuals we'll meet later when we read the whole book of

2 Kings include Joram, a widow, the woman from Shunem, Naaman, Gehazi, Hazael, Jehoram, Jehu, Jezebel, Jehoash, Amaziah, Jeroboam II, Uzziah, Zechariah, Shallum, Menahem, Pekahiah, Pekah, Jotham, Ahaz, Nebuchadnezzar, Jehoiachin, Zedekiah, and Gedaliah.

You can read 2 Kings three chapters a day in eight days.

Some sections of this book probably would be rated PG-13 for violence and other mature themes.

{Snapshot}

Second Kings records how the northern *kingdom* of Israel (ten tribes) and later the southern *kingdom* of Judah (two tribes) were decimated and taken into captivity by Assyria and Babylon respectively. This book concludes the first series of four books using a straightforward historical approach to review the four centuries when Israelite *kings* ruled Israel (and Judah).

From the Kings to the Exile (Priestly Perspective)

First Chronicles begins with an elaborate family tree and ends with a focus on worship. It presents the genealogies from Adam to David and his descendants down to the Babylonian captivity. It then presents highlights from the reign of King David, with an emphasis on his preparations for the building of the temple of God in Jerusalem.

The key chapters in 1 Chronicles are 15–17, 21–22, and 28–29. These chapters give a fresh perspective on David's reign. They tell how he brought the ark of the covenant to Jerusalem, decided to build the temple, and received a covenantal promise from the Lord. They also tell how David sinned by taking a census, repented before the Lord, stopped a plague, selected the location for the temple, instructed Solomon on how to build it, gave a final address to the nation, and commissioned the nation to help Solomon build the temple.

Additional key passages include the prayer of Jabez (4:9–10), the death of Saul (10:1–14), and the death of Uzzah when he touched the ark of God (13:1–14).

The key individuals we'll meet in this survey are David, Zadok, Abiathar, Michal, Nathan, Joab, Araunah the Jebusite, and Solomon.

Other individuals we'll meet later when we read the whole book of 1 Chronicles include Saul, David's "mighty men," and Uzzah.

You can read 1 Chronicles three chapters a day in ten days. If you decide to skim chapters 1–9 (genealogies) and chapters 23–27 (duties of the temple staff), however, you can easily read 1 Chronicles in one sitting.

A few sections of this book probably would be rated PG for violence. For the most part, however, this book skips over David's sins—in keeping with the book's focus.

{Snapshot}

First Chronicles is the first of two books telling about the reign of Israel's (and then Judah's) kings from a priestly perspective. This book goes back to the beginning, *chronicling* the names of the descendants of Adam to Abraham to David to the Babylonian exile. It then retells the story of King David's reign, with a focus on all of his preparations for temple worship.

Second Chronicles ends with the destruction of Judah. It tells about the reign of Solomon, records how the nation split into two kingdoms, and then recounts how the kings of Judah either followed or (more often) rebelled against the Lord. The book ends with the Babylonians' taking the people of Judah into captivity—and includes a postscript about their release seventy years later.

The key chapters in 2 Chronicles are 5–10, 14–16, 24–26, and 29–35. These chapters present the story of Solomon's rise and fall. They then show how Judah's best kings almost always fell away from the Lord toward the end of their lives, just like their ancestor Solomon. The conclusion? No matter how fervently you and I may have worshiped the Lord, we need to be very careful not to drift away from the Lord in the future.

Additional key passages in 2 Chronicles include the account of how King Jehoshaphat's faith saves Judah from destruction (20:1–30), how the Babylonians overthrow Judah and rule it (36:5–10), and how Judah rebels and is destroyed (36:11–19).

The key individuals we'll meet in this survey are Solomon, the queen of Sheba, Rehoboam, Jeroboam, Asa, Joash, Jehoiada, Amaziah, Uzziah, Hezekiah, Sennacherib, Isaiah, Manasseh, Josiah, Hilkiah, and Neco.

Other individuals we'll meet later when we read the whole book of 2 Chronicles include Hiram, Shemaiah, Abijah, Jehoshaphat, Ahab, Micaiah, Jehoram, Ahaziah, Athaliah, Jotham, Ahaz, Jehoahaz, Jehoiakim, Jehoiachin, Zedekiah, Nebuchadnezzar, and Cyrus.

You can read 2 Chronicles three chapters a day in less than two weeks.

Some sections of this book probably would be rated PG-13 for violence and other mature themes.

{Snapshot}

Second Chronicles retells the story of the rise, decline, and eventual destruction of the kingdom of Judah, which was ruled by descendants of David—from Solomon to Zedekiah—for four centuries. Both 1 and 2 Chronicles are written from a priestly point of view. It is possible Ezra may have written them while in exile, before he led a large group back to rebuild Jerusalem and help revive the nation of Israel.

The Babylonian Exile

Ezra begins the story of rebuilding. It tells its story using three empires as a backdrop. Over the course of two centuries, these empires have ruled the regions east of the Mediterranean Sea. The Assyrians destroyed Israel. The Babylonians crushed Judah. The Persians, however, do the opposite: they grant permission for the exiled Jewish people to return to Judah. Nearly fifty thousand Israelites return under Zerubbabel. Two generations later, thousands more return under Ezra.

The key chapters in Ezra are 3 and 6–7. Chapter 3 tells how Zerubbabel rebuilt the altar and began rebuilding the temple only to stop (536 BC). Chapter 6 tells how years later the Persian king Darius ordered the rebuilding of the temple, which was finally completed (515 BC). Chapter 7 tells how Ezra received the assistance of King Artaxerxes to completely restore the worship of the Lord in the temple (458 BC).

Additional key passages include Ezra and others' fasting and praying for three days before safely journeying to Jerusalem (8:21–32), Ezra's publicly mourning over the sins of the Jewish people (9:3–10:1), and the people's agreeing to repent of their sin of intermarriage with pagans (10:2–17).

The key individuals we'll meet in this survey are Zehozadak, Zerubbabel, Darius, Cyrus, Tattenai, Shethar-Boznai, Artaxerxes, and Ezra. Other individuals we'll meet later when we read the whole book of Ezra include Jeshua, Xerxes, Haggai, Zechariah, and Shecaniah.

You can read Ezra three chapters a day in three days.

Some sections of this book probably would be rated PG for violence and other mature themes.

{Snapshot}

Ezra is the first of three history books set after the Babylonian captivity. This book presents the story of the first wave of Israelites who returned to Jerusalem immediately after their release from captivity (chapters 1–6), and then of a second wave who returned eighty years later under the leadership of the great scribe *Ezra*, whose family had preserved the Scriptures. *Ezra's* great-grandfather, Hilkiah, rescued the only surviving copy of God's Word after the death of terrible King Manasseh (see 2 Kings 22:3–23:25; 2 Chron. 34:14–33).

Nehemiah finishes the story of rebuilding. It records how Nehemiah rebuilt the walls around Jerusalem and helped lead a religious revival, working closely with Ezra.

The key chapters in Nehemiah are 1–2, 4, and 6. These chapters record how Nehemiah earnestly prayed, asked the king for support, led a delegation to Jerusalem, inspected the situation, challenged the people to rebuild the city's walls, faced fierce opposition, and yet completed the wall in less than two months.

Additional key passages include the Water Gate revival (8:1–11), the celebration of the Festival of Shelters (8:13–18), the prayer of the Levites (9:5–37), and the dedication of Jerusalem's walls (12:27–43).

The key individuals we'll meet in this survey are Nehemiah, Artaxerxes, Sanballat, Tobiah, Geshem, and Shemaiah. Other individuals we'll meet later when we read the whole book of Nehemiah include Hanani, Hananiah, Ezra, and Eliashib.

You can read Nehemiah three chapters a day in four days.

Some sections of this book probably would be rated PG for limited violence.

{Snapshot}

Nehemiah records the story of the great leader *Nehemiah*, who mobilized the Israelites to rebuild the walls of Jerusalem, repent of their sins, and worship the Lord. *Nehemiah* focuses on the rebuilding of the wall (1:1–7:73), the repentance of the people (8:1–12:26), and the disciplining of the people (13:1–31).

Esther is an intriguing story of deliverance. It tells how one woman rescued the Jewish people throughout the Persian Empire from a plot to exterminate them.

The key chapters in Esther are 1–4. These chapters tell how King Xerxes chose a young Jewish woman, Esther, as his new queen. Esther's cousin, Mordecai, learns of a plot against the king's life—then later of a plot against his own life and the lives of every Jewish person in the Persian Empire. Esther agrees to risk her life by speaking to the king and revealing her Jewish identity.

Additional key passages include, well, the rest of the story!

The key individuals we'll meet in Esther are Xerxes, Vashti, Mordecai, Esther, and Haman.

You can read Esther three chapters a day in three days. Then again, you may want to read it all in one sitting!

Some sections of this book probably would be rated PG-13 for violence, sexuality, and other mature themes.

> **{Snapshot}**
>
> Esther tells the intriguing story of how God worked behind the scenes to save the Israelite people scattered throughout the known world. Had they not been saved, the line of the Messiah would have been wiped out. Although God isn't mentioned by name, Hebrew readers can find the Lord's name—YHWH—repeated in acrostic form four times in the original text.

❑ ❐

You can read Joshua through Esther three chapters a day in two and a half months. You can carefully survey all twelve of these Old Testament history books in one month.

After you finish the first half of the Old Testament, get ready for some completely new kinds of books in the second half!

Ahead, you'll enjoy five kinds of Hebrew literature:

- a full-length drama
- 150 worship lyrics
- hundreds of wise sayings
- a reflective homiletic essay
- a sensuous love song

So whatever you do, don't stop reading!

how do i read the middle of
MY BIBLE?

A cold rain drove against the courtyard bricks and whipped up against the windows at every fit of wind. Kendall found herself staring out at the rhythmic pounding of raindrops, distracted from the conversation between Daniel, Erik, and Maria. Sure, she'd managed to squeeze in her Bible reading this week between classes, papers, and an extra heavy internship assignment. And even though reading portions of the Psalms felt comforting, it seemed as if she were reading someone's spiritual diary. She couldn't quite get it to fit.

What bothered her, she decided, was more in her head. Trying to figure out life and the human condition was not getting her anywhere. Maybe she thought too much. All this analyzing was exhausting. Maybe she needed to skip reading the news blogs for a while and tune out the political debates in class. But surely there were *some* answers to her questions! She didn't need to have them all—just a few.

"Hey, Kendall." Maria nudged her. "Are you okay?"

"Sorry," Kendall murmured. "I guess my mind is in the Twilight Zone. What have I missed while I was gone?"

"Not much," Maria assured her. "Daniel was preaching on the foreshadowing of the Messiah in the Psalms—and it's quite normal to fall asleep during a sermon!"

Kendall laughed. "Did I miss the singing of the 'Ave Maria' too?"

"Maybe that's what brought you back! Seriously, after my 'sermon,' Erik and Maria were reading verses they had highlighted from the Psalms. Did you have any you wanted to share?" Daniel asked.

Kendall surveyed the small group through her wire-rimmed glasses. How much did they really want to know? "I hope it's okay, but the Psalms we chose to read just didn't do it for me. I'm not in this sensitive, emotional state—I'm just trying to figure out life and how it works and how God fits into it. I'm having a hard time getting my head wrapped around it all."

To her relief, none of the others seemed shocked at her less-than-spiritual answer. Kendall continued, "And Job didn't do much for me either. I've heard that it's this great piece of literature, but reading only the opening and closing chapters of the book was a little confusing. Not to mention trying to figure out what the deal was with his friends. I mean, what was that all about?"

"That's why it will be so great when we actually read the entire Bible through after Christmas," Maria answered. "Reading the book and getting the whole picture is going to make so much more sense."

{ Today's First Question: }
What's So Important About the Book of Job?

"Exactly," Daniel agreed. "But let's get back to Kendall's questions. If we figure out what the book of Job is all about, we might just find some answers to the other questions too."

"Okay," Erik said, "what *is* so important about the book of Job?"

"First, my apologies again that we only had time to read a few chapters. That's definitely unfair! Job is a brilliant piece of Hebrew poetry—a drama, really. The most amazing thing about it is that it deals with the overarching question that each person faces at some point in his life: *Why do really horrible things happen to truly good people?*"

"So is the answer in the chapters we didn't read?" Kendall asked.

"The Bible isn't a formula book, Kendall. God doesn't usually give out the answers like that. Take Job—he was a real person with real feelings, a real family, real friends, and real problems. We're sitting in the front row watching his life—thousands of years afterward—and as with any good play, we get hit in the gut with the point when we least expect it."

"So what was the point?"

"I'm getting there. The twist in the book of Job is that there is actually another play going on behind the scenes of the main play. Or vice versa. In the bigger play, the main characters are God and Satan. Satan appears to dare or bet God that people will love and serve him only for what they get out of it. God seems to take the crazy risk of letting Job prove otherwise."

Kendall was completely sincere in her response. "Fun for Job. Not everyone can be as 'patient as Job,' as they say. And not everyone gets a happy ending. I don't see how this answers the question of pain and suffering."

"Like I said, I wish I could give you a formula for that, but God doesn't work that way. He's much more honest, and he knows the full answer is much deeper than we can comprehend. But there are truths—principles—to give us a foundation for our lives so our faith isn't just about jumping over a cliff in the dark and hoping God catches us."

"Like what—from the book of Job, I mean?"

"Like the fact that there is a whole other universe going on out there. A universe where spiritual beings interact with each other—and interact with us. Like the fact that our actions actually have impact on that spiritual world. How I respond to pain and suffering may actually *mean* something to God and the angels. Like the fact that I don't have all the facts! Job really thought God was out to get him, when God was really cheering him on all the time!"

"So how does that work in the real world, Daniel?"

Daniel hesitated before stepping out of his usually cognitively oriented self. "I'm not saying I'm any expert on suffering, and I'm sure I have a lot more ahead of me in my life, but I really did wrestle with all this when my cousin died. I was fourteen, and we were best buddies. Tim was a year older than me, so he was always teaching me something new. He's the one who taught me how to dive and fish and rappel. He's the one who challenged me to read God's Word every day. One day he was rock climbing. Even though he was roped up and doing everything right, a snow bridge collapsed and he fell into a crevasse and died instantly."

Kendall asked quietly, "What made it make sense for you, Daniel?"

Daniel thought it over. "Besides all the heaven stuff, just knowing that God was bigger than I—that's the point he's making to Job when he's giving him that nature talk at the end of the story. I saw a poster at the time that said, 'If God were small enough to fit in my brain, he wouldn't be big enough to solve my problems.' It was like knowing somebody had the answer—even if it wasn't me. In the story, Job never got the answer either. And I just accepted that God was good, even if all the stuff happening around me wasn't. God loved Job, he believed in him, he blessed him. I learned that being loved by God didn't equal having life go well. So I guess I just trusted God more even if I didn't understand anything any better."

Maria nodded. "You know, my brother is on the street on drugs. It eats up my parents every day—me too—but it drove us to God as well. We don't like what's happening, but we would have ignored God otherwise. We just keep trusting because we know God knows the end of the story."

Kendall sighed. "I wish I could use those as arguments in my world history class. I guess you just have to experience it yourself."

"Or let the Holy Spirit use God's Word to make it real." Erik had been silent through the whole conversation, so his succinct observation brought each person to a moment of silence. Someone opened the nearby door, and a blast of wind rushed in. Everyone around the table turned to look. Outside, the rain continued its futile assault against the coffee shop.

{ A Second Look at . . . Today's First Question: }
What's So Important About the Book of Job?

Job is an elaborate play. It is an intense drama with a purpose. The story is real, the characters are true to life, and the question they debate is timeless: *Why in the world does God allow horrible things to happen to good people?* The ultimate answer isn't apparent until Jesus Christ's passion many, many hundreds of years later.

The key chapters are 1–3 and 38–42. These chapters introduce Job and his family, tell how Job lost almost everything, and begin a series of poetic laments and debates between Job and a small handful of his "wisest" friends. Then, toward the end of the book, God comes on the scene, silences everyone, demonstrates his sovereignty over all of creation, accepts Job's repentance, and prospers Job once again.

Additional key passages include verses about righteousness in God's eyes (4:17; 8:3), about the hope of life after death (14:14; 19:25–26), and about wisdom (11:7; 28:28).

When reading the book of Job, it's important to keep in mind that most of the book is a series of monologues by Job and his friends (chapters 3–37). Notice how careful they are not to interrupt each other. But they sure don't hesitate to argue with each other! In fact, Job's first three friends level many false accusations against him in their mistaken belief that personal sin is the chief or sole cause of suffering.

The key individuals we'll meet in this survey are God, Satan, Job, Job's children, and Job's wife. Other individuals we'll meet later when we read the whole book of Job include Job's friends Eliphaz, Bildad, and Zophar (who debate with Job in chapters 4–25) and Job's younger friend Elihu (who argues with the other three friends in chapter 32 and then presents his case against Job in chapters 33–37).

You can read Job three chapters a day in two weeks. You may prefer to read it like a full-length play, however, in one or two sittings.

Because this book doesn't gloss over human tragedy and anguish, Job probably would be rated PG-13.

Two questions to ponder as you read this first wisdom book:

1. After losing everything, Job worships God. While debating with his friends, however, Job sometimes speaks out against God in angry and bitter tones. Later, God rebukes Job. Is it ever right to be angry at God? Why or why not?

2. When the first three friends reach Job, they sit in silence for a week and don't say a word. As soon as Job begins to express his sorrow, however, they begin debating rigorously and condemning him. Later, God rebukes these three friends. Is it ever right to judge a friend who is suffering? Why or why not?

{Snapshot}

Job is the first of five Old Testament books of wisdom. The story of *Job* explores why the godly suffer. The book refutes three errors. First, it refutes Satan's assumption that people exercise righteousness only for reward (we should obey God for his sake alone). Second, it refutes Job's friends' assumption that only sin causes suffering (the more you sin, the more you suffer). Third, it refutes Job's assumption that some individuals aren't sinners (seen in Job's repentance, 40:4 and 42:6).

It's possible that a millennium or more may separate the story of Job and the writing of the next four Old Testament books.

Many clues within the book of Job suggest that Job may have lived before the time of Abraham. In any case, it's possible that he wasn't an Israelite. Still, it's clear that Job worshiped and revered the Lord God.

For the most part, Psalms, Proverbs, Ecclesiastes, and Song of Songs were written during the lifetimes of history's two most famous Israelites, David and Solomon.

{ **Today's Second Question:** }
What's So Important About the Rest
of the Old Testament's Wisdom Books?

In answering this question, it is helpful to look at an overview of all five Old Testament wisdom books. Each book represents a different literary form. The following table illustrates their similarities and differences.

Book	Type of Literature	Period of History	Primary Themes
Job	Dramatic poetry	Set c. 2000 BC; possibly written in final form many years later	Human suffering can have a divine purpose that we may not know this side of heaven.
Psalms	Poetry	Most written c. 1000 BC but range from c. 1450 BC to c. 450 BC	In 70 percent, the psalmists call out to God in the midst of crisis; many others offer praise to the Lord and his Word; some include prophecies about the coming Messiah.
Proverbs	Proverbs	Most written before 930 BC	Fear the Lord and seek wisdom with all your heart.

Book	Type of Literature	Period of History	Primary Themes
Ecclesiastes	Prose with wisdom poetry interspersed	Written before 930 BC	Apart from the Lord, life is meaningless.
Song of Songs	Prose with romantic poetry interspersed	Written before 930 BC	The beauties of romantic and marital love

This section of the Bible is sometimes called the *Books of Poetry.* It's also sometimes referred to as the *Books of Wisdom.*

We've already looked at Job, so let's take a quick look at these other books. Because truth is timeless, these books still have much to say to us today!

Psalms is an extensive collection of worship lyrics. Like any good collection of songs, these 150 psalms cover a wide variety of themes. Some present important truths. Some urge the congregation to praise God. Many call on the Lord to deliver the psalmist from the midst of his overwhelming circumstances. Others call on God to judge evildoers and vindicate the godly. A few confess the psalmist's sins against the Lord. More than a dozen psalms, like Psalm 22 for example, describe the coming Son of David, the Lord Jesus Christ.

The most famous chapters in this book are 1, 8, 19, 23 (the most loved, memorized, and quoted chapter in all Scripture), 51, 100, 103, and 139. These chapters speak of the value of Scripture, the dignity of humanity, and the praiseworthiness of God. They also speak of God's intimate knowledge of who we are, his gracious provision of all we need, and the joys of his forgiveness.

Other famous chapters include Psalm 119 (the longest psalm, with 176 verses on the value of Scripture), Psalm 117 (the middle chapter of the Bible and the shortest psalm with two verses of praise), Psalm 95 (used as a call and guide to worship from ancient times), Psalms 63 and 42 (describing the psalmist's intense desire to follow the Lord), Psalm 22 (foreshadowing Jesus Christ's passion a thousand years ahead of time), and Psalms 16:8–11; 17:15; and 23:6 (picturing the hope we have beyond the grave).

The key word in the Psalms, "praise," appears more than 210 times, compared with fewer than 130 occurrences in all the rest of Scripture combined. (Psalm 88 is the only psalm that ends without some sense of praise or hope in God.)

The word "selah" appears seventy-one times throughout Psalms, perhaps indicating that the reader should pause, keep reading, call the congregation to respond, or signal the musicians to play louder—the meaning is very uncertain.

Psalms 25, 34, 37, 111, 112, 119, and 145 are examples of acrostic Hebrew poetry. In these seven psalms, the first letter of each line, verse, or stanza begins with a successive letter of the Hebrew alphabet. Their acrostic nature isn't readily apparent in English translations. Psalms 9–10 form a broken acrostic, in keeping with their theme (about the psalmist's world falling apart as he waits for the Lord to appear and deliver him from his enemies).

When reading the book of Psalms, it's important to keep in mind that Hebrew poetry focuses on thought rhythms, not word rhymes. These thought rhythms in the second part of each verse echo, expand, or contrast the idea presented in the first statement. Most of the time, it's easy to follow what the psalmist is saying. Don't read too much into the second statement, however, if he's simply repeating what he just said. Also, remember that the psalmists frequently use figures of speech, historical and literary allusions, and other poetic devices.

The primary author of Psalms is David, who is credited with writing seventy-three of them. Actually, make that seventy-five, because Acts 4:25 confirms that David wrote Psalm 2, and Hebrews 4:7 confirms that he wrote Psalm 95.

Other authors include Moses (one), Solomon (two), Asaph (twelve), the sons of Korah (eleven, including Psalm 88, which is attributed specifically to Heman the Ezrahite, plus possibly Psalm 43), and Ethan the Ezrahite (one).

You can read Psalms five songs a day in a month.

Some sections of Psalms 1–150 probably would be rated PG for brief descriptions of violence.

Two questions to ponder as you read this second wisdom book:

1. Psalms 1, 15, 26, 101, and 112 speak of the wisdom of living a godly life. The first and last are anonymous. The other three were written by David, who passionately loved God but also broke half of the Ten Commandments. Was David spiritually schizophrenic? Why or why not?

2. In Psalms 38 and 51, David speaks of the terrible anguish he has experienced because he initially refused to confess his sins to the Lord. He may have written both of these psalms after his terrible actions against Uriah and

Bathsheba (2 Sam. 11). Did God abandon David during this period of time? Why or why not?

{Snapshot}

Psalms is an amazing collection of Hebrew *songs*. Traditionally, Psalms is divided into five books: Book I, Psalms 1–41; Book II, Psalms 42–72; Book III, Psalms 73–89; Book IV, Psalms 90–106; Book V, Psalms 107–150. Each book ends with a brief doxology (except Book V, where Psalm 150 serves as a conclusion to the Psalms). Book V features several shorter collections of psalms. Ezra may have been the final editor.

Proverbs is an extensive collection of wise sayings. It urges readers to fear the Lord and seek wisdom with all their hearts. It also urges readers to apply wisdom in scores of everyday situations.

The key chapters in Proverbs are 1–3. These chapters exalt the virtues and benefits of honoring God in heaven and actively acquiring wisdom for life here on earth.

Practical themes explored in Proverbs include the path to prosperity and a happy heart, the folly of spending time with the wrong crowd and committing adultery, and the value of a good wife and godly children and grandchildren.

When reading the book of Proverbs, it's important to keep in mind that each statement is a truism. That is, each proverb states how life usually works. None of the proverbs, however, presents a divine promise you and I can claim. For instance, Proverbs 3:7–8 says we can gain renewed health and vitality if we fear the Lord and turn our backs on evil. That's usually true! But it's not a promise from God that he will always heal us if we're ill.

You can read Proverbs three chapters a day in a week and a half. Or, since it has thirty-one chapters, you may want to read a chapter of Proverbs each day for a month. There's plenty of wisdom to absorb!

Some sections of this book probably would be rated PG-13 for descriptions of violence, sexual sins, and other mature themes.

Two questions to ponder as you read this third wisdom book:

1. Later in life, Solomon played the fool. He turned his back on the Lord, openly worshiped false gods, and sowed the seeds of his nation's destruction. Does the end of his biography discredit the value of what he wrote earlier in life? Why or why not?

2. Several sections of Proverbs were written by other men, at least two of whom may have been foreigners. Does the fact that these writers weren't Israelites, and had no apparent spiritual qualifications, discredit the value of what they wrote? Why or why not?

> **{Snapshot}**
>
> The primary author of Proverbs is Solomon. The first part of this book presents a series of lengthy wise sayings (chapters 1–9). Most of the book presents hundreds of very short sayings (10:1–22:16; chapters 25–29). One section contains a series of paragraph-sized sayings on thirty topics (22:17–24:22), plus a few bonus topics (24:23–34). The end of the book presents several more lengthy wise sayings (chapters 30–31) attributed to several other authors.

Ecclesiastes is a reflective essay full of wise sayings. It explores the nagging, age-old question, what is the meaning of life? This question is considered from the perspective of someone "under the sun," i.e., someone thinking in natural, not supernatural, terms. So instead of expounding on divinely revealed truths recorded in Scripture, Solomon's reflections in this essay are decidedly earthbound.

Solomon probably wrote this book at least halfway through his reign as king of Israel. Sometime after he finished this book, Solomon began drifting further and further from God.

The key chapters in Ecclesiastes are 1–5 and 12. These chapters describe Solomon's search for meaning in a variety of spheres of life, to no avail. In many ways, this essay reads like a philosophical sermon. The final chapter describes Solomon's conclusions: fear God and obey his commands from youth to old age. If only Solomon had heeded his own counsel!

Additional key passages in the second half of Ecclesiastes include

Solomon's remarks on the contemplation of the day of one's death (7:1–4), on God's blessings on those who fear him (7:18; 8:12–13), on the fact that everyone sins (7:20), and on the importance of working hard and using wisdom to succeed (9:10; 10:10).

When reading the book of Ecclesiastes, it's important to keep in mind that this book doesn't contain divine revelations. But it does allude to Solomon's basic beliefs in God's justice, graciousness, sovereignty, omniscience, transcendence, revelation, mystery, creative power, and eternal nature.

You can read Ecclesiastes three chapters a day in four days. Since it's a short essay, however, you may want to read it in a single sitting.

Because this book describes violence and other hardships of life and is rather pessimistic, Ecclesiastes probably would be rated PG-13.

Two questions to ponder as you read this fourth wisdom book:

1. Solomon may have assumed his readers knew God and were well-versed in his commands. If his primary readers were Israelites, do you think a majority of them got the point of this book? Why or why not?

2. Solomon may have distributed copies of this book to foreign visitors as a means of provoking their interest in the God of Israel. If his primary readers were non-Israelites, do you think a majority of them got the point of this book? Why or why not?

> **{Snapshot}**
>
> Ecclesiastes is a short homiletic essay. The theme of the book is the meaninglessness of life "under the sun," apart from God. This theme is developed in the introduction (chapter 1), discourse (chapters 2–6), reflections (chapters 7–11), and conclusion (chapter 12). If anyone could preach this sermon, it was Solomon, the one man in all of history who had everything: tremendous power, unlimited wealth, great wisdom, beautiful women, fabulous building projects, and international acclaim.

Song of Songs is a passionate duet. It celebrates the joys of romantic and marital love.

The key chapters in Song of Songs are 1–2. These chapters interweave the sensuous lyrics of a young woman and man. We also hear a few lines from a chorus of women. (Toward the end of the book, we also hear a few lines from the young woman's brothers.)

Key themes we hear repeated in Song of Songs include a heartfelt declarations of the other person's beauty (1:15; 4:1, 7; 7:6) and the warning not to awaken love until the time is right (2:7; 3:5; 8:4).

Some of the most famous lines include these:
- I am the rose of Sharon. (2:1)
- He brought me to the banqueting house. (2:4)
- Catch us the foxes. (2:15)
- My beloved is . . . / Chief among ten thousand. (5:10)
- I am my beloved's. (6:3; 7:10)
- Love is as strong as death. (8:6)
- Make haste, my beloved. (8:14)

When reading Song of Songs, it's important to keep in mind that it's a love song. So as with the book of Ecclesiastes, you won't find much formal theology in this book. While this duet isn't an allegory per se, many believe it pictures something of the Lord's love for his people.

You can read Song of Songs three chapters a day in three days. Because it's so short and so passionate, however, you may want to read it in one sitting. Over the millennia, the Jewish people have publicly read Song of Songs during their first and greatest festival of the year, Passover.

Since this book is full of sensuous language, Song of Songs probably would be rated PG-13 or R.

Two questions to ponder as you read this fifth and final wisdom book:

1. Song of Songs doesn't talk much about the Lord, worship, or other religious subjects. The same is true of Ruth and Esther, two other Old Testament books in which the main character is a young woman. It's also true of Proverbs and Ecclesiastes, in which the main character is a middle-aged man. What do you think about Scripture's taking page after page to talk about nonreligious themes? What do you think is God's purpose (or purposes) for these sections of Scripture?

2. Song of Songs talks a lot about love, romance, marriage, and sex. We've already seen all four subjects come up repeatedly in the first half of the Old

Testament, and we'll see them again as we continue reading through the Bible. Why do you think that Scripture takes page after page to talk about issues of sexuality?

{Snapshot}

Song of Songs is also called the *Song of Solomon*. Many biblical scholars believe that Solomon wrote this duet when he had sixty wives and eighty concubines and was taking new wives (6:8). They don't all agree, however, on the identity of the second main character—the man. Some believe Solomon was writing about himself. Others believe Solomon is describing someone else, a shepherd, who wins the young woman's heart despite Solomon's best efforts. Either way, this book presents a passionate story of true love.

❏ ❏

You can read Job through Song of Songs three chapters a day in two months. You can carefully survey all five of these Old Testament wisdom books in ten days.

After you finish this section, get ready for a completely new series of books in the last part of the Old Testament.

Ahead, you'll explore seventeen amazing prophetic books written hundreds of years before Jesus Christ. These books accurately predicted

- the futures of Israel and Judah,
- the futures of four world empires, and
- the coming of the Messiah, Jesus Christ.

These prophets clearly stated

- when and where Jesus Christ would be born,
- what Jesus would do during his ministry,
- what Jesus's message of good news would be,
- how much Jesus would suffer during his passion,
- that Jesus would rise from the dead, and
- that Jesus would sit at God the Father's right hand.

So be sure to keep reading!

how do i read the last part of
THE OLD TESTAMENT?

Maria sat cross-legged on the stiff plastic chair—not very comfortably, but as good as things were going to get in the busy Laundromat on a Saturday afternoon. Her dark hair hung over her face as she bent over her Bible.

Caught up in what she was reading, Maria let out an exclamation of joy—and was equally startled when the woman near her let out an expletive.

Jerking up her head, Maria met the gaze of the young woman sitting directly across from her. "I'm sorry," Maria said. "Did I bother you? I'm afraid I get involved in reading and forget that I'm in public."

The woman waved her hand. "Don't worry about it. It just startled me, and I'm already in a bad mood. But that's my problem, not yours."

Maria laid her Bible beside her and leaned toward the woman. "I'm sorry to hear you're having a bad day. My name's Maria. Besides making a lot of noise when I read, I actually have a lot of practice listening to people. What's bothering you? Can I ask your name?"

The woman seemed unsure whether to be irritated, confused, or relieved by this personal offer. "Nice to meet you, Maria. I'm Andrea. I'm not sure I'm used to unloading to strangers, but I do appreciate your concern."

Andrea's eyes picked up on the Bible next to Maria. "You know, I try to avoid personal conversations with religious people. There's a lot of bad stuff in my life, and God hasn't seemed to notice, much less do anything about it. Too bad he wasn't as interested in me as you seem to be."

Now Maria was fully engaged. Her dark eyes met Andrea's clouded blue eyes and carried the impact of her words. "Andrea, I meant what I said about listening. I volunteer at the women's shelter, and I doubt you have a story that's any worse than anything some of those women have lived through. I'm here for the duration of the rinse cycle and an hour of drying. If you don't have to go anywhere, the least I can do as a human being is be interested in you. The best I can do as a 'religious person' is represent God well by showing I care."

Andrea shifted her gaze away and looked as if she wished she could leave, but she couldn't come up with a polite excuse quickly. "Forget what I said about God, okay? But if you're really bored, I could give you something to listen to—I mean, if you're really that desperate. Is this free counseling or something?"

Maria laughed. "No, don't call it that! Do you think I want to get sued? Just tell me your story—tell me a little about yourself. Later I can tell you a little about myself to make it even."

"Like you're used to stories of little girls so neglected and abused that they end up on the street? That's not exactly how my story plays out."

Maria kept quiet and Andrea kept going. "I've managed to keep my life together just fine, thanks, but no thanks to God. My parents took me to church and I learned all the God stuff, but it was all talk. At home, my father went into fits of rage and my mom just went into hiding. She'd leave for days at a time to get away from him, but she'd leave me there to take it—in more ways than one.

"God never did rescue me from that hell. I finally just left. Trouble is, every man since then has been just the same—a total user. I woke up this morning and realized I'd done it again. My boyfriend just moved in last month, and I've already caught him with someone else. I wish I could say I felt like God cared—but I don't."

Maria spoke in a whisper. "Andrea, I can assure you that God does more than just care about you—he can completely relate. You might think you learned the Bible when you were a little girl, but no one probably told you about the parts where God is writhing in anguish because he's given his heart away and he's been rejected. You know how that feels, don't you?"

"Yeah, you're right. Where was that on my Sunday school memory list?"

"Right here where I'm reading in the Prophets. How are you and I supposed to read this last part of the Old Testament? As if it's all about God getting mad at people for breaking a few rules? No! Instead, it's about God being angry because his people have betrayed him and destroyed each other in the process. It's about God longing to have his beloved people back."

Maria paused briefly. "Listen to this, Andrea. This is what I was reading when I accidentally startled you earlier. It's from the book of Isaiah."

{ **Today's First Question:** }

What's So Important About Isaiah?

Maria picked up her Bible and read Isaiah 41:10–13.

> Fear not, for I am with you;
> Be not dismayed, for I am your God.
> I will strengthen you,
> Yes, I will help you,
> I will uphold you with My righteous right hand.
>
> Behold, all those who were incensed against you
> Shall be ashamed and disgraced;
> They shall be as nothing,
> And those who strive with you shall perish.
> You shall seek them and not find them—
> Those who contended with you.
> Those who war against you shall be as nothing,
> As a nonexistent thing.
> For I, the LORD your God, will hold your right hand,
> Saying to you, "Fear not, I will help you."

Maria looked up. "Can you believe it, Andrea? He knows your hurt. He hasn't abandoned you. He really does care."

Andrea shook her head. "I can't believe I've gotten this involved in a conversation with you. I must be getting desperate."

Maria reached across the aisle, and her hands encircled Andrea's. "Just promise me that you won't be afraid to let God speak to you. Your life isn't finished yet, and he has a lot more to say."

{ **A Second Look at . . . Today's First Question:** }

What's So Important About Isaiah?

Isaiah urges readers to humble themselves before "the Holy One of Israel." The key chapters are 1–2, 6, 40, and 52–55. These chapters begin with

God's stern warning to the kingdoms of Israel and Judah. In chapter 6, Isaiah flashes back to recall how God called Isaiah to serve as his prophet. Later God offers words of consolation to those who have gone into exile and then describes the long-awaited Savior, Jesus Christ.

Famous verses in Isaiah include:

- Your sins . . . shall be as white as snow. (1:18)
- The nations . . . shall beat their swords into plowshares. (2:4)
- Holy, holy, holy, is the Lord of hosts. (6:3)
- Lord, I'll go! Send me. (6:8 NLT)
- Behold, the virgin shall conceive and bear a Son. (7:14)
- For unto us a Child is born, / Unto us a Son is given. (9:6)
- You will keep him in perfect peace, / Whose mind is stayed on You. (26:3)
- These people . . . / . . . honor Me with their lips, / But have removed their hearts far from Me. (29:13)

Famous verses in the latter part of Isaiah include:

- Those who wait on the Lord / Shall renew their strength. (40:31)
- When you pass through the waters, / I will be with you. (43:2)
- How beautiful . . . / Are the feet of him who brings good news. (52:7)
- All we like sheep have gone astray. (53:6)
- So are My ways higher than your ways. (55:9)
- All our righteousnesses are like filthy rags. (64:6)

When reading the book of Isaiah, it's important to keep three things in mind:

1. Chapters 7–35 contain extensive warnings of God's pending judgment of many other nations, not just Israel and Judah. These nations included Assyria, Philistia, Moab, Aram, Cush, Egypt, Babylon, Edom, Arabia, and Tyre.

2. Chapters 36–39 feature a historical interlude describing key events during the reign of King Hezekiah in Judah. These chapters talk about how the Lord spared Judah from the Assyrians and how the Lord predicted that the Babylonians would conquer Judah instead (more than a century later).

3. Chapters 40–66 weren't written for Isaiah's day. Near the end of this book, the Lord aptly promises, "Before they call, I will answer" (65:24). That promise is especially true of these chapters! They were written to bring much-needed comfort and consolation when the Jewish exiles in Babylon

called out to the Lord—more than a century after God inspired Isaiah to write these Scriptures.

Once you read the key chapters in Isaiah, you'll be tempted to go back and read the whole book. You can read it three chapters a day in three weeks. You may prefer to read it as you would a mystery, however, in three or four sittings.

Because this book doesn't gloss over sin and judgment, some parts probably would be rated PG-13 for violence.

Isaiah 52:13–53:12 describes the passion of Jesus Christ in amazing detail and speaks of his resurrection. Look for other messianic prophecies throughout this book!

{Snapshot}

Isaiah *prophesied* about Jesus Christ seven centuries before his birth. So remarkable are Isaiah's prophecies that the New Testament makes a special note that "he was given a vision of the Messiah's glory" (John 12:41 NLT). Matthew, Mark, Luke, John, Peter, Paul, and Jesus himself quoted from Isaiah's prophecies scores of times—far more than all the other Old Testament prophetic writings put together.

At least five other prophetic books were already penned by the time Isaiah finished his book around 680 BC. Approximately two and a half centuries later, the last pages of the Hebrew Scriptures were penned and the Old Testament canon was complete.

The Old Testament's books of prophecy are usually divided into two sections. The first section, Isaiah through Daniel, is commonly referred to as the Major Prophets. The second section, Hosea through Malachi, is often called the Minor Prophets. As we've mentioned, they're "minor" only because of their length, not because of their content or value!

Whether long or short, these prophetic books are all compelling. Imagine God telling you about things to come! Most important, these books repeatedly urge readers to stop rushing headlong to disaster—and instead turn from their sins, turn back to God, and enjoy his blessings.

{ **Today's Second Question:** }
What's So Important About the Other Old Testament
Prophetic Books?

In answering this question, it is helpful to look at an overview of seventeen Old Testament prophetic books. The following table illustrates their similarities and differences.

Book	Period of History	Occasion	Primary Themes
		Major Prophets	
Isaiah	740–681 BC	The kingdom of Judah's increasing paganism would end with the Babylonian captivity.	The first half of the book warns of judgment; the second half offers hope, consolation, salvation, and amazing prophecies about the coming Messiah.
Jeremiah	626–586 BC	Judah's refusal to repent would end in total disaster when the Babylonians destroyed the nation.	The theme of returning to God and repenting before it's too late recurs nearly fifty times.
Lamentations	586 BC	The destruction of Jerusalem	This book contains the lyrics of a series of sad, sorrowful songs crying out to the Lord in grief and pain.
Ezekiel	593–571 BC	The Babylonian captivity	The theme "Know that I am the LORD" appears dozens of times; the phrase speaks of the Lord's great desire to love and be loved by his people.

Book	Period of History	Occasion	Primary Themes
Major Prophets			
Daniel	605–537 BC	The Babylonian captivity	The narrative and prophetic sections of this book both emphasize that God is directing all of history and in the end will judge each of us.
Minor Prophets			
Hosea	c. 745–710 BC	The kingdom of Israel was acting increasingly unfaithful to God (committing spiritual adultery).	The theme of returning and repenting recurs nearly two dozen times.
Joel	c. 800 BC	A serious drought and locust plague	This book urges readers to repent, for "the day of the LORD" is on its way.
Amos	c. 755 BC	The kingdoms of Israel and Judah and surrounding nations faced God's coming judgment.	This book urges readers to pursue righteousness and justice, since "faith without works is dead."
Obadiah	Uncertain	The nation of Edom faced God's coming judgment.	This ungodly nation would be completely destroyed.
Jonah	c. 760 BC	The city of Ninevah faced God's coming judgment.	This ungodly city repented, so the Lord didn't judge it, proving his love for all peoples, not just the Jews.

Book	Period of History	Occasion	Primary Themes
Micah	750–686 BC	The kingdom of Israel faced God's coming judgment.	This book urges readers to pay attention to the Lord's warnings of impending disaster.
Nahum	663–612 BC	The city of Ninevah faced God's coming judgment again.	More than a century after it turned to God, this city had grown extremely corrupt and evil.
Habakkuk	c. 607 BC	The kingdom of Judah faced God's coming judgment.	This book features a unique dialogue between the Lord and the best-known "doubting Thomas" of the Old Testament.
Zephaniah	c. 640–630 BC	Judah and other surrounding nations faced God's coming judgment.	This book urges readers to repent, for "the day of the LORD" is on its way.

After the Babylonian captivity

Book	Period of History	Occasion	Primary Themes
Haggai	520 BC	The temple hadn't been rebuilt yet.	This book urges readers to repent of their mis-placed priorities and rebuild the temple.
Zechariah	520–518 BC	The temple hadn't been rebuilt yet.	This book urges readers to repent, finish rebuild-ing the temple, and look forward to the coming Messiah.

Book	Period of History	Occasion	Primary Themes
Malachi	c. 430 BC	The Israelites had drifted away from the Lord once again.	This book urges readers to quit playing games with God.

Four Hundred Silent Years

This section of the Bible is usually called the *Books of Prophecy*. But "prophecy" doesn't mean their focus was always foretelling the future. They often reminded readers of what the Lord had done in the past and urged them to live for God in the present.

We've already looked at Isaiah, so let's take a quick look at the other sixteen prophetic books. Listen to what the Lord has to say to *you*!

Major Prophets

Jeremiah urges readers to come back to the Lord—before it's too late.

The key chapters in Jeremiah are 1–5. These chapters describe Jeremiah's call to be a prophet and the first series of messages that the Lord gives him.

Famous verses in Jeremiah include these:

- They . . . [say], "Peace, peace!" / When there is no peace. (6:14)
- Has this house, which is called by My name, become a den of thieves in your eyes? (7:11)
- Do not pray for this people. (7:16; 11:14; 14:11)
- The summer is ended, / And we are not saved! (8:20)
- Let him who glories glory in this, / That he understands and knows Me. (9:24)
- Can a leopard change his spots?/ In the same way . . . you cannot change and do good. (13:23 NCV)
- The heart is deceitful above all things. (17:9)

Other famous verses include these:

- [The Lord's] word burns in my heart like a fire. (20:9 NLT; see 23:29)
- Take your choice of life or death! (21:8 NLT)
- I will place a righteous Branch on King David's throne. (23:5 NLT; see 30:9; 33:14–26)

- For I know the plans I have for you. (29:11 NLT)
- I have loved you, my people, with an everlasting love. (31:3 NLT)
- I will make a new covenant. (31:31)

When reading the book of Jeremiah, it's important to keep in mind that it's not arranged in chronological order. After Jeremiah wrote all his prophecies over the course of several decades, he rearranged them thematically. So you'll find all of his prophecies against foreign nations near the end of his book in chapters 46–51. Everything before that focuses on Judah's pending destruction. The appendix, chapter 52, includes a historical report of Babylon's conquering Jerusalem and taking the people into captivity.

You can read Jeremiah three chapters a day in two and a half weeks.

Some sections of this book probably would be rated PG-13 for violence and other mature themes.

In 23:6, Jeremiah predicts that King David's descendent will be the Savior.

{Snapshot}

Jeremiah is known as the "weeping prophet." Like Isaiah, he wrote his lengthy book before the fall of Judah. Unlike Isaiah, he suffered ongoing personal rejection and persecution. During the course of his ministry, Jeremiah dictated new prophecies to his scribe, Baruch. After they had compiled many of them, King Jehoiakim burned the scroll (Jer. 36:21–25). Jeremiah immediately dictated all of the prophecies again—and a few new ones!

Lamentations records the lyrics of a series of sad, sorrowful songs that Jeremiah wrote after Jerusalem was destroyed.

The key chapter in Lamentations is 3. This chapter describes Jeremiah's faith in God (3:21ff.) despite all the tragedy, heartache, pain, and grief that he has suffered and witnessed in Jerusalem's streets.

Famous verses in Lamentations include these:

- Behold and see / If there is any sorrow like my sorrow. (1:12)
- The LORD has caused / The appointed feasts and Sabbaths to be forgotten in Zion. (2:6)

- I am the man who has seen affliction. (3:1)
- This I recall to my mind, / Therefore I have hope. (3:21)
- The LORD is good to those who wait for Him. (3:25)
- Turn us back to you, O LORD, and we will be restored. (5:21)

When reading the book of Lamentations, it's important to keep in mind that it is a superb set of Hebrew poems often referred to as *dirges, laments,* or *funeral songs.* The first four of these carefully and beautifully crafted poems were written as acrostics (using the twenty-two letters of the Hebrew alphabet). These poems weren't written in a day!

You can read Lamentations three chapters a day in two days. Or you may want to read it in a single sitting. Just be sure to take enough time to absorb what Jeremiah is saying!

Some sections of this book probably would be rated PG-13 for violence and other mature themes.

{Snapshot}

Lamentations is a *dirge,* a poetic expression of Jeremiah's grief after Judah's capital city was decimated. Jeremiah writes as an eyewitness to the horrible atrocities his people suffered at the hands of the invading Babylonian soldiers.

Ezekiel urges readers to know that Yahweh is the Lord.

The key chapters in Ezekiel are 1–3, 18, and 33. These chapters describe Ezekiel's first visions of God and his calling to serve as a "watchman." God made it very clear that his prophetic ministry was a matter of life and death.

Additional key passages include Ezekiel's visions of God's departing glory (8:4; 9:3; 10:4, 18–19; 11:22–23; but also see 43:2–5), the Lord's warnings that he will judge the people for their actions (7:3, 9, 27; 18:30; 24:14; 33:20; 36:19; 39:24), and God's promises to restore his people if they repent (11:16–20; 18:31; 36:26–28; 43:11).

Famous verses in Ezekiel include these:

- The fathers have eaten sour grapes, / And the children's teeth are set on edge. (18:2)

- I have no pleasure in the death of one who dies. . . . Turn and live!
  (18:32; see 33:11)
- I sought for a man among them who would . . . stand in the gap. (22:30)
- I Myself will search for My sheep and seek them out. (34:11)

When reading the book of Ezekiel, it's important to keep in mind that he wrote the last section (chapters 40–48) more than a dozen years after Jerusalem's fall. Ezekiel describes a vision of a massive new temple being built—and filled with the Lord's glory—if only the exiled Jewish people would truly repent (43:11). Sadly, that didn't happen.

You can read Ezekiel three chapters a day in sixteen days.

Some sections of this book probably would be rated PG-13 or R for violence, graphic sexual descriptions, and other mature themes.

In 37:24–25, Ezekiel prophesies that the Messiah will be David's son and a king.

{Snapshot}

The book of Ezekiel features signs, visions, direct prophecy, parables, poems, proverbs, and conditional promises to urge the people of Judah to repent and know the Lord. It also features an account of how the Lord transported Ezekiel from Babylonia back to Jerusalem on September 17, 592 BC (chapters 8–11). It was an intense experience Ezekiel never forgot!

Daniel urges readers to remember that God is directing all of human history and in the end will judge each of us.

The key chapters in Daniel are 1–2 and 4–6. These chapters tell the epic stories of Daniel's dramatic encounters with three of the most powerful rulers of the known world between 605 and 537 BC.

In chapter 3, Daniel tells another epic story about three of his closest friends—Shadrach, Meshach, and Abed-Nego.

In chapters 7–12, Daniel presents an astounding series of prophecies about the Babylonian, Medo-Persian, Greek, and Roman empires. These prophecies supplement what Daniel already has told Nebuchadnezzar and Belshazzar, the first and last rulers of the Babylonian Empire.

When reading the book of Daniel, it's important to keep in mind that he starts the book as a young man and wraps up the book nearly seventy years later. You'll need to keep a wide spectrum of portraits of Daniel in your mind's eye. He wasn't a young man, for instance, when he was thrown into the lions' den. Just the opposite—Daniel was well past eighty years old.

You can read Daniel three chapters a day in four days.

Some sections of this book probably would be rated PG for mature themes.

In 7:13–14, Daniel vividly portrays the promise of the coming of the "Son of Man."

{Snapshot}

Daniel is the last major prophet. While his book is relatively short, it's probably the best-known prophetic book. The first half contains a series of fascinating narratives focused on God's glory. The second half contains a series of prophecies about human history, counting down to the days of the coming Messiah.

Because these next twelve books are relatively short, we'll keep each synopsis as concise as possible. There's something for you in every book!

Minor Prophets

Hosea urges readers to come back to the Lord—before it's too late.

The key chapters in Hosea are 1–4. These chapters explain how Hosea's unfaithful wife, Gomer, is a picture of the spiritual unfaithfulness of the Israelites and the profound lovingkindness of God.

Key verses in Hosea include these:

- It shall be said to them, / "You are sons of the living God." (1:10)
- I will also cause all her mirth to cease, / Her feast days, / Her new moons, / Her Sabbaths— / All her appointed feasts. (2:11)
- Come, and let us return to the Lord. (6:1)
- Let us know, / Let us pursue the knowledge of the Lord. (6:3)
- But like men, they transgressed the covenant; / There they dealt treacherously with Me. (6:7)

- They return, but not to the Most High. (7:16)
- They sow the wind, / And reap the whirlwind. (8:7)
- Plow up the hard ground of your hearts, for now is the time to seek the Lord. (10:12 NLT)

When reading the book of Hosea, it's important to keep in mind that his wife became a prostitute and that some of her children apparently were fathered by other men. Hosea adopted those children and later redeemed Gomer from slavery.

You can read Hosea three chapters a day in five days.

Some sections of this book probably would be rated PG-13 or R for sexuality and other mature themes.

Hosea 11:1 foretells that Jesus will return from Egypt (this was fulfilled when he was still a young boy).

{Snapshot}

Hosea is the first of the Minor Prophets. Hosea called the kingdom of Israel to repentance before its fall. Hosea's theme is the enduring love of God despite his people's spiritual idolatry and adultery. This theme is portrayed against the backdrop of Hosea's enduring love for his unfaithful wife.

Joel urges readers to repent, for "the day of the LORD" is on its way. The key chapter in Joel is 2. This chapter warns of coming judgment, calls the people to repentance, declares the Lord's promise of restoration, and speaks of the day when the Lord will give the Holy Spirit to his people.

Key verses in Joel include these:

- Whoever calls on the name of the Lord / Shall be saved. (2:32)
- Beat your plowshares into swords / And your pruning hooks into spears. (3:10)
- There are huge numbers of people in the Valley of Decision. (3:14 NCV)

When reading the book of Joel, it's important to keep in mind that his prophecies address events in his own day, other events during the founding of the church, and still other events at the climax of history.

You can read Joel in one day.

Some sections of this book probably would be rated PG-13 for descriptions of violence and other mature themes.

{Snapshot}

Joel warned the kingdom of Judah of coming judgment. The setting of his prophecies is a terrible drought and locust plague.

Amos urges readers to pursue righteousness and justice.

The key chapter in Amos is 3. This chapter describes God's coming judgment on the kingdom of Israel.

Key verses in Amos include these:

- Can two walk together, unless they are agreed? (3:3)
- Prepare to meet your God. (4:12)
- Hate evil, love good; / Establish justice in the gate. (5:15)
- But let justice run down like water, / And righteousness like a mighty stream. (5:24)
- I will send a famine . . . of hearing the words of the Lord. (8:11)

When reading the book of Amos, it's important to keep in mind that his opening two chapters begin with God's judgments on Israel's neighbors, getting closer and closer until God announces his judgments on Judah and Israel.

You can read Amos three chapters a day in three days.

Some sections of this book probably would be rated PG-13 for descriptions of violence and other mature themes.

In 9:11–12, Amos declares that Gentiles will believe in the coming Messiah.

{Snapshot}

Amos warned the kingdom of Israel that faith without works is dead. He spoke out strongly against corrupt worship and social injustice.

Obadiah warns of the Lord's coming judgment on the nation of Edom. The key verses in Obadiah are these:

- The pride of your heart has deceived you, / You who dwell in the clefts of the rock. (1:3)
- You will really be ruined! (1:5 NCV)
- But on Mount Zion there shall be deliverance, / And there shall be holiness. (1:17)
- And the kingdom shall be the LORD's. (1:21)

When reading this very short book, it's important to keep in mind that the sins of the Edomites included acting arrogantly, deserting the kingdom of Judah, plundering Judah's wealth, killing those who tried to escape, and handing over survivors to Judah's enemies.

Other important Scriptures about Edom include Numbers 20:14–22; Psalm 137:7; Isaiah 21:11–12; 34:5–10; Jeremiah 49:7–22; Lamentations 4:21–22; Ezekiel 25:12–14; 35:1–15; Amos 1:6, 9, 11–12; and Malachi 1:2–4.

Some sections of Obadiah probably would be rated PG-13 for descriptions of violence and other mature themes.

{Snapshot}

Obadiah's prophecy was fulfilled to the last detail. The nation of Edom disappeared; only its abandoned ruins remained.

Jonah urges readers to embrace the fact that God loves the world and wants everyone to believe in him. Surprisingly, Jonah is the last person in the world who wants to hear this message. Even so, his book is one of the world's best-known and best-loved Bible stories.

The key chapter in Jonah is 1. In this chapter God calls Jonah to preach to the people of Nineveh, Jonah decides to run from God, and he ends up in the belly of a great fish for three days.

Key verses in Jonah include these:

- His psalm of repentance inside the fish (2:1–9)
- His prophecy: "Forty days, and Nineveh shall be overthrown!" (3:4)

- The king's declaration: "Who can tell if God will turn and relent, and turn away from his fierce anger?" (3:9)
- The result: "Then God saw their works, that they turned from their evil way; and God relented from the disaster that He had said He would bring upon them." (3:10)
- Jonah's lament: "Was not this what I said when I was still in my country? . . . I know that You are a gracious and merciful God, slow to anger and abundant in lovingkindness." (4:2)

When reading the book of Jonah, it's important to keep in mind that it's not a fable. Even the Lord Jesus spoke of Jonah's three days in the fish as a historical fact (Matt. 12:39–41).

You can read Jonah in a day.

Some sections of this book probably would be rated PG for limited violence and predictions of disaster.

Jonah 1:17 foreshadows the fact that the Messiah will be in the grave for three days and nights.

{Snapshot}

The book of Jonah tells how the city of Nineveh repented before God's judgment fell. This story is a dramatic reminder of God's desire that none perish but that all come to repentance (2 Pet. 3:9).

Micah urges readers to pay attention to the Lord's warnings of impending judgment.

The key chapters in Micah are 1–2. These chapters speak of the sins and rebellion of Israel and Judah, of the certainty of God's judgment, of Micah's deep sorrow and mourning, and of the Lord's promise of future restoration of the remnant who are left.

Key verses in Micah include these:

- Listen! (1:2; see also 3:1, 9; 6:1, 2, 9)
- For her wounds are incurable. (1:9)
- But you, O Bethlehem Ephrathah, / Though you are little among the

thousands of Judah, / Yet out of you shall come forth to Me / The One to be Ruler in Israel. (5:2)

- He has shown you, O man, what is good; / And what does the LORD require of you / But to do justly, / To love mercy, / And to walk humbly with your God? (6:8)
- You will give truth to Jacob / And mercy to Abraham. (7:20)

When reading the book of Micah, it's important to keep in mind that Micah was a contemporary of Isaiah. Like Isaiah, Micah doesn't hesitate to denounce the corrupt rulers, priests, false prophets, and others who filled the kingdoms of Israel and Judah. Like Isaiah, Micah pictures the Lord putting his people on trial. And like Isaiah, Micah contrasts the paganism of his day with the glorious future ahead.

You can read Micah three chapters a day in two days.

Some sections of this book probably would be rated PG for descriptions of violence and other mature themes.

In 5:2, Micah says the Messiah will be born in the city of Bethlehem.

{Snapshot}

The book of Micah has been called a "little Isaiah." Micah warned the people of Israel and Judah of the consequences of their rebellion against God. His prophecies also speak of the birthplace of the coming Messiah and his future reign on earth.

Nahum warns of the Lord's coming judgment on the city of Nineveh.

The key chapter in Nahum is 1. This chapter describes how awesome the Lord is and how wrong Nineveh is to continue to rebel against him.

Key verses in Nahum include these:

- The LORD is slow to anger and great in power. (1:3)
- The LORD is good, / A stronghold in the day of trouble; / And He knows those who trust in Him. (1:7)
- What do you conspire against the LORD? / He will make an utter end of it. (1:9)

When reading the book of Nahum, it's important to keep in mind that his warnings come more than a century after the capital of Assyria repented in response to the preaching of Jonah. Sadly, the city slowly grew more corrupt than ever.

You can read Nahum in a day.

Some sections of this book probably would be rated PG-13 for descriptions of violence and other mature themes.

{Snapshot}

Nahum foretold God's coming judgment on the city of Nineveh. His prophecies were fulfilled in dramatic fashion in 612 BC.

Habakkuk urges readers to continue trusting the Lord when evil overruns the world.

The key chapter in Habakkuk is 1. This chapter describes a unique dialogue between the Lord and the best-known "doubting Thomas" of the Old Testament.

Key verses in Habakkuk include these:

- I will stand my watch / And set myself on the rampart, / And watch to see what He will say to me. (2:1)
- The just shall live by his faith. (2:4; see Rom. 1:17; Gal. 3:11; Heb. 10:38)
- For the earth will be filled / With the knowledge of the glory of the Lord, / As the waters cover the sea. (2:14; see 3:3)
- In wrath remember mercy. (3:2)
- Though the fig tree may not blossom . . . / Yet I will rejoice in the Lord. (3:17–18)

When reading the book of Habakkuk, it's important to keep in mind that he wasn't surprised when God said he would judge his people. But he was shocked when the Lord said he would ask the wicked Babylonians, the new superpower of the ancient world, to ransack their kingdom.

You can read Habakkuk in a day.

Some sections of this book probably would be rated PG-13 for descriptions of violence and other mature themes.

{Snapshot}

Habakkuk upheld the integrity of God despite his plan to use a foreign nation to judge the kingdom of Judah. His dialogue with God is a dramatic reminder that the Lord isn't afraid of our toughest questions.

Zephaniah urges readers to repent, for "the day of the LORD" is on its way.

The key chapter in Zephaniah is 3. This chapter speaks of Jerusalem's rebellion, punishment, redemption, and future restoration.

Key verses in Zephaniah include these:

- Be silent in the presence of the Lord GOD; / For the day of the LORD is at hand. (1:7)
- Seek the LORD. . . . / It may be that you will be hidden / In the day of the LORD's anger. (2:3)
- For the LORD their God will intervene for them, / And return their captives. (2:7)
- The LORD . . . will do no unrighteousness. / Every morning He brings His justice to light; / He never fails. (3:5)

When reading the book of Zephaniah, it's important to keep in mind that the sins of Judah included prolific wickedness, rampant idolatry, astrology, child sacrifice, anarchy, shamelessness, pride, and complete indifference to the things of the Lord.

You can read Zephaniah in a day.

Some sections of this book probably would be rated PG-13 for descriptions of sin and violence.

{Snapshot}

Zephaniah warned the kingdom of Judah and other nations of God's coming judgment. His repeated use of the phrase "the day of the LORD" echoes the older book of Joel.

Haggai urges readers to repent of their misplaced priorities.

Key verses in this short book include these:

- Consider your ways! (1:5, 7; see 2:15, 18)
- "Be strong, all you people of the land," says the LORD, "and work; for I am with you." (2:4; see 1:13)
- Once more . . . I will shake heaven and earth. (2:6; see 2:21)
- "I will fill this temple with glory," says the LORD of hosts. (2:7)
- The glory of this latter temple shall be greater than the former. (2:9)

When reading the book of Haggai, it's important to keep in mind that Haggai was the first prophet to declare the word of the Lord after the Babylonian exile. The Lord gave Haggai a series of five urgent messages for the leaders of the Jewish nation.

You can read Haggai in a day.

Some sections of this book probably would be rated PG for mature themes.

{Snapshot}

Haggai called God's people to finish building the new temple after their return from exile. He rebuked them for their self-absorbed materialism and failure to do what God said. Haggai praised God when the people repented and went to work. They finished the temple less than five years later!

Zechariah urges the people to repent, finish building the temple, and look forward to the coming Messiah.

The key chapters in Zechariah are 1–2. These chapters contain the first two messages and first three visions that Zechariah received from the Lord. They emphasize God's concern for the Jewish people during their exile and his promise to restore and bless their nation.

Key verses in Zechariah include these:

- "Return to Me," says the LORD of hosts, "and I will return to you." (1:3)
- "Not by might nor by power, but by My Spirit," / says the LORD of hosts. (4:6)

- Who has despised the day of small things? (4:10)

Other key verses that contain messianic prophecies include:

- Rejoice greatly, O daughter of Zion! / Shout, O daughter of Jerusalem! / Behold, your King is coming to you; / He is just and having salvation, / Lowly and riding on a donkey, / A colt, the foal of a donkey. (9:9)
- They weighed out for my wages thirty pieces of silver. (11:12)
- And the LORD said to me, "Throw it to the potter"—that princely price they set on me. (11:13)
- Then they will look on Me whom they pierced. Yes, they will mourn for Him as one mourns for his only son. (12:10)
- In that day a fountain shall be opened for the house of David . . . for sin and for uncleanness. (13:1)
- Strike the Shepherd, / And the sheep will be scattered. (13:7)
- And the LORD shall be King over all the earth. (14:9)

When reading the book of Zechariah, it's important to keep in mind that he and Haggai were working together (see Ezra 5:1ff.).

You can read Zechariah three chapters a day in five days.

Some sections of this book probably would be rated PG-13 for descriptions of violence and other mature themes.

In 9:9, we learn that the coming ruler (Messiah) will ride on a donkey. This was fulfilled when Jesus entered Jerusalem triumphantly, riding on a donkey.

{Snapshot}

Zechariah received a series of prophetic messages from the Lord addressing events near at hand, events during the Messiah's first coming (more details than any other prophet except Isaiah), and still other events at the climax of history.

Malachi urges readers to quit playing games with God.

The key chapter in Malachi is 1. He challenges the insincerity and corruption of his people with hard-hitting exhortations. Many of these exhortations take the form of a dialogue between the Lord and the Jewish people. In these dialogues, the Lord makes a statement only to be countered by his people—"Really? How?"

Key verses in Malachi include these:

- I wish one of you would close the Temple doors. (1:10 NCV)
- I promised them life and peace so they would honor me. (2:5 NCV)
- Do not break your promise to the wife you married when you were young. The LORD God of Israel says, "I hate divorce." (2:15–16 NCV)
- For I am the LORD, I do not change; / Therefore you are not consumed, O sons of Jacob. (3:6)
- Bring all the tithes into the storehouse . . . / And try Me now in this / . . . I will . . . open for you the windows of heaven. (3:10)

Other key verses that contain messianic prophecies include these:

- Behold, I send My messenger, / And he will prepare the way before Me. (3:1; see 4:5)
- And the Lord, whom you seek, / Will suddenly come to His temple. (3:1)
- But to you who fear My name / The Sun of Righteousness shall arise / With healing in His wings. (4:2)
- Behold, I will send you Elijah the prophet / Before the coming of the great and dreadful day of the LORD. (4:5)
- And he will turn / The hearts of the fathers to the children. (4:6)

When reading the book of Malachi, it's important to keep in mind that, like the book of James, Malachi is a rapid-fire series of mini-sermons on practicing true religion, honoring the Lord's name, obeying God's Word, teaching what is right, doing what is just, fearing the Lord, and loving him with all one's heart, soul, strength, and mind.

You can read Malachi in a day.

Some sections of this book probably would be rated PG-13 for descriptions of sin and corruption.

Malachi 4:5–6 describes the Messiah's forerunner, an "Elijah" who will make the way clear for the Messiah.

{Snapshot}

Malachi rebuked God's people for their spiritual apathy and social injustices. His book was the last prophecy added to the Old Testament canon. Four hundred years of silence followed until the birth of the Messiah, Jesus Christ.

❏ ❏ ❏

You can read Isaiah through Malachi three chapters a day in twelve weeks. You can carefully survey all seventeen of the Old Testament's prophetic books in only two weeks.

After you finish the Old Testament, you'll be three-fourths of the way through the Bible. Now get ready for everything that's coming in the New Testament!

Everything in the Old Testament is pointing toward the coming of Jesus Christ, the Messiah and Savior of the world. His coming will turn the world upside down and split history in two.

After his resurrection, Jesus Christ will instruct his followers to take the good news to "everyone." Despite external persecutions and internal strife, the emerging church will take the gospel throughout the known world. The church will long for the day when Jesus Christ returns.

To say the least, the New Testament is powerful, even life-changing!

Ahead, you'll enjoy four sets of books:

1. four Gospels by Matthew, Mark, Luke, and John;

2. the Acts of the apostles by Luke;

3. twenty-one letters by Paul, James, Peter, John, and Jude; and

4. the Revelation by John.

So whatever you do, don't stop reading!

how do i read
THE NEW TESTAMENT?

The looming prospect of finals and the biting December cold filled the espresso shop with more than the usual number of people seeking warmth and comfort. The Thursday afternoon Bible reading group found itself scrounging chairs to pull around a small table in the far corner.

Erik motioned to Daniel to take his seat. "I'm tall enough; if I need to, I can sit on the floor and still see you all."

"Thanks, Erik," Daniel said and laughed, "but we're still going to need to squeeze in two more chairs. Krista asked me if she and Hamid could drop in on us today. I hope that won't throw you all off."

Kendall shrugged as she unwound her scarf from her neck and draped it over the back of another chair. "I'm sure we'll get a whole new perspective on the New Testament after hearing a few questions from a Muslim."

Maria nodded. "Here they are now."

Hamid strode in and Krista came in a few steps behind, both stopping once or twice to greet people who were used to seeing them on the other side of the counter. When they reached the crowded corner table, Hamid offered his hand to each one. "May I extend my greetings and appreciation that you allow me to join your group today. I've watched your conversations with interest. My only regret is that you are not reading the Koran as well."

Daniel said, "It's nice to talk to you about something besides coffee! I think all six of us are at the same place in our survey reading—about halfway through the New Testament. Any questions or ideas come up for you guys during your reading this last week?"

Hamid laughed. "Of course, everyone is looking at me. But please, go ahead, and I will ask my questions later."

"As long as you promise not to let me monopolize the conversation, I'll jump in," said Maria. "Reading through the Bible quickly has closed some of the gap I had in my mind between the Old and New Testaments. When I read the Prophets as God longing to have his people return, it made sense that the next step would be his sending Jesus to come and get us."

Kendall nodded thoughtfully. "That's what I've been thinking about too. I'm trying to see the Bible as a whole book, a complete story. I think I was taught that there was this one crabby God in the Old Testament and then he changed into this nice God in the New Testament. Of course, that's far from the truth. Now I can see that God had an awesome plan of redemption from the very beginning."

"You mean about sending Jesus?" Erik asked.

{ Today's First Question: }
What's So Important About the Book of Matthew?

"Of course. That's what is so cool about the Gospel of Matthew. I never saw it before," Kendall explained. "Before, I always skipped all that genealogy stuff and got confused by the obscure Old Testament quotes. Now I see that Matthew is connecting with everything the Jewish people had experienced. Everything that came before prepared them to understand that Jesus was the answer they had been looking for."

"Like they—or we—wouldn't have even known what questions to ask," Maria said.

"Or what we needed," Krista added.

Hamid asked, "Is this just about Jewish people?"

Daniel opened his Bible to Ephesians 2:14–15. "Listen to this: 'For He Himself [referring to Jesus] is our peace, who has made both one, and has broken down the middle wall of separation, having abolished in His flesh the enmity, that is, the law of commandments contained in ordinances, so as to create in Himself one new man from the two, thus making peace.' There's a lot more, but these two verses are talking about God's eternal plan to bless the whole world through Jesus. In the New Testament, God unveils that his family is going to include all people who trust in Jesus."

Hamid leaned forward, his demeanor intent. "You know my people accept Isa, Jesus, as a great prophet, but only as a prophet. We believe the last and greatest prophet was Mohammed. Yet when I read the Injil, the 'New Testament' as you call it, I cannot get away from Jesus. He seems like so much more. . . ."

"Yes, that's it, Hamid. No matter what your race or religion or political stand, you can't get away from Jesus. The New Testament is all about Jesus—his life here on earth in a physical body."

"But what about all these books and letters after the story of Jesus?"

"Those are all about Jesus too—his life here on earth in his people—what we call his body, the church."

"That clicks for me, Daniel," Krista interrupted, "but I'm not sure that makes sense to Hamid's vocabulary or worldview. Better back it up a bit."

Hamid joked, "Are you saying I'm not educated enough, Krista? What do you think they've been teaching me at this American university?"

Krista smiled back and said, "Not Christianity, that's for sure! Don't forget what I keep telling you—*American* does *not* mean *Christian!*"

Hamid allowed himself one more serious moment. "All I know is that when I began reading this holy book, I thought it was a dead book. But I feel betrayed. You didn't tell me this Bible is alive! It pursues me and tears at my heart. I pray to Allah to show me what is truth."

{ A Second Look at . . . Today's First Question: }
What's So Important About the Book of Matthew?

Matthew is the first of four Gospels.

This first book in the New Testament challenges us to trust Jesus Christ as our loving Savior and obey him as our rightful Lord.

The key chapters in Matthew are 1–2, 5–7, 17, and 26–28. These chapters contain Jesus's famous Sermon on the Mount, show a few key events in Jesus Christ's later ministry, and then present what is commonly called the passion of Jesus Christ: his arrest, torture, crucifixion, death, and burial and then his resurrection and ascension to heaven.

The most important individual we'll meet in this survey is Jesus! In addition, we'll meet his three closest disciples: Peter, James, and John. In the midst of the passion, we'll also meet Judas Iscariot, who betrayed Jesus, and Pilate, who condemned him to death on a Roman cross.

Other individuals we'll meet later when we read the whole book of Matthew include Mary and Joseph, the wise men, John the Baptist, the rest of Jesus's disciples, Jesus's brothers, and of course the many, many people who flocked to see Jesus during the three years he ministered throughout Palestine.

We'll also meet the enemies of Jesus: the Pharisees, Sadducees, and other religious and political leaders who violently opposed the idea that Jesus could be the long-awaited Messiah. They followed Jesus wherever he went, sneering and plotting. In the end, just as they feared, Jesus rose from the dead.

As one of Jesus's original twelve disciples, Matthew writes as an eyewitness of Jesus's itinerant ministry, death, and resurrection. Tradition says the apostle traveled far and wide proclaiming the good news of Jesus for more than thirty years—until he was martyred for his faith.

Many of Matthew's original readers may have wondered if Jesus truly was the long-awaited King of the Jews. In this Gospel, Matthew frequently refers back to the Old Testament writings to prove that Jesus is indeed the Messiah.

Once you read these key chapters, you'll be tempted to go back and read the entire Gospel of Matthew. You can read it three chapters a day in nine days. You may prefer to read it like a novel, however, in one or two sittings.

Because this book doesn't gloss over Jesus's sufferings, the last few chapters probably would be rated R for violence.

{Snapshot}

Matthew was a despised Jewish tax collector who worked for the Romans before he became a disciple of Jesus Christ. Matthew wrote his gospel for the Jewish people. The "kingdom of God" is in focus throughout the book, including God's plan to allow Gentiles to join it. Matthew clearly presents the resurrection of Jesus Christ as the capstone of our faith.

Matthew is only the first of four Gospels that tell us about Jesus Christ.

Why four Gospels? Though they are similar in many ways, the Gospels give us four distinct perspectives on the life, ministry, teachings, miracles, passion, death, and resurrection of Jesus Christ.

The Gospels give us a more balanced, complete picture of Jesus Christ, just as four television cameras located at various angles in a stadium can give us more complete coverage of each play during a ball game.

Watch closely whenever Mark, Luke, or John replays something Jesus said or did. Pay attention to what these other three Gospel writers choose to highlight or omit.

{ **Today's Second Question:** }
What's So Important About the Other Gospels?

In answering this question, it is helpful to look at an overview of all four Gospels. The following table illustrates their similarities and differences.

Book	Audience	Focus on Christ	Distinctives
		Synoptic Gospels	
Matthew	Jews	Jesus Christ the King	Matthew keeps the "kingdom of God" in focus throughout the book, including God's plan to allow Gentiles to join it.
Mark	Romans	Jesus Christ the Servant	Mark uses crisp, quick writing and frequently uses the word "immediately." His Gospel is the shortest by far. Jewish details are often omitted because of his Roman readership.
Luke	Greeks	Jesus Christ the Son of Man	As a doctor, Luke records many things from a medical point of view. He describes the birth of Jesus in detail and puts special focus on women and prayer.

Book	Audience	Focus on Christ	Distinctives
		Non-Synoptic Gospel	
John	Everyone	Jesus Christ the Son of God	John doesn't record any parables of Jesus and omits almost everything else that the synoptic Gospels say. John focuses on Jesus's divinity, specific miracles, Jesus's interactions with individuals, his words in the Upper Room before his crucifixion, and his words to the disciples and others after his resurrection.

This section of the New Testament is often called the *good news of Jesus Christ*. The first three Gospels overlap in many ways, so they're known as the synoptic Gospels. All three were written within a generation of Jesus's resurrection.

The last Gospel rarely overlaps with the others until its closing chapters. Even then, we receive many new insights into Jesus's sufferings, death, burial, resurrection, and appearances to the disciples.

We've already looked at Matthew, so let's take a quick look at the other Gospels. Ask the Lord to move your heart as you reflect on these three books.

Mark challenges us to consider Jesus's life and then choose for or against him.

The key chapters in Mark are 1–4, 10, and 15–16. These chapters talk about the start and explosive growth of Jesus's ministry, present a sampling of his interactions as he traveled through Palestine, then show Mark's perspective of Jesus's betrayal, arrest, interrogations, beatings, crucifixion, burial, resurrection, and instructions for his disciples to proclaim the good news to everyone, everywhere.

Mark was a close associate of the apostle Peter, so his Gospel retells many of

Peter's stories about Jesus's ministry and the final days before and after his death. Mark wrote his Gospel with an emphasis on Jesus's actions and other people's reactions. You'll find more than 160 such reactions in this brief Gospel!

The key verse of Mark is "For even the Son of Man did not come to be served, but to serve, and to give His life a ransom for many" (10:45).

You can read Mark three chapters a day in five days. Since it's by far the shortest Gospel, however, you may want to read it in one or two sittings.

Like Matthew, the last few chapters of Mark probably would be rated R for violence.

{Snapshot}

Mark's full name was John Mark. He wrote for a Roman audience and knew they were more interested in what Jesus did than in where he came from or what he said. So while Luke takes 183 verses to introduce Jesus's public ministry, Mark takes only thirteen. And while Matthew uses eleven chapters to recount several of Jesus's most important sermons, Mark uses only one and a half. Mark's crisp writing style still appeals to many readers today.

Luke challenges us to take the time to carefully consider Jesus's life, ministry, teachings, death, burial, resurrection, and ascension.

The key chapters in Luke are 1–2, 4–6, 8–10, and 22–24. These chapters present Luke's telling of the Christmas story, dramatic accounts from Jesus's public ministry, and Luke's perspective of the days immediately before and after Jesus's crucifixion.

You can read Luke three chapters a day in eight days.

Like the other Gospels, the last few chapters of Luke probably would be rated R for violence.

{Snapshot}

Luke was a Gentile doctor who served on the apostle Paul's missionary team. Jesus's mother, Mary, seems to have aided Luke in

> writing his Gospel. Luke also interviewed other eyewitnesses. His
> focus is on Jesus Christ the Son of Man. His Gospel is the longest
> by far. Luke also wrote the book of Acts, which serves as a sequel
> to the four Gospels.

John calls us to "believe that Jesus is the Christ, the Son of God, and that believing you may have life in His name" (20:31).

The key chapters in John are 1, 3–4, 13–17, and 19–21. These chapters include John's introduction of Jesus as God's Son, his explanation of why Jesus came to earth, and the account of how John the Baptist encouraged his disciples to become disciples of Jesus. These chapters also feature extended accounts of Jesus' talking with a Jewish leader and with a Samaritan woman, an extensive report on what Jesus said to his disciples the night before his crucifixion, and then John's perspective of what happened before and after Jesus's death.

The most loved, memorized, and quoted verse in all of Scripture is found in this Gospel: "For God so loved the world that He gave His only begotten Son, that whoever believes in Him should not perish but have everlasting life" (3:16).

Another often-quoted verse from John is "I have come that they may have life, and that they may have it more abundantly" (10:10).

You can read John three chapters a day in a week. You may want to read it more than once, however, since this Gospel is so packed with truths about living in Jesus.

Like the other three Gospels, the last few chapters of John probably would be rated R for violence.

{Snapshot}

John and his brother James were hot-tempered fishermen before they became disciples of Jesus Christ. The last week of Jesus Christ's life takes up a major portion of John's Gospel. John emphasizes Jesus Christ's work to make fellowship with the Gospel possible for anyone and everyone. The key word in John is "believe."

Of course, the New Testament doesn't stop after Jesus ascended to heaven. Before he left, Jesus promised to send the Holy Spirit to indwell everyone who believes in him. The minute the Holy Spirit came, the disciples became bold witnesses for Jesus.

Over the next three decades, the early Christians took the good news of Jesus Christ throughout the known world. As an expert reporter and close associate of the apostle Paul, Luke tells the story of the early church's birth and expansion with dramatic flair.

Get ready for an exciting adventure!

(Today's Third Question:)
What's So Important About the Book of Acts?

Acts is often called *the Acts of the Apostles* or *the Acts of the Holy Spirit*. It's both!

The book of Acts shows the fulfillment of Jesus's last words: "But you shall receive power when the Holy Spirit has come upon you; and you shall be witnesses to Me in Jerusalem, and in all Judea and Samaria, and to the end of the earth" (1:8).

The most important verse in this book is this: "Nor is there salvation in any other [besides Jesus], for there is no other name under heaven given among men by which we must be saved" (4:12).

What does that verse mean? Simply that God's wonderful gift of freedom from sin, guilt, and shame, and his gift of life, love, joy, and peace, isn't found in Abraham, Moses, David, Solomon, Nebuchadnezzar, Alexander, or Caesar. Instead, it's found only in Jesus, God's Son, who died on the cross for our sins and rose from the dead to offer us new, eternal life.

No wonder the disciples were so bold!

The key chapters in Acts are 1–4, 8–10, and 12–15. These chapters present Jesus's last words to the disciples, the coming of the Holy Spirit, the preaching of the gospel in Jerusalem, and the disciples' scattering throughout Palestine after persecution breaks out. These chapters then present the conversion of Saul, who became an apostle, helped lead the first missionary journey, became known as the *apostle Paul*, and participated in the first church council in Jerusalem.

Of course, every chapter in the book of Acts is exciting, so you'll want to read it all! You can read Acts three chapters a day in nine days. You may want to read it as you would a novel, however, in one or two sittings.

Some sections of this book probably would be rated PG-13 for violence and other mature themes.

{Snapshot}

In the book of Acts, Luke records the growth of the early church. Luke draws his outline from the last words of Jesus at the end of Acts 1:8. Jesus predicted that the gospel would be proclaimed first in Jerusalem (chapters 1–8), then throughout Judea and Samaria (chapter 8), and then to the ends of the earth (chapters 9–28). Luke abruptly stops the story while the apostle Paul is under house arrest in Rome. It's possible that Luke gave the original manuscripts of his Gospel and Acts to a high-ranking Roman official to seek assistance in Paul's defense.

As the church grew, so did the need for authoritative writings by the apostles regarding church teachings and practices. Most of these writings took the form of letters to churches or church leaders. These letters addressed emerging questions, concerns, and problems Christians faced throughout the Roman Empire.

The apostle Paul was the primary author of these letters, but the New Testament also features compelling letters by two other apostles (Peter and John) and two of Jesus's half brothers (James and Jude), who became outstanding Christian leaders after Jesus's resurrection.

If you're a Christian, you'll want to glean everything you can from these pivotal books!

{ Today's Fourth Question: }
What's So Important About the New Testament Letters?

In answering this question, it is helpful to look at an overview of all twenty-one letters. The following table illustrates their similarities and differences.

Book	Audience	Brief Synopsis
		The Letters of Paul to Churches
Romans	Christians in Rome	Detailed doctrinal explanation of the life-changing gospel of Jesus Christ (chapters 1–8), detailed explanation of God's plan for the Jewish people, detailed instructions on living out the Christian faith in the world and within the church, and instructions on the freedom to disagree within the church when it comes to secondary issues.
1 Corinthians	Christians in Corinth	Correction of errors about how to live as Christians, then correction of errors about worship, spiritual gifts, and the resurrection of the dead; includes an entire chapter about love.
2 Corinthians	Christians in Corinth	Explanation and defense of Paul's apostolic ministry as an ambassador of Christ, instructions on taking up a promised offering for the persecuted Christians in Jerusalem, then contrast of Paul and the false apostles who sought to corrupt the Corinthian church.
Galatians	Christians in Galatia	Contrast of the gospel of Jesus Christ with the false gospel message they had heard, defense of Paul's message as the true gospel message confirmed by the apostles of Jesus Christ, and teaching about the freedom of living by the Spirit.
Ephesians	Christians in Ephesus	Essential teachings about the Christian faith and practical teaching about living out the Christian faith; includes a section on the relationship of Jesus Christ and the church and of husbands and wives.
Philippians	Christians in Philippi	Encouragement to remain steadfast, be shining witnesses of Jesus Christ, and grow in faith despite the threat of further persecution; includes a section on Jesus Christ's divinity, humility when he became a man, and exaltation when he ascended back to heaven; a key theme in this letter is joy.

Book	Audience	Brief Synopsis
Colossians	Christians in Colosse	Contrast of the supremacy of Jesus Christ over every other authority in heaven and earth; encouragement not to be led astray by false teachers; then practical teachings on living the Christian life.
1 Thessalonians	Christians in Thessalonica	Encouragement to remain steadfast in their new-found Christian faith despite persecution; includes sections on the hope of heaven and the reality of Jesus's promise to return.
2 Thessalonians	Christians in Thessalonica	Encouragement to remain steadfast despite false teaching and persecution; includes section on Jesus's promise to return.

The Letters of Paul to Individuals

Book	Audience	Brief Synopsis
1 Timothy	The leader of the church in the city of Ephesus, Timothy	Encouragement to remain steadfast in the ministry; instructions for leading public worship and appointing elders and deacons; teaching on Christian faith and living.
2 Timothy	The leader of the church in the city of Ephesus, Timothy	Encouragement to remain steadfast in the ministry despite the perilous times; teaching on Christian faith and living; includes Paul's final written words of instruction and challenge.
Titus	The leader of the church on the island of Crete, Titus	Instructions for appointing elders and opposing false teachers; instructions for Christian faith and living; includes emphasis on "doing good."
Philemon	A leader of the church in the city of Colosse, Philemon	Encouragment to forgive his former slave and accept him back as a brother in Christ.

Book	Audience	Brief Synopsis
The Letters by Various Apostles		
Hebrews	Jewish Christians and seekers who were tempted to turn back to Judaism	Contrast of the supremacy of Jesus Christ over the Old Testament law and sacrificial system and over the greatest Old Testament heroes; encouragment to persevere in their faith because God's Word is sure, because all the great heroes of the faith persevered, and because great rewards await the faithful in heaven and terrible judgment awaits those who reject Jesus Christ.
James	Jewish Christians scattered throughout the Roman Empire	A series of rapid-fire mini-sermons on important issues of Christian faith and practice; many verses echo important themes that Jesus addressed in his earthly ministry.
1 Peter	Christians living in five Roman provinces	Encouragement to embrace the Christian life fully and be willing to suffer for Jesus Christ; includes instructions for elders and other Christian men.
2 Peter	The church at large	Encouragement to keep growing in the Christian faith and embrace the Scriptures and apostles' teachings so they won't stumble or fall away; exposes the ungodliness and impure motives of false teachers, who face God's judgment; further encouragement to live godly lives, remembering what Jesus said about the future.
1 John	The church at large	Encouragement to be pure in their faith and loving in their relationships with other Christians despite intense pressures from false teachers; emphasis on "love," "light," and "life."
2 John	An anonymous group of Christians	Warning to watch out for false teachers and to have nothing to do with them.

Book	Audience	Brief Synopsis
3 John	A Christian leader named Gaius	Encouragement to continue showing hospitality to itinerant Christian teachers despite opposition from a corrupt church leader named Diotrephes.
Jude	The church at large	Encouragement to stand firm for the Lord despite false teachers; this letter echoes several themes in Peter's longer letters.

These twenty-one letters are sometimes called *epistles*. From the very beginning, these letters were copied and distributed to many other recipients, often churches in other cities throughout the Roman Empire.

The apostle Peter spoke of Paul's letters and "the rest of the Scriptures" (2 Pet. 3:16), recognizing that his letters were part of the emerging New Testament Scriptures. Eventually, the apostles and other important early church leaders recognized twenty-one letters by Paul, Peter, John, and Jude as part of the new canon.

These letters were all written during the first century AD, but their instructions, encouragements, and warnings have served the church well down through the centuries. We would be wise to read each letter with an open heart to what the Lord wants to say to us today!

The Letters of Paul to Churches

Romans answers many basic questions about Christian life and practice.

The key chapters in Romans are 5–8 and 12. These chapters present important teachings about embracing the truths of the gospel of Jesus Christ, living in freedom from habitual sins, experiencing the power of the Holy Spirit in one's life, anticipating the glories of life with the Lord in heaven, and resting in the assurance that nothing can separate us from God's love. The last chapter provides practical encouragement and instruction for living as a Christian.

Key verses in Romans explaining the gospel of Jesus Christ include these:
- There is none righteous, no, not one. (3:10)
- For all have sinned and fall short of the glory of God. (3:23)

- Therefore, just as through one man sin entered the world, and death through sin, and thus death spread to all men, because all sinned. (5:12)
- For the wages of sin is death, but the gift of God is eternal life in Christ Jesus our Lord. (6:23)

Over the years, many Christians have used the following verses to explain the gospel to others. They have been nicknamed *the Romans Road to Salvation.*

- But God demonstrates His own love toward us, in that while we were still sinners, Christ died for us. (5:8)
- If you confess with your mouth the Lord Jesus and believe in your heart that God has raised Him from the dead, you will be saved. (10:9)
- Whoever calls on the name of the Lord shall be saved. (10:13)

Other key verses in Romans include these:

- I am not ashamed of the gospel of Christ, for it is the power of God to salvation for everyone who believes. (1:16)
- And we know that all things work together for good to those who love God, to those who are the called according to His purpose. (8:28)
- Present your bodies a living sacrifice, holy, acceptable to God, which is your reasonable service. (12:1)
- Do not be conformed to this world, but be transformed by the renewing of your mind, that you may prove what is that good and acceptable and perfect will of God. (12:2)

You can read Romans three chapters a day in five days.

Some sections of this book probably would be rated PG.

{Snapshot}

The letter to the Roman believers has three distinct parts. Chapters 1–8 present core Christian beliefs. Chapters 9–11 answer important questions about God's plan for the Jewish people in the past, at that point in history, and in the future. Chapters 12–16 describe how Christians should live.

First Corinthians answers many tough questions about living out the Christian faith as a church.

The key chapters in 1 Corinthians are 1–2 and 13. These chapters contrast the wisdom of God and the world and then present Paul's famous description of Christian love, which is more important than wisdom, wealth, leadership positions, spiritual gifts, or other human credentials.

Key verses in 1 Corinthians include these:

- Eye has not seen, nor ear heard, / Nor have entered into the heart of man / The things which God has prepared for those who love Him. (2:9)
- You are not to associate with anyone who claims to be a Christian yet indulges in sexual sin, or is greedy. (5:11 NLT)
- But now your sins have been washed away, and you have been set apart for God. You have been made right with God. (6:11 NLT)
- Knowledge puffs up, but love edifies. (8:1)

Other key verses include these:

- I have become all things to all men, that I might by all means save some. (9:22)
- So run to win! (9:24 NCV)
- God is faithful, who will not allow you to be tempted beyond what you are able. (10:13)
- Whatever you do, do all to the glory of God. (10:31)
- Be steadfast, immovable, always abounding in the work of the Lord. (15:58)

You can read 1 Corinthians three chapters a day in five days.

Some sections of this book probably would be rated PG-13 for mature themes.

{Snapshot}

First Corinthians contains important Christian teachings about taking communion (11:23–32), about using various spiritual gifts by the power of the Holy Spirit to build up and strengthen the unity of the church (chapters 12 and 14), about the essential gospel message (15:1–8), and about the resurrection of the dead (15:12–57).

Second Corinthians presents important Christian teachings and contrasts the authority of Paul with that of false teachers.

The key chapters in 2 Corinthians are 4–5 and 8–9. These chapters contrast our fragile bodies on earth with the glorious new bodies we will have in heaven someday, talk about the wonder that God indwells our temporal bodies, and speak of our role as ambassadors of Jesus Christ in this world. The latter two chapters encourage believers to give generously to the Lord and to the needs of persecuted Christians.

Key verses in 2 Corinthians include these:

- He [God] comforts us in all our tribulation, that we may be able to comfort those who are in any trouble. (1:4)
- Our only power and success come from God. (3:5 NLT)
- Even though our outward man is perishing, yet the inward man is being renewed day by day. (4:16)
- For we must all appear before the judgment seat of Christ, that each one may receive the things done in the body, according to what he has done, whether good or bad. (5:10)
- Therefore, if anyone is in Christ, he is a new creation; old things have passed away; behold, all things have become new. (5:17)
- We are ambassadors for Christ. (5:20)

Other key verses include these:

- Now is the day of salvation. (6:2)
- Don't team up with those who are unbelievers. (6:14 NLT)
- God loves a cheerful giver. (9:7)
- God can give you more blessings than you need. (9:8 NCV)
- We use God's mighty weapons, not mere worldly weapons, to knock down the Devil's strongholds. (10:4 NLT)
- My grace is sufficient for you, for My strength is made perfect in weakness. (12:9)
- Examine yourselves as to whether you are in the faith. (13:5)

You can read 2 Corinthians three chapters a day in four days.

Some sections of this book probably would be rated PG-13 for mature themes.

> **{Snapshot}**
>
> Second Corinthians has three distinct parts. In chapters 1–7, the apostle Paul presents key teachings on victorious Christian living. In chapters 8–9, Paul encourages believers to give generously. In chapters 10–13, Paul contrasts his apostolic ministry with false teachers who had set themselves up as "superapostles" and urges the Corinthian believers to re-embrace true Christianity.

Galatians contrasts the message of Paul with that of false teachers.

The key chapters in Galatians are 5–6. These chapters describe our freedom in Christ, the power of being filled with the Holy Spirit, and the importance of always doing what is good and pleasing to God.

Key verses in Galatians include these:

- It is no longer I who live, but Christ lives in me. (2:20)
- There is no longer Jew or Gentile, slave or free, male or female. For you are all Christians—you are one in Christ Jesus. (3:28 NLT)
- But when the fullness of the time had come, God sent forth His Son. (4:4)
- God has sent the Spirit of his Son into your hearts, and now you can call God your dear Father. (4:6 NLT)
- Christ has made us free . . . do not be entangled again with a yoke of bondage. (5:1)
- Walk in the Spirit. (5:16)

Two of the most famous verses in Galatians are these:

- But the fruit of the Spirit is love, joy, peace, longsuffering, kindness, goodness, faithfulness, gentleness, self-control. Against such there is no law. (5:22–23).

Other key verses include these:

- If a man is overtaken in any trespass, you who are spiritual restore such a one in a spirit of gentleness, considering yourself lest you also be tempted. (6:1)
- For whatever a man sows, that he will also reap. (6:7)
- Don't get discouraged and give up, for we will reap a harvest of blessing at the appropriate time. (6:9 NLT)

- Therefore, as we have opportunity, let us do good to all, especially to those who are of the household of faith. (6:10)

You can read Galatians three chapters a day in two days.

Some sections of this book probably would be rated PG-13 for mature themes.

{Snapshot}

Galatians has three distinct parts. Chapters 1–2 confirm the authenticity of Paul's presentation of the gospel of Jesus Christ. Chapters 3–4 contrast Christianity with the teachings of false teachers, who sought to enslave the Galatian believers. Chapters 5–6 present the real way to live the Christian life.

Ephesians may have been a circular letter that Paul sent to many cities throughout the Roman Empire. Its grand themes, majestic prayers, and practical instructions have made it a favorite of many Christians down through the ages.

The key chapters in Ephesians are 4–6. These chapters present important teachings on being a part of the church, living in the light and shining bright in a dark world by the power of the Holy Spirit, having Spirit-guided relationships, and on taking on the whole armor of God.

Key verses in Ephesians include these:

- God . . . has blessed us with every spiritual blessing in the heavenly places in Christ. (1:3)
- The Spirit is God's guarantee that he will give us everything he promised. (1:14 NLT)

Three more important verses in Ephesians are these:

- For by grace you have been saved through faith, and that not of yourselves; it is the gift of God, not of works, lest anyone should boast. For we are His workmanship, created in Christ Jesus for good works, which God prepared beforehand that we should walk in them. (2:8–10)

Other key verses in Ephesians include these:

- [God] is able to do exceedingly abundantly above all that we ask or think. (3:20)

- There is one body and one Spirit, just as you were called in one hope of your calling; one Lord, one faith, one baptism. (4:4–5)
- Use every chance you have for doing good, because these are evil times. (5:16 NCV)
- Yield to obey each other because you respect Christ. (5:21 NCV)
- Whatever good anyone does, he will receive the same from the Lord. (6:8)

You can read Ephesians three chapters a day in two days.

Some sections of this book probably would be rated PG.

{Snapshot}

Ephesians has two distinct parts. Chapters 1–3 focus on important Christian teachings. These chapters contain several majestic prayers. Chapters 4–6 focus on matters of practical Christian living. These chapters contain a strong focus on living in the Holy Spirit's power.

Philippians is perhaps the most encouraging book in the New Testament.

The key chapters in Philippians are 2 and 4. The second chapter of Philippians talks about why we Christians will get along well, be bright witnesses in a dark world, and be exemplary Christian leaders if (!) we imitate the example of Jesus Christ, who, being God, humbled himself to the fullest extent. The last chapter reiterates those themes and then urges us to pray for peace, fix our thoughts on what is pure, trust God in every situation, and be generous in our giving.

Key verses in Philippians include these:

- He who has begun a good work in you will complete it until the day of Jesus Christ. (1:6)
- For to me, to live is Christ, and to die is gain. (1:21)
- Let this mind be in you which was also in Christ Jesus. (2:5)
- Do all things without complaining and disputing, that you may become blameless and harmless, children of God without fault. (2:14–15)

- I also count all things loss for the excellence of the knowledge of Christ Jesus my Lord, for whom I have suffered the loss of all things. (3:8)
- I press toward the goal for the prize of the upward call of God in Christ Jesus. (3:14)

Other key verses include these:

- Be anxious for nothing, but in everything by prayer and supplication, with thanksgiving, let your requests be made known to God. (4:6)
- Whatever things are true, whatever things are noble, whatever things are just, whatever things are pure, whatever things are lovely, whatever things are of good report, if there is any virtue and if there is anything praiseworthy—meditate on these things. (4:8)
- I can do all things through Christ who strengthens me. (4:13)

You can read Philippians in a day.

A couple of sections of this book probably would be rated PG.

{Snapshot}

The key word in Philippians is "joy." Except for the first three verses of chapters 3 and 4, it doesn't speak of any problems in the church at Philippi. Many Bible teachers and pastors recommend reading this book when you're feeling discouraged. It works!

Colossians addresses some key intellectual questions facing the early church.

The key chapters in Colossians are 1 and 4. The first chapter begins with words of affirmation and prayer, presents a wonderful picture of the supremacy of Jesus Christ, and then presents the secret of the Christian life: "Christ lives in you" (1:27 NLT).

Key verses in Colossians include these:

- He is the image of the invisible God, the firstborn over all creation. (1:15)
- All things were created through Him and for Him. (1:16)
- God was pleased for all of himself to live in Christ. (1:19 NCV)

- In him all the treasures of wisdom and knowledge are safely kept. (2:3 NCV)
- For in Him dwells all the fullness of the Godhead bodily. (2:9)
- If then you were raised with Christ, seek those things which are above, where Christ is, sitting at the right hand of God. (3:1)

Other key verses include these:

- And let the peace of God rule in your hearts, to which also you were called in one body; and be thankful. Let the word of Christ dwell in you richly in all wisdom, teaching and admonishing one another in psalms and hymns and spiritual songs, singing with grace in your hearts to the Lord. And whatever you do in word or deed, do all in the name of the Lord Jesus, giving thanks to God the Father through Him. (3:15–17)

Still other key verses include these:

- And whatever you do, do it heartily, as to the Lord and not to men. (3:23)
- Continue earnestly in prayer, being vigilant in it with thanksgiving. (4:2)
- Walk in wisdom toward those who are outside, redeeming the time. Let your speech always be with grace, seasoned with salt, that you may know how you ought to answer each one. (4:5–6)

You can read Colossians in a day.

Some sections of this book probably would be rated PG.

{Snapshot}

Colosse must have been a college town. The apostle Paul contrasts the truth of Christianity with the false philosophies of the ancient world. Because of the reality that Jesus Christ is God-become-man, Paul warns them (and us): "Beware lest anyone cheat you through philosophy and empty deceit, according to the tradition of men, according to the basic principles of the world, and not according to Christ" (2:8).

First Thessalonians urges new believers to live for the Lord in the face of adversity.

The key chapters in 1 Thessalonians are 2 and 4. These chapters speak of Paul's ministry among and love for the Thessalonian believers and his encouragement to live in growing holiness and love for one another and to embrace the reality of the life to come.

Key verses in 1 Thessalonians include these:

- Your faith toward God has gone out, so that we do not need to say anything. (1:8)
- Walk worthy of God who calls you into His own kingdom and glory. (2:12)
- And may the Lord make you increase and abound in love to one another and to all. (3:12)
- For if we believe that Jesus died and rose again, even so God will bring with Him those who sleep in Jesus. (4:14)
- That whether we wake or sleep, we should live together with Him. (5:10)

Other short key verses include these:

- Rejoice always. Pray without ceasing, in everything give thanks. . . . Hold fast what is good. Abstain from every form of evil. (5:16–18, 21–22)

You can read 1 Thessalonians three chapters a day in two days.

Some sections of this book probably would be rated PG.

{Snapshot}

Paul probably wrote this letter shortly after he planted the church at Thessalonica and then was forced out of the city (Acts 17:1–10). He describes his ministry among them in tender parental terms: "But we were gentle among you, just as a nursing mother cherishes her own children" (2:7), and "You know how we exhorted, and comforted, and charged every one of you, as a father does his own children" (2:11).

Second Thessalonians urges confused believers to stand firm for the Lord despite persecution and false teachings.

The key chapter in 2 Thessalonians is 3. This chapter begins with a combination of Paul's requests for prayer and echoes of how he has been praying for the Thessalonian Christians. He then gives practical instructions about working hard every day even though Jesus Christ may come back at any time.

Key verses in 2 Thessalonians include these:

- Therefore we also pray always for you that our God would count you worthy of this calling, and fulfill all the good pleasure of His goodness and the work of faith with power. (1:11)
- Now may our Lord Jesus Christ Himself, and our God and Father, who has loved us and given us everlasting consolation and good hope by grace, comfort your hearts and establish you in every good word and work. (2:16–17)
- Pray for us, that the word of the Lord may run swiftly and be glorified, just as it is with you. (3:1)
- Now may the Lord of peace Himself give you peace always in every way. (3:16)

You can read 2 Thessalonians in a day.

Some sections of this book probably would be rated PG-13 for mature themes.

{Snapshot}

Paul wanted to correct the Thessalonian Christians' understanding about future things. In 1:7–10, he briefly explains what will happen *when* the Lord Jesus comes back. In 2:1–12, he describes what will happen *before* the Lord Jesus comes back. In 3:6–15, he describes what *we* should do every day before the Lord Jesus comes back.

The Letters of Paul to Individuals

First Timothy answers many of Timothy's basic questions about living out the Christian faith as a church leader. The apostle Paul had appointed Timothy to help strengthen the emerging church in the city of Ephesus. Paul considered Timothy his spiritual son.

The key chapters in 1 Timothy are 1 and 3. The first chapter warns Timothy against false teachers, reminds him how amazing God's mercy is, and urges him to hold tightly to his faith. This letter's third chapter describes the character qualities of church elders and deacons and then presents a brief summary of the gospel message.

Key verses in 1 Timothy include these:

- Christ Jesus came into the world to save sinners. (1:15)
- I exhort first of all that supplications, prayers, intercessions, and giving of thanks be made for all men. (2:1)
- Anyone wanting to become an elder desires a good work. An elder must not give people a reason to criticize him. (3:1–2 NCV)
- In the same way, deacons must be respected by others. (3:8 NCV)
- For bodily exercise profits a little, but godliness is profitable for all things, having promise of the life that now is and of that which is to come. (4:8)
- Let no one despise your youth, but be an example to the believers in word, in conduct, in love, in spirit, in faith, in purity. (4:12)
- Now godliness with contentment is great gain. For we brought nothing into this world, and it is certain we can carry nothing out. (6:6–7)

Other key verses in 1 Timothy speak of the gospel message:

- God our Savior . . . desires all men to be saved and to come to the knowledge of the truth. For there is one God and one Mediator between God and men, the Man Christ Jesus, who gave Himself a ransom for all, to be testified in due time. (2:3–6)
- God was manifested in the flesh, / Justified in the Spirit, / Seen by angels, / Preached among the Gentiles, / Believed on in the world, / Received up in glory. (3:16)

You can read 1 Timothy three chapters a day in two days.

Some sections of this book probably would be rated PG.

{Snapshot}

In 1 Timothy 4:1–5, Paul speaks prophetically of the "last times," which describe a period between Jesus Christ's ascension and return. Paul says that some will turn away from the Christian faith and follow lying spirits and demonic teachings. Paul describes the false teachers propagating these new teachings as hypocrites and liars with seared consciences. Among their false teachings: it's wrong to get married and it's wrong to eat certain foods.

Second Timothy urges Timothy to stand firm for the Lord despite persecution.

The key chapters in 2 Timothy are 3 and 4. In these chapters, Paul tells Timothy about the dangers of the "last times," describes his need to remain faithful to the Lord because of the certainty of what he's been taught, and exhorts him to actively serve the Lord.

Key verses in 2 Timothy include these:

- God has not given us a spirit of fear, but of power and of love and of a sound mind. (1:7)
- I am not ashamed, for I know whom I have believed and am persuaded that He is able to keep what I have committed to Him until that Day. (1:12)
- The things that you have heard from me among many witnesses, commit these to faithful men who will be able to teach others also. (2:2)
- Be diligent to present yourself approved to God, a worker who does not need to be ashamed, rightly dividing the word of truth. (2:15)
- Flee also youthful lusts; but pursue righteousness, faith, love, peace with those who call on the Lord out of a pure heart. (2:22)
- Everyone who wants to live as God desires, in Christ Jesus, will be hurt. (3:12 NCV)
- All Scripture is given by God and is useful. (3:16 NCV)
- Preach the word! Be ready in season and out of season. (4:2)

You can read 2 Timothy in a day.

Some sections of this book probably would be rated PG-13 for mature themes.

{Snapshot}

The end of 2 Timothy contains the last recorded words of Paul before his martyrdom in Rome. He could testify, "I have fought the good fight, I have finished the race, I have kept the faith" (4:7).

What kept him going in his darkest days? "There is laid up for me the crown of righteousness, which the Lord, the righteous Judge, will give to me on that Day" (4:8). He goes on to say, "And not to me only but also to all who have loved His appearing" (4:8). His example is a challenge to every Christian.

Titus answers many of Titus's questions about living out the Christian faith as a church leader. Paul has appointed Titus, like Timothy, to help lead an emerging church, this time on the island of Crete.

The key chapter in Titus is 2. This chapter challenges every Christian to make the truths of Christianity attractive to others by his or her godly living.

Key verses in Titus include these:

- An elder must not be guilty of doing wrong. (1:6 NCV)
- To the pure all things are pure. (1:15)
- He gave himself for us so he might pay the price to free us from all evil and to make us pure people who belong only to him—people who are always wanting to do good deeds. (2:14 NCV)
- But when the kindness and the love of God our Savior toward man appeared, not by works of righteousness which we have done, but according to His mercy He saved us, through the washing of regeneration and renewing of the Holy Spirit. (3:4–5)

You can read Titus in a day.

Some sections of this book probably would be rated PG-13 for mature themes.

{Snapshot}

Almost everywhere Paul went, false teachers soon followed (1:10–16; 3:9–11). Many of these false teachers deceptively used Jewish and Christian concepts to promote their own warped religious cults. These false teachers deliberately distorted the truth, tried to fleece money from sincere Christians, and caused trouble wherever they went.

Philemon is the first New Testament postcard epistle.

In this moving letter, Paul strongly urges a friend to forgive his runaway slave and accept him back as a brother in Christ. As such, it is a masterful example of persuasive writing.

{Snapshot}

Paul's friend Philemon was a Christian leader in the city of Colosse. His family hosted one of the city's house churches.

The Letters by Other Apostles

Hebrews presents the superiority of Jesus Christ.

The key chapters in Hebrews are 10–13. The preceding chapters present Jesus Christ as the perfect fulfillment of the Old Testament law, sacrificial system, and messianic prophecies. These latter chapters culminate that grand theme and continue the book's strong appeal to persevere in the Christian faith, no matter what. Chapter 11 is often called *the Hall of Faith*. The last chapter includes practical instructions for godly living.

Key verses in Hebrews include these:

- God, who at various times and in various ways spoke in time past to the fathers by the prophets, has in these last days spoken to us by His Son, whom He has appointed heir of all things, through whom also He made the worlds. (1:1–2)
- When He had by Himself purged our sins, [He] sat down at the right hand of the Majesty on high. (1:3)
- And now he [Jesus] can help those who are tempted, because he himself suffered and was tempted. (2:18 NCV)
- For the word of God is living and powerful, and sharper than any two-edged sword, piercing even to the division of soul and spirit, and of joints and marrow, and is a discerner of the thoughts and intents of the heart. (4:12)
- Let us therefore come boldly to the throne of grace, that we may obtain mercy and find grace to help in time of need. (4:16)

Other key verses include these:

- This hope we have as an anchor of the soul, both sure and steadfast, and which enters the Presence behind the veil. (6:19)
- So he is able always to save those who come to God through him because he always lives, asking God to help them. (7:25 NCV)
- It is appointed for men to die once, but after this the judgment. (9:27)
- You should not stay away from the church meetings, as some are doing, but you should meet together and encourage each other. Do this even more as you see the day coming. (10:25 NCV)
- Now faith is the substance of things hoped for, the evidence of things not seen. (11:1)
- But without faith it is impossible to please Him, for he who comes to God must believe that He is, and that He is a rewarder of those who diligently seek Him. (11:6)

Still other key verses include these:

- Therefore we also, since we are surrounded by so great a cloud of witnesses, let us lay aside every weight, and the sin which so easily ensnares us, and let us run with endurance the race that is set before us. (12:1)
- Be careful that no one fails to receive God's grace and begins to cause trouble among you. A person like that can ruin many of you. (12:15 NCV)
- For our God is a consuming fire. (12:29)
- Jesus Christ is the same yesterday, today, and forever. (13:8)
- Therefore by Him let us continually offer the sacrifice of praise to God, that is, the fruit of our lips, giving thanks to His name. (13:15)

You can read Hebrews three chapters a day in four days.

Some sections of this book probably would be rated PG-13 for mature themes.

{Snapshot}

Hebrews is the only anonymous New Testament letter. Many early church fathers attributed this letter to the apostle Paul. Others attributed it to Paul's colleagues—Barnabas, Apollos, or Priscilla and Aquila. In any case, the book itself was widely distributed, fully endorsed, and gladly accepted by the early church.

James is the only New Testament wisdom book.

The key chapters in James are 1–2. These chapters contain a series of mini-sermons about faith and endurance, faith and obedience, faith and love, and faith and good deeds.

Key verses in James include these:

- If any of you lacks wisdom, let him ask of God, who gives to all liberally and without reproach, and it will be given to him. (1:5)
- Blessed is the man who endures temptation; for when he has been approved, he will receive the crown of life which the Lord has promised to those who love Him. (1:12)
- Every good gift and every perfect gift is from above, and comes down from the Father of lights, with whom there is no variation or shadow of turning. (1:17)
- So then, my brethren, let every man be swift to hear, slow to speak, slow to wrath. (1:19)
- Pure and undefiled religion before God and the Father is this: to visit orphans and widows in their trouble, and to keep oneself unspotted from the world. (1:27)

Other key verses include these:

- For whoever shall keep the whole law, and yet stumble in one point, he is guilty of all. (2:10)
- Thus also faith by itself, if it does not have works, is dead. (2:17)
- But the wisdom that comes from above is first pure, then peaceable, gentle, willing to yield, full of mercy and good fruits, without partiality and without hypocrisy. (3:17)
- Therefore submit to God. Resist the devil and he will flee from you. (4:7)
- Instead you ought to say, "If the Lord wills, we shall live and do this or that." (4:15)
- Confess your trespasses to one another, and pray for one another, that you may be healed. The effective, fervent prayer of a righteous man avails much. (5:16)

You can read James three chapters a day in two days.

Some sections of this book probably would be rated PG.

{Snapshot}

James wasn't one of the twelve apostles of Jesus Christ but a half brother of Jesus who came to faith after Jesus's resurrection. Not surprisingly, many verses in James echo important themes that we find Jesus talking about in the four Gospels. If you read the words of Jesus and the letter of James side by side, you can find more than three dozen common themes and statements.

First Peter urges Christians to live for the Lord in the face of adversity.

The key chapters in 1 Peter are 1 and 5. The first chapter describes the priceless gift of salvation we've received thanks to Jesus Christ's death and resurrection. That gift provides us with great hope and the assurance of eternal life. In light of that wonderful gift, Peter says, we should live new, holy lives even if we suffer. In the last chapter, Peter reiterates these themes, with a special challenge for elders and younger men.

Key verses in 1 Peter include these:

- That the genuineness of your faith, being much more precious than gold that perishes, though it is tested by fire, may be found to praise, honor, and glory at the revelation of Jesus Christ. (1:7)
- But as He who called you is holy, you also be holy in all your conduct. (1:15)
- As newborn babes, desire the pure milk of the word, that you may grow. (2:2)
- But you are a chosen generation, a royal priesthood, a holy nation, His own special people, that you may proclaim the praises of Him who called you out of darkness into His marvelous light. (2:9)
- Dear friends, you are like foreigners and strangers in this world. I beg you to avoid the evil things your bodies want to do that war against your soul. (2:11 NCV)

Other key verses include these:

- For to this you were called, because Christ also suffered for us, leaving us an example, that you should follow His steps. (2:21)
- Who Himself bore our sins in His own body on the tree, that we, having died to sins, might live for righteousness—by whose stripes you were healed. (2:24)
- Do not do wrong to repay a wrong. (3:9 NCV)
- But sanctify the Lord God in your hearts, and always be ready to give a defense to everyone who asks you a reason for the hope that is in you, with meekness and fear. (3:15)
- Love will cover a multitude of sins. (4:8)

Still other key verses include these:

- Therefore humble yourselves under the mighty hand of God, that He may exalt you in due time, casting all your care upon Him, for He cares for you. Be sober, be vigilant; because your adversary the devil walks about like a roaring lion, seeking whom he may devour. (5:6–8)

You can read 1 Peter three chapters a day in two days.

Some sections of this book probably would be rated PG.

{Snapshot}

Peter intertwines three important themes throughout his first letter. With the first, Peter emphasizes how much we have received and have to look forward to for all eternity thanks to the gospel of Jesus Christ. In the second, Peter emphasizes how Jesus Christ set the standard for us if we're called to suffer on earth. In the third, Peter emphasizes our need to live under authority—good or bad.

Second Peter urges Christians to stand firm for the Lord despite false teachers.

The key chapter in 2 Peter is 1. This chapter promises that we will not stumble spiritually if we keep growing in our faith and hold fast to the Old Testament Scriptures and the teachings of the apostles.

Key verses in 2 Peter include these:

- His divine power has given to us all things that pertain to life and godliness, through the knowledge of him who called us by glory and virtue. (1:3)

- So make every effort to apply the benefits of these promises to your life. (1:5 NLT)
- Be even more diligent to make your call and election sure, for if you do these things you will never stumble. (1:10)
- For we did not follow cunningly devised fables when we made known to you the power and coming of our Lord Jesus Christ, but were eyewitnesses of His majesty. (1:16)

Other key verses include these:

- No prophecy of Scripture is of any private interpretation, for prophecy never came by the will of man, but holy men of God spoke as they were moved by the Holy Spirit. (1:20–21)
- The Lord knows how to deliver the godly out of temptations. (2:9)
- But, beloved, do not forget this one thing, that with the Lord one day is as a thousand years, and a thousand years as one day. (3:8)
- The Lord is not slack concerning His promise, as some count slackness, but is longsuffering toward us, not willing that any should perish but that all should come to repentance. (3:9)

You can read 2 Peter in a day.

Some sections of this book probably would be rated PG-13 for mature themes.

{Snapshot}

In 2 Peter 1:12–15, Peter tells Christians that he knows he will be martyred soon. He explains that he wrote this letter to remind them about important truths that will help them stand firm in the faith. "I want you to remember them long after I am gone," Peter concludes (NLT). Thanks to God's inspiration and preservation of his letter, Christians have remembered Peter's final written words for nearly two thousand years.

First John urges Christians to be pure in their faith and loving in their practice despite intense pressures from false teachers.

The key chapters in 1 John are 1–2. These chapters begin by echoing the opening paragraphs of the Gospel of John, lifting up Jesus Christ as God's Son. John then applies the gospel of Jesus Christ to sin in the lives of Christians. We should love each other, not this evil world and all it offers. Evil abounds in this world, and many seek to lead us astray, but we can remain faithful because the Holy Spirit indwells us and helps us do what is right.

Key verses in 1 John include these:

- But if we walk in the light as He is in the light, we have fellowship with one another, and the blood of Jesus Christ His Son cleanses us from all sin. (1:7)
- If we confess our sins, He is faithful and just to forgive us our sins and to cleanse us from all unrighteousness. (1:9)
- Do not love the world or the things in the world. If anyone loves the world, the love of the Father is not in him. (2:15)
- Behold what manner of love the Father has bestowed on us, that we should be called children of God! Therefore the world does not know us, because it did not know Him. Beloved, now we are children of God; and it has not yet been revealed what we shall be, but we know that when He is revealed, we shall be like Him, for we shall see Him as He is. (3:1–2)

Other key verses include these:

- But whoever has this world's goods, and sees his brother in need, and shuts up his heart from him, how does the love of God abide in him? (3:17)
- You are of God, little children, and have overcome them, because He who is in you is greater than he who is in the world. (4:4)
- This is what real love is: It is not our love for God; it is God's love for us in sending his Son to be the way to take away our sins. (4:10 NCV)
- Perfect love casts out fear. (4:18)
- He who has the Son has life; he who does not have the Son of God does not have life. (5:12)
- Now this is the confidence that we have in Him, that if we ask anything according to His will, He hears us. (5:14)

You can read 1 John three chapters a day in two days.

Some sections of this book probably would be rated PG.

> ## {Snapshot}
>
> John intertwines three important themes throughout his first letter. With the first, John emphasizes the *life* we have in Jesus Christ; the contrast is death and eternal separation from God. With the second, John emphasizes the *light* we can walk in as Christians; the contrast is darkness and a rejection of God's truth. With the third, John emphasizes the *love* we can enjoy and express as Christians; the contrast is hatred of God and anyone who loves God.

Second John is the second New Testament postcard epistle.

In this short yet urgent letter, John warns his readers to watch out for false teachers and to have nothing to do with them.

> ## {Snapshot}
>
> John wrote his second letter to a group of Christians—either an extended family or a local church.

Third John is the third New Testament postcard epistle.

In this short yet urgent letter, John praises his friend Gaius for showing hospitality to Christian teachers and urges him to continue to do so despite opposition from a corrupt church leader named Diotrephes.

> ## {Snapshot}
>
> "Dear friend, I pray that you may enjoy good health and that all may go well with you, even as your soul is getting along well" (3 John 2 NIV) has been quoted in letters between Christians for many centuries.

Jude is the fourth and final New Testament postcard epistle.

In this short yet urgent letter, Jude urges confused Christians to stand firm for the Lord despite false teachers.

{ Today's Fifth Question: }
What's So Important About the Book of Revelation?

Revelation is the New Testament's only book of prophecy.

It is an apocalyptic vision of the future. Like Isaiah and other Old Testament prophetic books, Revelation speaks of days both near at hand and far into the future. In several remarkable passages, Revelation clearly and compellingly presents a vision of Jesus Christ's future kingdom and of the new heavens and earth.

Revelation deliberately weaves in many themes from the book of Genesis to portray paradise restored after God's wrath is fully revealed against Satan, death, and sin. It also masterfully weaves in many other themes from the Old and New Testaments. Once you read Revelation, you'll be tempted to go back and begin reading the Bible all over again.

The key chapters in Revelation are 19–22. These chapters describe the worship in heaven when Jesus Christ returns to rule the earth, the ultimate defeat of Satan, the judgment of humanity, and the glories of the new heaven and earth. The final verses encourage Christians to look forward to seeing Jesus Christ face-to-face.

Key verses in Revelation include these:

- Blessed is he who reads and those who hear the words of this prophecy, and keep those things which are written in it; for the time is near. (1:3)
- Behold, I stand at the door and knock. If anyone hears My voice and opens the door, I will come in to him and dine with him, and he with Me. (3:20)
- The four living creatures, each having six wings, were full of eyes around and within. And they do not rest day or night, saying, "Holy, holy, holy, / Lord God Almighty, / Who was and is and is to come!" (4:8)

- And they sang a new song, saying, / "You are worthy to take the scroll, / And to open its seals; / For You were slain, / And have redeemed us to God by Your blood / Out of every tribe and tongue and people and nation." (5:9)
- Behold, I am coming as a thief. Blessed is he who watches, and keeps his garments, lest he walk naked and they see his shame. (16:15; see 3:3)
- These will make war with the Lamb, and the Lamb will overcome them, for He is Lord of lords and King of kings; and those who are with Him are called, chosen, and faithful. (17:14; see 19:16)

Other key verses include these:

- And I saw the dead, small and great, standing before God, and books were opened. And another book was opened, which is the Book of Life. And the dead were judged according to their works, by the things which were written in the books. (20:12)
- Now I saw a new heaven and a new earth, for the first heaven and the first earth had passed away. Also there was no more sea. (21:1)
- And I heard a loud voice from heaven saying, "Behold, the tabernacle of God is with men, and He will dwell with them, and they shall be His people. God Himself will be with them and be their God." (21:3)
- I am coming quickly! (22:7, 12, 20)

You can read Revelation three chapters a day in a week.

Some sections of this book probably would be rated PG-13 or R for descriptions of catastrophic judgment and other mature themes.

{Snapshot}

The book of Revelation is outlined in 1:19, which says, "Write the things which you have seen, and the things which are, and the things which will take place after this." Chapter 1 is "what you have seen." Chapters 2–3 are "what is now." Chapters 4–22 are "what will take place later."

Once we've seen the key themes of each section of the Bible, it's time to begin looking at the Scriptures more closely.

{ part three }

what do i look for
WHEN I'M READING?

ey, Daniel!" Daniel looked up to see Tyler Carns approaching. Daniel didn't know Tyler well—they'd had one class together and he knew that Tyler was on the newspaper staff, but they were barely acquaintances.

"Hi, Tyler. What's up?"

"Got a minute, Daniel? I'm doing a piece for the paper, and I'd like to interview you."

Daniel raised his eyebrows. "I've got a class in half an hour, but I'm not sure I have anything to say that will fill up that much time."

Tyler sat down in the nearest chair. "Great. Sit down, and we'll get started. Say, is this where you have your little Bible reading group?"

"Yeah. How did you hear about that?" Daniel wasn't sure where the conversation was going. The rest of the group had just left, so he was on his own.

"Martin mentioned it to me. He heard you talking about it, and since I'm doing a piece on small, radical groups on campus, he thought you might give me some material."

{ Today's First Question: }
When It Comes to Reading a Book,
What's Different About the Bible?

"A few friends and I are reading through the Bible, so we meet once a week to talk about what we've read. We embrace it as the Lord's written revelation of himself. We believe it is God's inspired message to all of humanity. We believe it's more true than any textbook ever published. Does that count as being a small, radical campus group?"

Tyler smiled. "Don't you want to be a radical, Daniel? Jesus was, wasn't he?"

"It still depends on how you define *radical*. We don't have any plans to take over the world, but I hope reading the Bible makes us different enough—in a good way—to change the world."

"Okay, so you're not as exciting as some of the groups, but that's a great quote. Can you say that again?"

Daniel complied and tried to hurry along the conversation. "What else do you want to know, Tyler?"

"The usual. Who all is in this group? What is your purpose? Where and when do you meet? Are you open to new members?"

"Really, we're just a group of friends meeting to discuss reading the Bible. We're not a club you can join—though I'd be happy to talk to anyone who is serious about reading the Bible. Now that the winter quarter has started, we've been meeting on Wednesdays instead of Thursdays. But like I said, we're not trying to gather a crowd."

"I hear that you have a Muslim in your group."

Daniel thought carefully before answering. "We have a Muslim friend who has sat in with us from time to time, but you'd really have to ask him if he considers himself part of our group. I really can't speak for him or his experience in reading the Scriptures."

"How about some details about what you're reading? Where are you guys at in this venture?"

Daniel explained the quick survey reading they had finished at the end of fall term. Because they would have extra time for reading, they had agreed to start reading Genesis through Leviticus over the break.

Tyler was attempting to act interested, but Daniel could tell he was a bit bored. He hoped Tyler wouldn't try to spice up the details for his article.

"Okay, so you guys are reading this book my grandma keeps on the shelf. Do any of you have degrees in this stuff? How do you know what it means?"

"Well, Tyler, you tell me."

"Tell you what?"

"What do they teach you to do when you're learning basic reporting?"

"Like, what questions do you ask when you want to find out information? Is that what you're asking? You already know the answer to this, Daniel—or do you really need me to give it to you?"

"At least tell me so I can make sure I haven't missed any. We were talking about observation just a few minutes ago."

Tyler rolled his eyes and quickly rattled off, "The six questions every journalist asks are who, what, when, where, why, and how."

{ Today's Second Question: }
What Are You Looking for When You Read the Bible?

Daniel shrugged. "That's it. You start by asking the same questions you would about any topic. Basically you simply read and ask questions."

Tyler was definitely disappointed. "No fancy codes, no secret messages?"

"Sorry. The only messages are those anyone can find by looking and asking good questions. It might take time, but it's not magic."

{ A Second Look at . . . Today's First Question: }
When It Comes to Reading a Book,
What's Different About the Bible?

Daniel is right: the Bible is truer than any other book ever published.

The Bible was written by God. It will *never* be out of date.

Our belief in the Bible is based on the fact that God *always* tells the truth.

It is a book of *unquestionable facts about eternal realities.*

In the Bible, we find two kinds of facts: *simple* truths (easily grasped facts) and *complex* truths (facts that exceed our grasp). You and I will never plumb the depths of the Bible's complex truths. God's thoughts far exceed the collective brainpower of *all* humanity (Isa. 55:8–9).

It's no wonder that God doesn't pretend to tell us everything (Deut. 29:29). It's also ridiculous to think we can contribute one microscopic atom of truth to what God has known before the beginning of time (Rom. 11:33).

As we examine how Jesus and the apostles viewed the Old Testament, we come to understand that they believed the Scriptures are not only a revelation *from* God but also a revelation *of* God. They accepted the factual details in the Bible at face value, then saw the spiritual implications of those details.

As we read the Bible, we need to remember that even the smallest details (say, a person's name) often have spiritual undertones.

Person	Biblical Insight	Spiritual Implications
Adam	His name means "man."	Adam was the first man. He represents all of humanity. In Hosea 6:7, Romans 5:12ff., and other passages, we see that all of Adam's descendants are sinners, just as he was.
Abraham	His name means "father of many nations."	Abraham was the father of all who believe in the Lord God (Rom. 4:9–18). He is one of the most highly regarded men of all human history.
Moses	His name means "to draw out."	Moses was the founder of the Israelite nation. In Exodus, we read how he drew out two million Israelites from Egypt, releasing them from centuries of slavery and oppression. Nearly thirty-five hundred years ago, Moses was drawn out of the Nile River by Pharaoh's daughter (Exod. 1).
David	His name means "beloved."	David was the greatest king of Israel. In Acts 13:22, we read that David was a man after God's own heart. God's love for David, and David's love for God, has been renowned for three thousand years.
Jesus	His name means "Yahweh saves."	As the Savior of the world, Jesus's name is very appropriate! His name reminds us that Yahweh is the God of the Old Testament as well as the New. He truly is "God our Savior" (Titus 2:13).
Christ	This title means "Messiah" or "Anointed One."	Jesus Christ's coming to earth was the fulfillment of prophecies that go all the way back to the Garden of Eden (Gen. 3:15). The biggest surprise: Jesus is the Messiah of *all* peoples, including you and me!

As we read the Bible, we also need to remember that other small details (say, a place's name) can have spiritual undertones.

Place	Biblical Insight	Spiritual Implications
Eden	This term refers to the place where God planted a lush garden for the first man and woman.	Since the beginning of history, Eden has represented Paradise lost. Thankfully, that Paradise one day will be restored (Rev. 21–22).
Egypt	This term refers to an ancient world power, not the modern nation we think of as Egypt.	The ancient Israelites were mixed in their views of Egypt. It was a place of temporary refuge but often became a place of trial and suffering. Still, God wanted the Egyptians to become one of his chosen peoples (Isa. 19:18–25; 27:13). So Egypt wasn't always considered "bad."
Wilderness	This term describes remote areas in biblical lands, including the desert areas between Egypt and the Promised Land.	After their exodus from Egypt, the Israelites rebelled against the Lord and were stuck in the wilderness for forty years, until the entire older generation (except Joshua and Caleb) died. The wilderness almost always represents a place of testing and trials, even in New Testament times (Matt. 4:1–4).
Promised Land	This phrase describes the region that the Lord gave to Abraham and his descendants.	Only during the reigns of David and Solomon did the Israelites truly enjoy living in the Promised Land. Even then, at the height of the nation's glory, they never possessed all of the land God had offered them (Gen. 15:18–21).
Bethlehem	The name of this town means "House of Bread."	It has been known for three thousand years as the City of David. Because it was King David's place of birth, Bethlehem is mentioned frequently in the Old Testament. The last reference prophesies that it will be the birthplace of the Messiah, Jesus Christ (Mic. 5:2).

The reality is that we need to remember that just about anything in the Bible can have spiritual undertones.

Item	Definition	Spiritual Implications
Fruit	This term often—but not always—is used in a positive sense of goodness.	Biblically, only one kind of fruit in the Garden of Eden was forbidden. Every other kind of fruit was good! It wasn't because of hunger that Eve and Adam ate from the Tree of the Knowledge of Good and Evil. Thousands of years later, God came to earth and was crucified on a tree in our place (1 Pet. 2:24).
Serpent	This term is sometimes used as a symbol for Satan.	Most people view this creature negatively. Biblically, the serpent in the Garden of Eden was the devil in disguise, deceiving Eve (2 Cor. 11:3).
Seed	This term speaks of someone's descendants.	Biblically, the "seed" in Genesis 3:15 and the "seed" of Abraham in Galatians 3:16 speak of the promised Messiah, Jesus Christ.

So when we read the Bible, we need to do so with our spiritual eyes wide open. How do we do that?

First, we can come to God in prayer. We can worship God, thank him for his Word, and then ask him to remove anything that would cloud our hearts and minds as we read the Bible.

Second, we can ask God for the Holy Spirit's illumination as we read (and reread) each passage of Scripture. We can read the same section of the Bible twenty, thirty, forty, or more times and still make new discoveries with each new reading.

Third, we can come to the Bible with a strong sense of expectancy, determination, and persistence. We need to look closely at Scripture. The goal of such careful observation is to discover more and more of what God's Word says.

We're not talking about a superficial once-over, like taking a cursory glance around the room to look for your shoes. Instead, we're talking about looking intently at Scripture.

{ **A Second Look at . . . Today's Second Question:** }
What Are You Looking for When You Read the Bible?

So what *do* we look for as we read the Bible?

Here's where you get to turn into a not-so-mild-mannered reporter. Pull out your press card and get ready to ask a stream of questions worthy of the best journalist.

Here is a fairly comprehensive list of *Who? What? When? Where? Why?* and *How?* questions you and I can ask repeatedly as we read through God's Word.

Feel free to add your own journalistic questions to the following lists. In fact, we've added extra space for you to do just that. You won't ask all of these questions every time you read a verse. But you can ask the most pertinent questions that come to mind after reading Scripture. We've provided the list below to stimulate your questions!

Who?

Who is the author?

- What do we know about the author?
- What is his purpose for writing?
- What is his point of view?
- What didn't the author know at the time that the Bible tells us later?

Who are the readers?

- What do we know about the readers?
- How well did they know the author?
- How well did they know the Lord?
- What struggles did they face?
- What did they hope to gain from this writing?

Whom do we read about in this passage?

- Who are the main characters? Who are the secondary characters? What do we learn about each person?
- Is the devil, or are angels or demons, present? If so, what do we learn about each?
- More important, is God the Father, Jesus Christ, or the Holy Spirit in the picture? If so, what do we learn about and from God?

What?

What did the biblical characters say? *What* happened in this passage? *What* strikes you as you're reading?

- What stays the same? What changes progressively?
- What things seem similar? Different?
- Are any words, phrases, concepts, or actions repeated?

What surprises you?

- What side remarks and digressions does the author make?
- Is there anything not said that you'd like to know?
- What questions does this Scripture raise?

What doesn't make sense to you?

- Are there any words or phrases you'd like to define?
- Are there any word pictures or symbols you'd like to explore?
- Are there any social customs you have questions about?

What is the passage's context and purpose?

- What is the overall context of this passage of Scripture?
- What is the immediate context of this passage?
- What appears to be the writer's primary message?
- What compelled the writer to pen this passage?

What is the style of writing?

- Is it narrative? If so, what happens? What conflicts arise? Are the conflicts resolved? If so, how?
- Is it another literary form? If so, is it wisdom literature? Prophecy? A letter?
- If it is wisdom literature, what are its most important themes? Which of those themes are still relevant today?
- If it is prophecy, what does it tell us about history and the future?
- If it is a letter, what does it tell us about the church and the Christian life? How can you and I apply that today?

What have you learned?

- Any new truths? If so, how important are they? Which is the most important?
- Any new commands? If so, do any of them apply to you? If so, which one(s)?
- Any new examples? If so, are there one or two you should heed?

(Okay, we're getting a little ahead of ourselves with those last few questions. We'll come back to them in the next few chapters.)

When?

When is the passage set?

- Is it historic? If so, during what time period?
- Is it prophetic? If so, is it speaking of events near at hand or far into the future?
- Is it general? If so, how much of it relates to life today?

Where?

Where is the passage set?

- Is it set in heaven or on earth?
- If earth, is it set in the Promised Land? If so, is it set before or after Israel was divided into the separate kingdoms of Israel and Judah?
- Is it set in other parts of the Middle East? If so, in Egypt? Assyria? Babylonia? Samaria? The Roman Empire? Elsewhere?
- What is the significance of this particular setting?

Where is the passage going?

- Does it talk about a second location? If so, what is the significance of this new location?

Why?

Why is this section important?

- Does it tell us anything about God the Father, Jesus Christ, or the Holy Spirit?
- Does it tell us anything about trusting God, living for him, and remaining faithful to the end?

- Does it tell us anything about this life, death, or the afterlife?
- Does it tell us anything else of lasting importance?

Why is this passage written the way it is?
- Why did the author say what he said?
- Why did the author not say other things?
- What was God's agenda for this Scripture passage?

How?

How is this section important?
- Does it present any truths we can affirm?
- Does it present any commands we can obey?
- Does it present any examples we can heed?

(Again, we're getting a little ahead of ourselves with these last three questions.)

Most Christians today think it's easy to discern the facts of a Scripture passage. That's often the case, but not always!

Open to the middle of your Bible and take Psalm 49, for instance. Granted, it's not one of the most accessible psalms. That's all the more reason to blitz every verse with as many questions as possible, right? You can ask 145 questions over the course of the first six verses alone. Of those 145 questions, only twenty-four can be answered by observations made within the immediate content. The other 121 questions require interpretative answers. (Thankfully, those interpretative answers exist!)

Here's a quick look at verse one.

Looking Intently at Psalm 49:1
For the director of music.
Of the Sons of Korah. A psalm.

Hear this, all you peoples; listen, all who live in this world. (NIV)

Questions and Answers
Q. Of whom is Psalm 49?
A. *"Of the Sons of Korah"*
Q. Who wrote Psalm 49?
A.
Q. Who are the Sons of Korah?
A.

Q. What is a psalm?

A.

Q. In what ways is a psalm different from other writings included in the book of Psalms?

A.

Q. Who are to "hear?"

A. *"All you peoples"*

Q. What are "all you peoples" to hear?

A. *"This"*

Q. To what does "this" refer?

A. *Psalm 49, particularly verses 4–20*

Q. Who are "all you peoples"?

A.

Q. Who are to "listen"?

A. *"All who live in this world"*

By asking lots of *Who? What? When? Where? Why?* and *How?* questions, we get a much better idea of what any given Scripture passage says. We also get a good idea of what it *doesn't* say and what we're not yet sure it's saying. (Those interpretative questions are what the next chapter is all about.)

The key thing to remember is that the goal of Bible reading isn't simply to look intently at each passage of Scripture. James 1:25 reminds us, "But he who looks into the perfect law of liberty and continues in it, and is not a forgetful hearer but a doer of the work, this one will be blessed in what he does."

The exciting news is that throughout Scripture God promises to bless the person who reads his Word, looks intently at it, *then* interprets it correctly (chapter 11), personalizes it (chapter 12), and applies it to his or her life (chapter 13).

Reading the Bible carefully is very important.

But there's more!

how do i make sense of
WHAT I'M READING?

It was well after midnight when Daniel ventured into the kitchen for a snack. His other housemates were sprawled out in the living room, watching an old movie. He was surprised to see Erik hunched over the kitchen table, books spread around and papers stacked on a chair next to him.

"Hey, do you usually set up shop here?"

Erik looked up from his Bible and grinned. "Bad habit my mom could tell you all about. My room is such a mess that I can't concentrate, but I don't have time to clean it. I can't study in the living room while the movie's going. Besides, it's closer to the refrigerator in here."

"Anything good left in the cupboards?"

"Mainly peanuts and cereal—if you don't mind eating it with chocolate milk."

"I'll pass, thanks." Daniel leaned against the counter as he scooped some nuts from the bottom of a can. "What's the big project?"

"Oh, just a chemistry lab write-up. Nothing too exciting. But I am having a challenge with our Bible reading. I was catching up just now, because if I don't just make it part of my homework routine, it never happens."

"What's the problem?"

{ Today's First Question: }
What Does a Particular Passage of Scripture Mean?
How Can I Know for Sure?

Erik pushed back his chair and leaned against the wall, his Bible in his lap. "Okay. I'm reading in 1 Samuel and I can't figure out what God wants. First, he's not happy that the people want a king, then he lets them have a king and he tells them how he can bless the king if he obeys. Then he reaffirms Saul as

177

king—and tells them he's still unhappy they have a king. Then Saul gets axed from God's plan and God is sorry he ever let Saul be king—but then he picks another king and promises to bless his dynasty forever. What in the world does God want here? Does he know? Is he changing his mind? I don't understand what I'm reading!"

Daniel laughed and sat down at the table. "Well, at least you're doing great on your observation skills, Erik! You've got the story straight—now to answer a few questions, right?" He picked up a stray paper. "Is this okay to scribble on?"

"Go ahead."

Daniel sketched a quick diagram. "You've done the first step—reading. Like we talked about before, the second step would be—more reading. Say ten or twenty times. But I'll spot you for that tonight, okay?

"We've got the *who*—God, the Israelites, Samuel, and Saul. We've got the *what*—they want a king. We've got the *when*—after Samuel has been a good judge his whole life, but his sons are worthless. We've got the *where*—Israel, various towns.

"We've also got the *why*—the Israelites want a king because Samuel's sons won't be good judges—and because all the other nations have one. But God tells us what their real reason is: they don't want God for their king.

"And the *how*—Samuel has to approve the one God chooses, because God is going to let them have what they want and learn the hard way. So God chooses the king *they* want. He follows their personal want ad and picks Saul."

"Great, Daniel. But what does it mean when it says God 'regrets' that he did it?"

"Okay, so here's where we take everything we just covered and look at that verse again. Do you have it there? Read it to me."

Daniel listened as Erik read 1 Samuel 15:24–35.

Then Saul said to Samuel, "I have sinned, for I have transgressed the commandment of the LORD and your words, because I feared the people and obeyed their voice. Now therefore, please pardon my sin, and return with me, that I may worship the LORD."

But Samuel said to Saul, "I will not return with you, for you have rejected the word of the LORD, and the LORD has rejected you from being king over Israel."

And as Samuel turned around to go away, Saul seized the edge of his robe, and it tore. So Samuel said to him, "The LORD has torn the kingdom of Israel from you today, and has given it to a neighbor of yours, who is better than you. And also the Strength of Israel will not lie nor relent. For He is not a man, that He should relent."

Then he said, "I have sinned; yet honor me now, please, before the elders of my people and before Israel, and return with me, that I may worship the LORD your God." So Samuel turned back after Saul, and Saul worshiped the LORD.

Then Samuel said, "Bring Agag king of the Amalekites here to me." So Agag came to him cautiously.

And Agag said, "Surely the bitterness of death is past."

But Samuel said, "As your sword has made women childless, so shall your mother be childless among women." And Samuel hacked Agag in pieces before the LORD in Gilgal.

Then Samuel went to Ramah, and Saul went up to his house at Gibeah of Saul. And Samuel went no more to see Saul until the day of his death. Nevertheless Samuel mourned for Saul, and the LORD regretted that He had made Saul king over Israel.

"So?"

"If you look back at verse 10, Erik, you'll see that twice God says he's sorry that he made Saul king. He regrets doing it. We could jump to the conclusion that God is hitting himself on the head for making a stupid mistake—like he didn't know what was going to happen.

"But we read the surrounding verses, the context, again, and we see that God rejected Saul and he's not going to change his mind about it! That tells us something important about God. He's not a human who vacillates. So scratch the idea of God kicking himself for his decision. He's not like us in that way.

"Now we look at the bigger context of the story. What is it that God wants? It says right here in the same chapter—God wants obedience from the heart. Saul would not give that to God, and God was grieved.

"Of course, we look at the bigger context of the whole Bible and we get more information. We find that there are times that God does seem to change his mind—with Moses, for instance, and with Abraham when he keeps lowering the minimum requirement for righteous people. Or we can go back further and see that in Noah's day, God regretted making man. We look at those stories within their contexts, and we find that the issue or the goal is again obedience.

"Then we look at even more passages and find that God knows everything about everything. He is never caught off guard. He was making choices from before the creation of the world—even with *our* sinful choices in mind—and he has a plan that will ultimately come to pass."

"So what does it mean?"

"You tell me, Erik."

"Man, Daniel, it's after midnight. But if I think it through, it would seem to mean that God's 'regretting' means that he experienced pain because Israel rejected him and Saul disobeyed him. He knew they were going to do it, but it hurt him anyway."

"That's a good interpretation. What else?"

"Okay, push me harder, will you? How about the fact that when the guy was writing the book, he already knew that David was going to be the king God chose? So this part of the story just sets up that doing it *their* way instead of *God's* way was a detour to disaster."

"Wow! That's great! And it's only a short jump to drawing out a principle for us to apply. . . ."

"Whoa! Slow down. Save it for the next meeting, Daniel! Besides, I still would like to understand more why it says God 'regretted' it. That seems like such strong language."

"That's when you pull out your concordance or an Old Testament dictionary or a good commentary or two. Believe me, a few people through the centuries have thought about this."

Erik stood up and stretched. "Thanks for the mental workout, Daniel. I think I'll hit the sack now. I knew it would be good for me to get out of the country and come to the big city for some reason."

"You going back after graduation?"

"I think so. When I was in high school, there was nothing there for me but drinking and driving around. After I became a Christian, I wanted to get away from all that, so I vowed I'd stay away. But I really am a country boy, and I'll probably go back and work for my uncle's company. Besides, I think God has a place for me there."

"Well, it's okay for you to change your mind, Erik—you're human! And you know what really matters to God."

"Yes, at least that's clear from my Bible reading! God wants obedience from the heart."

⟨ A Second Look at . . . Today's First Question: ⟩
What Does a Particular Passage of Scripture Mean?
How Can I Know for Sure?

Thankfully, there's no secret code or formula for understanding the Bible.

The world's best seller is written so people listening to or reading it can grasp what God is saying to them. True, it's possible to *misunderstand* Scripture—people have done that from day one. Still, the Lord wants you and me to *know* what he's saying!

The "golden rule" of biblical interpretation says God is not trying to mess with our minds. The same goes for Moses, David, Ezra, Malachi, Matthew, Mark, and all the other biblical writers. They expected listeners and readers to understand the meaning of what they wrote.

True, you and I may not catch everything the first time through. That's why we enjoy listening again to a favorite new song, why we want to watch a rerun on television, and why we stop to reread something that's profound.

Because God isn't trying to trick us, when we're reading Scripture we shouldn't try to "decode" it. Unless there's a compelling reason, we should accept the facts the Bible states at face value and embrace the normal meaning of its truths.

When it comes to understanding Scripture correctly, there are six important things to remember.

1. Primary Meaning. Like any great writer, God had specific facts and truths in mind for every sentence in Scripture. The important question isn't, what does this say to me? Instead, the question we need to ask is, what did God mean?

Take the famous statement by Jesus, "The truth shall make you free" (John 8:32). I could come up with any of a dozen *misinterpretations* of that verse. But in the end, it doesn't matter what *I* want that verse to mean.

If I consider myself an intellectual, I may want "The truth shall make you free" to mean that the more I know and learn, the better my life will be. If I consider myself an enlightened hedonist, I may want it to mean that I'm free to do whatever I want whenever I want as long as it doesn't hurt anyone else. But these popular *misinterpretations* are *not* what Jesus was saying!

As we read the Bible, we need to keep asking, what did God mean by this statement? If you're not sure, that's okay! Just write down your questions and then look up the answers later in a study Bible or a couple of good Bible commentaries. Reading the Bible isn't a matter of *my* interpretation. Instead, you and I want to embrace the church's orthodox understanding of Scripture.

If you don't have a study Bible, by the way, it's time to buy one! If you run into several tough questions, ask your pastor for permission to drop by his office to look up the answers in his Bible commentaries. Not all commentaries are created equal. In fact, some of them attack the Christian faith. If you're reading a commentary that doesn't (1) worship God, (2) praise the Lord Jesus Christ, and (3) show tremendous respect for God's Word, drop it fast and look for a better one!

Even the best Bible commentators don't have all the answers—not by a long shot. Not every statement in Scripture is clear-cut. Some are so poetic that it's hard to tell what the verse or paragraph means. Often, it's as we keep reading Scripture that we think, *There's the answer to one of my questions!*

Do your best to discover what *God* wants you to know. Most of the answers are right there in his Word. In the end, however, it's okay to have a list of unanswered questions.

In many cases, we'll have to wait until heaven to ask Moses, David, Ezra, or Paul, "What did you mean by this?" or "What did you mean by that?"

{Top Ten Questions to Ask in Heaven}

10. Paul, did you write the book of Hebrews?

9. Luke, as a doctor, what did you think the first time you saw Paul perform a miracle of healing?

8. Jonah, why didn't you write one more chapter explaining how God straightened you out?

7. Isaiah, how vivid was your vision of the passion of Jesus Christ?

6. Solomon, who is the second main character in Song of Songs?

5. David, how soon before Solomon's birth did Nathan rebuke you?

4. Job, did anyone else hear what the Lord told you in chapters 38–41?

3. Ruth, what was your first impression of your husband, Boaz?

2. Joshua, how did God make the sun stand still?

1. Moses, did you write Numbers 12:3: "Now Moses was a very humble man, more humble than anyone else on the face of the earth" (NIV)?

2. Secondary Meaning. Like any great writer, God occasionally has added an important second layer of meaning to a particular word, phrase, sentence, or longer section of Scripture. But that second layer of meaning always builds on—and never contradicts—the primary meaning.

In the Old Testament, we see a secondary layer of meaning most often in passages that look forward to the coming of the Messiah, Jesus Christ. Thankfully, Jesus himself pointed out many of these passages to his disciples after his resurrection (Luke 24:26–27). The apostles studied the Hebrew Scriptures diligently after Jesus's ascension (Acts 1:15–22). The apostle Paul did the same thing after his conversion (Acts 9:20–22).

If you think there might be a secondary meaning to a specific Old Testament verse, that's great! Write down your question and then look up the answer in your study Bible or a good commentary.

Just be careful not to spend too much time focused on or worried about possible secondary layers of meaning as you read the Bible. Unless something jumps out at you, keep your focus on the main thing God meant to say.

Passage	Primary Meaning	Secondary Meaning
Psalm 22	David tells the Lord vividly about a particularly painful, devastating time in his life.	Many statements in this psalm vividly describe Jesus Christ's experience on the cross, including: • what others said to insult him (Matt. 27:43)

Passage	Primary Meaning	Secondary Meaning
		• what Jesus said (Mark 15:34)
		• the fact that Jesus's hands and feet were pierced (Luke 24:38–40)
		• the kinds of pain and torture Jesus experienced during those six hours (John 19:1–37)
Hosea 1:2–3	Hosea obeyed God and married a woman named Gomer, who proved to be an adulterous wife.	The lurid lifestyle of Hosea's wife, Gomer, clearly pictured the extreme spiritual adultery of the kingdom of Israel.

3. Figures of Speech. Like any great writer, God used hyperbole, simile, metaphor, and other figures of speech throughout the Old and New Testaments. Not surprisingly, during his time on earth, the Lord Jesus repeatedly used figures of speech whenever he spoke to the crowds.

True, figures of speech sometimes confuse listeners and readers. But they're memorable and often cause readers to stop and wonder, *What did Jesus mean by that?* Thankfully, figures of speech usually *do* have a known meaning.

If you run across a figure of speech in the Bible that you haven't heard before, try looking it up in your English language dictionary. Many English figures of speech have biblical roots. If that doesn't work, look it up in your study Bible or commentary.

Biblical Figure of Speech	Type	Primary Meaning
You are the light of the world.	Metaphor	Christians reflect some of God's glory to others.
As the deer pants for water, so my soul pants for you, O God.	Simile	The psalmist greatly desired God.
Those who fall asleep	Euphemism	Those who die

Biblical Figure of Speech	Type	Primary Meaning
The setting of the sun	Word picture	The time of day when the sun appears to slip over the horizon

4. Key Words. Like any great writer, God used a rich vocabulary. So, not surprisingly, God's Word will stretch even the most avid reader's vocabulary.

Thankfully, Bible scholars down through the centuries have known what almost every word in the Bible means. Researchers in the past few centuries have carefully examined the known biblical manuscripts, looked at how the early church translated biblical words into Latin and other ancient languages, and reviewed how nonbiblical authors used the same words writing in Hebrew, Aramaic, and Greek. So it's easier than ever to find an answer to the question, what does this word mean?

The good news is you can use a standard collegiate dictionary to look up the meaning of most words you'll find in the Bible. That's especially true if your Bible translation and dictionary were published within a few years of each other. After all, the English language *does* change quickly!

Still, you'll run into words that you'll find only in a twenty-five-pound unabridged dictionary. Instead of running to your local library, see if your study Bible tells you what it means. Also, read the same verse in one or two other contemporary Bible translations. You may even want to look up the word in a Bible concordance. The concordance will give you a list of other verses that use the same word.

It's important to remember that the author determines the meaning of a given word. Earlier in this chapter, Erik was struggling with the meaning of the word "regrets." The problem was, he was thinking about only one meaning for that word. A good dictionary, however, may list five possible definitions. The Bible may add a sixth meaning.

Like William Shakespeare, Mark Twain, and Ernest Hemingway, God sometimes chose to use an old word in a new way. We see this in the New Testament letters Paul wrote. He used the word "mystery" a lot. That word already had several definitions. If you look up all of Paul's uses of the word, you'll discover it refers to the new revelations that God had given through Jesus Christ and the Holy Spirit to the apostles.

One of those new revelations is the "mystery" that God designed the church to be composed of *all* people—Jewish or Gentile (anyone who's not Jewish), male and female, slave and free. In other words, God wants everyone to turn from his or her sins, turn to God, trust Jesus Christ, and instantly become a member of the church, which includes everyone who is a real Christian. We take that for granted today, but it was a brand-new idea two thousand years ago!

Other times, God chose to cut and paste parts of old words to create a new word. Again, we see this in the letters Paul wrote. In Galatians 3:8, he used a word that in Greek combines the words "before" and "gospel." We don't find this compound word anywhere else in the Bible. That doesn't mean the early church didn't talk about it! If you look it up in your Bible, you'll discover it means "preached the gospel beforehand." To communicate that concept succinctly, Paul used what may have been a new word to many of his readers. It was his shorthand way of saying a lot in one power-packed term.

If you look really hard, you'll find only a small handful of biblical words where translators have had to add a footnote saying, in effect, "We don't know for sure what this word means." Many of these words are Hebrew musical terms.

Only one undefined word appears frequently in the Bible, and then almost exclusively in one book. It's the word "selah," which appears in the text of thirty-nine psalms. Translators have offered several possible meanings for *selah*. Whenever you run into the word assume it means, "Think about what God is saying in this psalm. Pay attention. Now, keep reading!"

Word	Dictionary Options	Biblical Meaning
Righteous	Appears in every dictionary; has several definitions, including slang usage	In Romans 3:10, this word means pure, faultless, sin-free, or "right."
Propitiation	Appears only in unabridged or biblical dictionaries	In Romans 3:25, this word means payment to satisfy God's wrath and restore relationship. Many translations use a phrase to translate this power-packed word.

5. Context. Like any great writer, God wrote every word and verse in context. He didn't write in a random, arbitrary manner. God has clearly communicated the meaning of most words and virtually all sentences and paragraphs within the same chapter, book, or section of the Bible.

In many cases, you can figure out what God meant if you keep reading.

In the Gospels, Jesus declared, "I am the bread of life" (John 6:35). Without even reading the context, we know Jesus is using a figure of speech. Every figure of speech has a known meaning. We can determine that meaning by reading what Jesus said in context. The immediate context tells us that Jesus was saying, "I have come from God to offer you new, eternal life. You can receive that life by believing me."

When we can't figure out the meaning of a statement in its immediate context, we may need to look at the broader context.

In the Ten Commandments, God declared, "You shall not murder" (Exod. 20:13; Deut. 5:17). Does this verse mean "Don't kill any life form"? No. The broader context is clear. Does it mean "God is against all killing, including war and capital punishment"? No. This commandment says it's against God's law for an individual to maliciously kill another human being. The broader context even goes on to say what to do if someone accidentally kills another human being.

Like Shakespeare, Twain, and Hemingway, God sometimes says something that we don't understand until later in the book.

In Genesis 37, we meet Joseph as a seventeen-year-old and are immediately told about two God-inspired dreams. Both have a single interpretation that inflames the hatred of his brothers, who sell Joseph into slavery in Egypt. Joseph's dreams are utterly destroyed. Worse, after being falsely accused of a terrible crime, Joseph spends years in prison.

More than a decade later, two of Joseph's fellow prisoners tell him about their dreams. The dreams sound similar, but Joseph interprets them in two very different ways. Two years later, Joseph is called before Pharaoh to interpret two very disturbing dreams.

This dream motif continues until we get to the climax of Joseph's story in Genesis 45. Finally, trembling and bowing before Pharaoh's right-hand man in Egypt, absolutely afraid for their lives, Joseph's brothers receive the shock of their lives. Joseph's teenage dreams had come true before their very eyes!

Like any great book, the Bible is meant to be read over and over. Better yet, think of it like watching one of your all-time favorite movies. Remember all the "Aha!" moments you had the second time you watched the movie? You can have "Aha!" moments every time you read through the Bible if you keep looking at the context.

Text	Focus of Pssage	Don't Miss This Detail
Luke 22:1–46	The last night before Jesus's crucifixion, when he celebrated the Passover with his disciples, then prayed on the Mount of Olives for the Father to "take this cup from me" if it was the Father's will.	You'll find the word "cup" used repeatedly in this chapter. Traditionally, the Jewish people celebrated the Passover by sharing several cups of wine. Each cup had special significance. Today we usually associate only one cup with the Last Supper, but Luke makes it clear that wasn't the case. What is the significance, if any, of the extra cups?

6. Comparison. Like any great writer, God wrote more than one work. Since the Bible is a collection of sixty-six books God inspired, with a unified theme and purpose, it's well worth our time comparing one Scripture passage with other related passages.

Many study Bibles provide a list of cross-references for any given Scripture verse. The cross-references show how other verses address the same theme.

Verse	Cross-Reference	Common Theme
Deuteronomy 4:29; 6:5; 30:2, 6, 10	Matthew 22:37; Mark 12:30; Luke 10:27	Love the Lord with all your heart, soul, strength, and mind.
Job 28:28	Psalm 111:10; Proverbs 1:7; 9:10; 15:33	The fear of the Lord is the beginning of wisdom.
Isaiah 65:17; 66:22	2 Peter 3:13; Revelation 21:1	Someday God will make new heavens and a new earth.

In addition, most study Bibles let you know whenever there's a parallel passage to the one you're reading.

- You'll find that Moses covers many of the events and laws in Exodus, Leviticus, and Numbers all over again in Deuteronomy.
- You'll find many of the events in 1 and 2 Samuel and 1 and 2 Kings covered again from a different perspective in 1 and 2 Chronicles. It's also worthwhile to read the corresponding psalms and related passages in the Prophets.
- You'll find many direct and indirect Old Testament quotations throughout the New Testament. Many show how Jesus is the promised Messiah.
- You'll find a number of Jesus's miracles and teachings covered from different perspectives in two or three Gospels. You'll find only the rare exception—Jesus feeds the five thousand—covered in all four Gospels. You'll also find that all four Gospels cover the passion of Jesus Christ in great detail.
- You'll find a number of the apostles' teachings and instructions covered from different perspectives in multiple New Testament letters.

Passage	Parallel	Theme
Exodus 20:18–19	Deuteronomy 5:23–27	How the Israelites reacted when the Lord gave the Ten Commandments.
2 Samuel 6:12–23	1 Chronicles 15:27–16:3	How David and others reacted when the ark of God was brought to Jerusalem.
Psalm 110:1	Matthew 22:44; Mark 12:36; Luke 20:42–43; Acts 2:34–35; Hebrews 1:13	This often-quoted verse speaks of the Messiah's sharing the Lord's authority and sitting at his right hand in heaven.
Matthew 14:13–21	Mark 6:32–44; Luke 9:10–17; John 6:1–13	Jesus feeds a multitude of people with a little boy's lunch: five small barley loaves and two fish.
1 Corinthians 10:3	Colossians 3:17	Whatever you do, do all for the glory of God.

So far, we've sought to address the literary challenges to correctly understanding Scripture. The good news is that the more time you spend seeking to understand Scripture correctly, the easier it gets. God designed it that way!

Before we wrap up this chapter, there are ten more challenges you and I need to seek to overcome. Thankfully, Christian publishers have produced a wealth of excellent Bible reference tools you and I can use to find the answers to our most important questions.

{ Today's Second Question: }
What Else Do I Need to Know About Understanding Scripture?

The following chart illustrates seven challenges that everyone today faces when seeking to understand the Bible.

It also lists tips you can use to answer most questions fairly quickly.

Challenge	Important Questions
1. Literary	What did God and the original author mean by this verse? What does this figure of speech or this key word mean? What can I learn from the context and other Scriptures? *Tip: Use the six factors just outlined. Also use a Bible concordance, Bible dictionary, Bible commentary, or study Bible notes if you run into a question you can't answer.*
2. Geographical	Where does this Scripture passage take place? What is the broader geographic context of this passage? What is the distance between locations? How were political boundaries changing during this period of history? *Tip: Start with the facts you find in Scripture. Also use a Bible atlas, maps in the back of your Bible, or study Bible notes.*
3. Biological	What do I need to know about people's living conditions? What do I need to know about animals in that region? What do I need to know about that area's plants? *Tip: Start with the facts you find in Scripture. Also use a Bible dictionary, Bible handbook, or study Bible notes.*
4. Historical	What historical background information do I need to know about the author's nation? About his audience's nation?

	About other surrounding nations? What other historical insights do I need to know? *Tip: Start with the facts you find in Scripture. Also use a Bible commentary, Bible dictionary, Bible handbook, or study Bible.*
5. Cultural	What cultural background information do I need to know about the cultures of the time? What did the author think about those cultures? What did God think about those cultures? *Tip: Start with the facts you find in Scripture. Also use Bible reference books or study Bible notes.*
6. Philosophical	How did people view God, the world, themselves, and others? What kind of philosophy of life did they have? How did God view their philosophy? *Tip: Start with the facts you find in Scripture. Also use Bible reference books or study Bible notes.*
7. Psychological	What was the author's frame of mind while writing this Scripture? Do I have any clues? If so, what do those clues suggest? What was his audience's frame of mind? Do I have any clues? What was the frame of mind of the main characters? *Tip: Start with the facts you find in Scripture. Also use Bible reference books or study Bible notes.*

When it comes to correctly understanding Scripture, you and I must face three other personal challenges. Thankfully, the more we can learn about the Bible *and* about ourselves, the better!

Challenge	Important Questions
1. National	How does my twenty-first-century citizenship in this nation, in this part of the world, color my perceptions of what Scripture says in the context of the ancient world?
2. Worldview	How does my modern or postmodern view of the universe, this world, reality, and truth collide with the outlook of the main characters in Scripture?
3. Personal	How does everything I feel, think, know, and think I know today make it difficult for me to hear what God has said in his Word?

While it's important to address all of these challenges, nothing replaces the importance of the Holy Spirit's illuminating our hearts and minds. Jesus sent the Spirit to take up residence in every Christian for that very reason.

The Holy Spirit's greatest desire is to bring God's Word alive within us so we wholeheartedly will love the Lord, worship him, and do what he says.

It's essential to correctly understand what Scripture says, but that's not enough.

There's still more!

how do i personalize
WHAT I'M READING?

K endall's fingers barely missed a beat on her computer keyboard as she picked up her cell phone on the first ring.

"Hello?"

"Kendall?" Her older sister's voice brought her to full attention. "It's Lauren. Is this a good time to talk?"

Kendall closed her document and moved to the couch. "Lauren, you know I wish you called me more often. I'd rather talk to you than write up business reports any hour. This will be my official mental health break for the day. What's up?"

Kendall heard a deep sigh. "While you're studying your head off, I'm counting little heads around here and wishing I was someplace else. Right this minute Julie is taking a nap and Max is searching the kitchen floor for remnants of leftover lunch."

Kendall laughed, visualizing her year-old nephew crawling about, nose to the ceramic tile. "Anything else wrong besides the afternoon doldrums of a mother of preschoolers?"

Lauren's voice got soft, and Kendall could almost see her, head hung down, hand running through her short, dark hair. "You know that business deal John was supervising? It looks like there's going to be a lawsuit, and I'm so afraid that he's going to get burned. We can't trust anyone at that office to tell the truth or look after anyone but themselves. Losing his job is the least of his worries—getting framed for someone else's mess up could mean losing everything."

"Oh, Lauren, I'm so sorry. I wish I could do something. I wish I was there to give you a hug."

"I know you do. I thought just talking to you would remind me that we're not alone in all this. John is handling this much better, but I'm finding myself trying to figure out how to handle the unfairness of it all."

"Have you talked to Mom?"

Lauren chuckled. "Of course I have. You know what she told me."

"'Read a few Psalms and call me in the morning'?"

{ Today's First Question: }
Is Scripture Relevant to My Life? If So, Why?

"Something to that effect. I've tried that, but I keep feeling like I'm reading someone else's mail. I'm not a shepherd or a king, and things are bad, but no one's trying to kill me. I just keep trying to figure out how it's relevant to my life."

Kendall was nodding even though she knew her sister couldn't see her. "I know that feeling. I always felt guilty that the Bible didn't speak to me the way it did to other people, so I just kept wondering how to personalize what I was reading. I mean, without making it up."

"Maybe I can send anonymous e-mails with verses about God's judgment to all the jerks involved in this mess—but that would probably be a little out-of-bounds."

"Not to mention increasing John's risk of getting nailed for something!"

Kendall reached over and pulled her Bible toward her. "This might sound flaky, but I've really starting getting more out of those verses Mom made us memorize. Remember that reading group at school? We're reading the whole Bible through, and this time it's coming alive to me personally."

"What do you think has made the difference?" Lauren asked.

{ Today's Second Question: }
How Do You Personalize a Particular Scripture? What's the Secret?

"Well, just reading everything, for one. Being challenged to let God speak to me, for another. But recently, something Daniel said has given me a grid for putting it together. First, he challenged us to read everything with an eye to *look for truths*—and then affirm our belief in those truths. I started seeing everything the Bible says about God—what he was like, what he did for people. As I realized that I believed what I read about God, it became more personal. And the same went for what the Scriptures say about people. I can now see the world through God's eyes and get some perspective."

"So do you have a verse for me, Kendall? Something to give me perspective before I go crazy with anxiety?"

Kendall knew Lauren wouldn't ask unless she was serious. "Here is something I read last week. I remembered thinking it was so true to life in the business world. Listen to this from Psalm 37:

> Don't be upset because of evil people.
> Don't be jealous of those who do wrong,
>   because like the grass, they will soon dry up.
> Like green plants, they will soon die away. . . .
>
> The wicked make evil plans against good people.
> . . . The wicked draw their swords
>   and bend their bows
> to kill the poor and helpless,
>   to kill those who are honest.
> But their swords will stab their own hearts. . . .
>
> Think of the innocent person,
>   and watch the honest one.
> The man who has peace
>   will have children to live after him.
> But sinners will be destroyed;
>   in the end the wicked will die. [vv. 1–2, 12, 14–15, 37–38 NCV]

Lauren laughed. "That sounds a little violent, Kendall. Sounds like I'm supposed to send those e-mails! Are you sure you want me to personalize that?"

"Well, the truth to affirm is that, eventually, people who try to hurt others will get what's coming to them. Mostly in this life, we hope, but God promises to take care of it one day for sure. So I remind myself that I believe God will not let wicked people succeed forever. The Bible doesn't promise bad things won't happen, but it lets off a lot of pressure on my end."

"And in the meantime?"

"I read this and remind myself that God is taking care of me—that's something about who he is, so I can personalize it even if I'm nothing like the person writing Psalm 37."

"Oh, Kendall, you know we always have to do something about everything—function at our highest potential, remember? I just want to know what I can *do* about it!" Kendall heard Max let out a little wail, and she knew Lauren wanted to do a little wailing of her own.

"That's exactly what I love about the rest of the personalizing process. Daniel encouraged us to read each Scripture passage a second time to *underline all the action verbs*. I did that last week with Psalm 37. Wouldn't Mom be proud? Then I made a list of everything I could *do* in response: Not worry. Do good. Turn from anger. Watch for God to act. I need to figure out exactly how that looks every day, but I have a list—and at least I'm starting down the path."

"Wait a minute—Max, don't eat that! Are you sure this is the same little sister we sent off to college three years ago? I'm glad you're finally growing up so you can pay me back for all the free advice I gave you all those years. Ouch! Max, stop pulling my earring! I really wish you were closer, but it sounds like the move has been good for you. I gotta go now—just keep me in your prayers, okay?"

"Keep me posted, Lauren—I'll be waiting!"

{ A Second Look at . . . Today's First Question: }
Is Scripture Relevant to My Life? If So, Why?

Kendall is right: Scripture *is* relevant.

No wonder it's so important to keep reading Scripture so we don't forget what it says!

After all, the Word of God is more than merely words on a page. It's not simply a best seller year after year, millennium after millennium. The Bible contains truths, commands, and examples that speak directly to our lives in the twenty-first century.

According to 2 Timothy 3:16–17, *all* Scripture is inspired by God and is useful, profitable, beneficial, practical, and full of rewards for the person who makes it his or her life's Global Positioning System (GPS).

Sometimes the trick, however, is determining how to read it when we're in a particular situation. The problem? We're often in a hurry to know which way to turn! How much better to slow down and check our God-given GPS. Even better, why not plot our course ahead of time? After all, the road ahead isn't about to move!

Thankfully, whatever the world's first GPS says about *God, humanity,* or *eternity* is relevant to everyone, all the time.

Three all-encompassing GPS realities:

1. God is great. We see this from page 1 on. You can't find ten words more powerful than the opening line: "In the beginning God created the heavens and the earth" (Gen. 1:1). Talk about *great*! On the sixth day, he made man (Gen. 1:26–27). Yet miracles are only ripples of God's first words. He isn't finished speaking yet! No matter what challenges we face between here and heaven, God is big enough to meet our needs. He'll never say, "Whoa! Now *that's* a problem. You're on your own this time, kid."

2. God is good. We see this from pages 2 to 1,002. Forget honeymooning on a remote South Pacific isle. You can't ask for anything better than the Garden of Eden (Gen. 2:8–25). Talk about *good*! Adam and Eve had it made. Yet Paradise is only God's first act. He's saving his best for last! From now until eternity, God will always do what is truly best for us. He'll never be tempted to say, "I'm tired of all this righteous stuff. I feel like changing all the rules today. Watch out, world!"

3. God is gracious. We see this throughout the Bible. Forget getting out of jail free. You can't thank God enough for showing mercy and promising a redeemer (Gen. 3:14–21). Talk about *gracious*! The wages of humanity's sin was death (Rom. 3:23). Yet forgiveness is only God's first gift. He's promised us so much more! We can always count on the fact that God has much more than salvation in store for us. He will always be glad to say, "Can I tell you again how much I love you? I'm so glad you're my child."

That's not all!

Scripture is full of countless amazing truths about *God himself, our lives,* and *things to come*. It's a GPS that works everywhere, every time.

And it's not just the Old and New Testaments that speak to us. It's not just Bible books and chapters. Individual Scripture paragraphs and verses are relevant too.

{ **A Second Look at . . . Today's Second Question:** }
How Do You Personalize a Particular Scripture? What's the Secret?

The good news: There is no secret to personalizing paragraphs and verses of Scriptures. It's just a matter of asking a few simple questions.

Interestingly, the simplest questions are sometimes the most profound. This is especially true when we're considering what God has to say to us in his Word. Sadly, many Christians feel personalizing Scripture has to be complicated. Nothing is further from the truth!

These six questions can quickly transform ordinary Bible reading into a life-changing experience.

As you read a phrase, verse, or short paragraph of Scripture, ask yourself:

Personalize	Apply
What Truths does this passage teach?	Do I Affirm them?
What Commands does the Lord give?	Do I Obey them?
What Examples does Scripture present?	Do I Heed them?

This is the TA-CO, EH? (Truths to Affirm, Commands to Obey, Examples to Heed) approach to personalized Scripture reading. It works great no matter where you live (Mexico or Canada, in between or overseas), how you prefer to talk (*sí*, eh, or yes), or what you like to eat.

In this chapter, we'll focus on the left column—on *personalizing* Scripture truths, commands, and examples. For most people, this is the missing jewel of Bible reading.

In the next chapter, we'll quickly springboard over to the right column—into instantly and actively *applying* Scripture to our lives.

Personalizing a Verse

Let's start with a verse almost everyone knows: "For God so loved the world that He gave His only begotten Son, that whoever believes in Him should not perish but have everlasting life" (John 3:16).

That's a fantastic verse. But what does it mean to you and me? Let's ask today's three TA-CO, EH? questions.

1. Truths to Affirm. First, what Truths to Affirm (TA) does this verse teach? Looking at the verse itself, we discover some important truths:

- God loves the world.
- God loves us so much he sent his only Son.
- Whoever believes in him will not perish.
- Whoever believes in him will have everlasting life.

These basic truths, however, don't tell us everything we need to know. If it's so important to believe in God's only Son, who is he? Where was he sent? And why?

Looking at this same verse from an informed New Testament perspective, we can affirm:

- God loves the world (everyone, including us).
- God loves us so much he sent his only Son (Jesus Christ, who died on a Roman cross in our place for our sins).
- Whoever believes in him (Jesus Christ) will not perish (remain spiritually dead here on earth and afterward go to hell).
- Whoever believes in him (Jesus Christ) will have everlasting life (enjoy spiritual life here on earth and afterward go to heaven).

No wonder John 3:16 is the most famous and loved verse in all Scripture! Let's look at the verse itself again: "For God so loved the world that he gave his one and only Son so that whoever believes in him may not be lost, but have eternal life" (NCV). Okay, it's time for our next TA-CO, EH? question.

2. Commands to Obey. Second, what Commands to Obey (CO) does the Lord give in this verse?

The verse itself doesn't contain any commands, but it implies the most important command the Lord gives in all Scripture. This is a command we find throughout the New Testament, especially prevalent in John's writings. The implied command is this: *believe in Jesus Christ.*

Again, John 3:16 doesn't state a direct command: "The Lord says to everyone, everywhere, for all of time, 'Believe in my only Son, Jesus Christ.'" But that imperative is imbedded at the core of the verse in the phrase "believes in him."

Whenever we see a powerful verb in Scripture, we need to ask ourselves, *Does this verb imply a biblical command I should obey? If so, what is that command?*

If you're reading the Bible for the very first time, and you've read only snatches here and there, you may not be able to *see* the implied commands of Scripture. With time, however, you'll see them on every page!

Okay, let's look at John 3:16 one more time: "God loved the world so much that he gave his one and only Son so that whoever believes in him may not be lost, but have eternal life" (NCV). It's now time for our last TA-CO, EH? question.

3. Examples to Heed. Third, what Examples to Heed (EH) does this verse present?

In this single verse, we find two important examples:

- God loves the world.
- God sent his only Son.

What do these examples show us? The rest of John's Gospel makes it clear:

- Just as God loves the world, so I should love all people, whether or not they believe in Jesus Christ yet.
- Just as God sent his only Son, so I should give sacrificially so others can accept God's love, believe in Jesus Christ, and receive eternal life.

After Jesus Christ's resurrection and ascension to heaven, the apostle John himself embraced both of these examples and faithfully lived them out for the rest of his life. They're worthy examples to imitate in our own lives today (we'll have more to say about that in the next chapter).

Now let's step beyond John 3:16 and take a more in-depth look at how to use these three *personalization* questions.

Taking a Closer Look

As you ask the three TA-CO, EH? questions during your Bible reading, you'll want to keep the following caveats in mind.

Truths to Affirm. Not all truths are created equal. Scripture accurately records outright lies, straightforward historical details, insights about how life works, and divinely revealed truths. The Bible itself places the most value on the latter.

Inspired Scripture	Divine Truth?	Fact of Life?	Simple Detail?	False Notion?
Genesis "In the beginning God created the heavens and the earth" (1:1).	X			
"God said, 'Look, I have given you all the plants that have grain for seeds and all the trees whose fruits have seeds in them. They will be food for you'" (1:29 NCV).		X		
"But the snake said to the woman, 'You will not die'" (3:4 NCV).				X
"When Enoch was 65 years old, he had a son named Methuselah" (5:21 NCV).			X	
Joshua "After the death of Moses the servant of the LORD, it came to pass that the LORD spoke to Joshua the son of Nun, Moses's assistant" (1:1).			X	
"Then the woman took the two men and hid them. So she said, 'Yes, the men came to me, but I did not know where they were from'" (2:4).				X
"So the men answered her, 'Our lives for yours, if none of you tell this business of ours. And it shall be, when the LORD has given us the land, that we will deal kindly and truly with you'" (2:14).		X		

Inspired Scripture	Divine Truth?	Fact of Life?	Simple Detail?	False Notion?
"Then the priests who bore the ark of the covenant of the LORD stood firm on dry ground in the midst of the Jordan; and all Israel crossed over on dry ground" (3:17).	X			
Job "There was a man in the land of Uz, whose name was Job; and that man was blameless and upright" (1:1).		X		
"With Him are wisdom and strength / He has counsel and and understanding" (12:13).	X			
"You have sent widows away empty, / And the strength of the fatherless was crushed" (22:9).				X
"But it is the spirit in a man, / the breath of the Almighty, that gives him understanding" (32:8 NIV).	X			

Commands to Obey. Not all commands are created equal. Some commands are perpetual, other commands have clearly expired, and still others are for someone else—not for you and me.

Inspired Scripture	Command to Obey?	Not for Me?	Out of Date?
Exodus "Take your sandals off your feet, for the place where you stand is holy ground" (3:5).		X	

Inspired Scripture	Command to Obey?	Not for Me?	Out of Date?
"On the tenth day of this [first] month each man must get one lamb for the people in his house" (12:3 NCV).			X
"Honor your father and your mother, that your days may be long upon the land" (20:12).	X		
Leviticus "You must be holy because I am holy" (19:2 NCV).	X		
"When you sacrifice a fellowship offering to the LORD, sacrifice it in such a way that it will be accepted on your behalf" (19:5 NIV).			X
"When you reap the harvest of your land, do not reap to the very edges of your field" (19:9 NIV).		X	
Numbers "He [a Nazirite] must let the hair of his head grow long" (6:5 NIV).		X	
"Present a cake from the first of your ground meal and present it as an offering from the threshing floor" (15:20 NIV).			X
"If a man makes a promise to the LORD or says he will do something special, he must keep his promise" (30:2 NCV).	X		

Examples to Heed. Not all examples are created equal. Some examples are positive, some are negative, and some don't apply to you or me.

Inspired Scripture	Example to Follow?	Example to Avoid?	Not for Me?
Genesis Abram questions how God could fulfill his promises in Abram's lifetime (15:2–3).		X	
Abram believes God wholeheartedly (15:6).	X		
Abraham offers a sacrifice to God (15:10).			X
Ruth Elimelech and his family move to another country during a famine (1:1).			X
Elimelech's daughter-in-law, Ruth, wholeheartedly puts her faith in God (1:16).	X		
Ruth's mother-in-law, Naomi, blames God for the tragedies in her life (1:21).		X	
Esther Haman plans to kill all of the Jewish people in the Persian Empire (3:6).		X	
Esther is willing to trust God and risk her life to try to save others from death (4:16).	X		
Esther authorizes the Festival of Purim to celebrate the deliverance of her people (9:29).			X

{ **Today's Third Question:** }
How Do I Personalize Broader Sections of Scripture?
Is That Even Possible?

With practice, you can learn how to apply the three TA-CO, EH? questions to longer paragraphs and chapters of the Bible.

This works even for whole books of the Bible. Take the book of Psalms, for instance. One of the overarching *examples* we see in the Psalms is how to pray in the midst of crisis.

Beginning with Psalm 3, and over and over again until Psalm 149, we find the psalmist crying out to the Lord in various dire circumstances.

- How many are my foes!
- Give me relief from my distress.
- Listen to my cry for help.
- Away from me, all you who do evil.
- Save and deliver me from all who pursue me.

In seven out of every ten psalms, the writer is either crying out to the Lord for physical salvation, thanking God for sparing his life, reminding himself of the differing fates of the righteous and evildoers, or renewing his allegiance to God and his Word in the face of rampant wickedness.

If the book of Psalms teaches us anything, then, it's *how* to turn to God in times of trouble and distress.

Here's a brief synopsis with specific examples from various psalms.

1. Call out to the Lord . . .

Hear my cry, O God;
> listen to my prayer. (Ps. 61:1 NIV)

2. . . . And ask for help!

Make haste, O God, to deliver me!
Make haste to help me, O Lord! (Ps. 70:1)

3. Tell God about your troubles . . .

O God, the nations have invaded your inheritance;
> they have defiled your holy temple,

they have reduced Jerusalem to rubble.
They have given the dead bodies of your servants
    as food to the birds of the air,
      the flesh of your saints to the beasts of the earth.
They have poured out blood like water
    all around Jerusalem,
      and there is no one to bury the dead.
We are objects of reproach to our neighbors,
    of scorn and derision to those around us. (Ps. 79:1–4 NIV)

4. . . . And admit if you feel abandoned or forsaken.

How long, LORD?
Will You hide Yourself forever?
Will Your wrath burn like fire?
Remember how short my time is;
For what futility have You created all the children of men? (Ps. 89:46–47)

5. Describe what you want God to do . . .

Make us glad according to the days in which You have afflicted us,
    The years in which we have seen evil.
Let Your work appear to Your servants,
    and Your glory to their children.
And let the beauty of the LORD our God be upon us,
    And establish the work of our hands for us;
Yes, establish the work of our hands. (Ps. 90:15–17)

6. . . . And explain why he should act on your behalf.

Let this be written for a future generation,
    that a people not yet created may praise the LORD:
"The LORD looked down from his sanctuary on high,
    from heaven he viewed the earth,
to hear the groans of the prisoners
    and release those condemned to death."
So the name of the LORD will be declared in Zion

and his praise in Jerusalem
when the peoples and the kingdoms
    assemble to worship the LORD. (Ps. 102:18–22 NIV)

7. Give a candid appraisal of your enemy . . .

With words of hatred they surround me;
    they attack me without cause.
In return for my friendship they accuse me,
    but I am a man of prayer.
They repay me evil for good,
    and hatred for my friendship. (Ps. 109:3–5 NIV)

8. . . . And ask God to put that foe in his place.

Appoint an evil man to oppose him;
    let an accuser stand at his right hand.
When he is tried, let him be found guilty,
    and may his prayers condemn him.
May his days be few;
    may another take his place of leadership.
May his children be fatherless
    and his wife a widow. (Ps. 109:6–9 NIV)

9. Honestly evaluate your guilt or innocence . . .

I have chosen the way of truth;
    Your judgments I have laid before me.
I cling to Your testimonies;
    O LORD, do not put me to shame! (Ps. 119:30–31)

10. . . . And confess any known sins.

I have gone astray like a lost sheep;
    Seek Your servant,
For I do not forget Your commandments. (Ps. 119:176)

11. Affirm your implicit trust in the Lord . . .

I will lift up my eyes to the hills—

From whence comes my help?
My help comes from the LORD,
    Who made heaven and earth. (Ps. 121:1–2)

12. . . . And then praise God for his deliverance.
    Blessed be the LORD,
    Who has not given us as prey to their teeth.
    Our soul has escaped as a bird from the snare of the fowlers;
    The snare is broken, and we have escaped.
    Our help is in the name of the LORD,
    Who made heaven and earth. (Ps. 124:6–8)

You may not be facing a crisis today—but crises will come. When they do, turn to Psalms, where you'll find comfort, solace, encouragement, joy, and strength to face each day.

In turn, God will begin to use you to share truths, commands, and examples from Scripture with family and friends, associates and acquaintances.

Before you put down this book, however, there's one last chapter you *have* to read. It's on how to apply God's Word so you can enjoy his blessing in every sphere of life. The rewards of Bible reading can be yours! Just turn the page. . . .

what do i do
AFTER I READ?

Hamid propped open the heavy glass door and let in the warmth of the early June afternoon. Most customers were grabbing iced drinks to take into the sunshine. The usual Wednesday Bible reading group had claimed the leather chairs, but so far, their conversation didn't seem to be getting too serious.

Daniel was proposing a toast with a tall caramel machiatto. "Here's to each of you—you can now say you've completely read through the world's foremost best seller! May you enjoy many more journeys through it!"

Kendall, Erik, and Maria raised their glasses. "Here's to a great guide," Erik offered. "I definitely would have given up or gotten lost on the trail without you, Daniel."

"Hey, you guys have taught me a lot this year. Fresh eyes sometimes see things better. I just wish we were going to be closer this summer. You'll keep in touch, won't you?"

Kendall set down her cappuccino to pick up her Bible. "Believe it or not, I think I'll go back and try using that biographical reading plan this summer. I'll keep you all posted on what I discover."

"That sounds like a great idea," Maria said. "I'll do it, too, so we can compare notes."

"Speaking of comparing notes—anyone have any moments of divine illumination this week?" Daniel motioned to Kendall, since she looked the most ready and prepared.

"Thanks, Daniel, but I'll let someone else go first. Just because I'm the first one to open my Bible doesn't mean I have the most meaningful things to say. I didn't promise that I had any great insights today!"

"I don't know about insights, but if you give me a minute, I can try to find that verse I've been thinking about all day." Maria quickly flipped through her Bible to the book of James. "I love this book because James is so straightforward. You don't have to do much guesswork to figure out what commands you're supposed to obey!

"Of course, his concern for the poor resonates with me—but I found another verse that I'm trying to apply to my life these days. It's this one, chapter 1, verse 20: 'Man's anger does not bring about the righteous life that God desires' (NIV).

"The principle's obvious—I don't use my anger to achieve God's purposes—but the application is a bit harder. Right now I'm really angry at the way the staff is treating one of the volunteers at the shelter. I really lost it the other day and gave the supervisor a piece of my mind. I even threatened to drop all my shifts."

"Doesn't the Bible also say to 'be angry and sin not'? Isn't it okay to be angry—like Jesus was—when people are doing wrong things?" Kendall asked.

"Believe me, I thought about that. But afterward I came back to this verse. I know that anger has a place, but I realized that this time I was definitely using my own anger and my own power to try to push something through."

"The previous verse says to 'be quick to listen, slow to speak, and slow to become angry,'" Erik noted.

"Yeah, I noticed that too. I decided to go back. Besides apologizing—that was sure hard—I actually asked some questions and then gave myself some time before I responded. I don't know if it will make any difference. I'm going to talk to the head supervisor tomorrow. But I feel like I'm at least letting *God* power me, not my own anger."

"Wow." Daniel shook his head. "That's powerful. You never cease to amaze me, Maria. I'm going to have to take some time to apply that verse myself."

At that moment, Hamid appeared with a tray of generous samples of double-chocolate brownies and lemon pound cake. "Things are slow this afternoon—can I interest you all in a sample of our specialties? I sliced them extra big since I knew you were celebrating."

"Hamid! I wish you could join us! Didn't you read the Bible for the first time this year too?"

{ Today's First Question: }
How Do I Apply Scripture to My Life? Does It Just Happen?

Hamid smiled. "Well, yes, though I wasn't able to fully complete the reading. Perhaps this summer. I'm still trying to understand what difference these Scriptures make today."

Daniel leaned forward and helped himself to a brownie while keeping his eyes locked on Hamid's. "Hamid, you said yourself that the Bible is a living book. The difference it makes is that it tells you how to have life with God—'eternal salvation,' we call it. Did you see that as you read through the Gospels?"

"Ah, now, Daniel, don't try to convert me! I cannot see how one man can die for another man's sins. You know that the Prophet gave us a clearer message from God that the Injil contains."

"I don't know about that, Hamid. I just want to make sure of one thing. When you want to have complete assurance that God accepts you, you will find it in the Bible—in Jesus."

{ Today's Second Question: }
Does Scripture Apply to All of Life? If So, How?

"In Jesus? Well, I do value my Bible, Daniel, and I promise I will keep reading it. I just wish I knew why you feel it applies to your whole life."

Daniel smiled and helped himself to another brownie. "What do you think, Maria?"

{ A Second Look at . . . Today's First Question: }
How Do I Apply Scripture to My Life? Does It Just Happen?

Without application, Scripture makes no more difference in your life than water in a cooler, coffee behind the counter, or a fruit-flavored energy drink commercial on TV. Nothing happens without deliberate *action*.

As we saw in chapter 12, there are six simple questions that can quickly transform ordinary Bible reading into a profound, life-changing experience.

Again, as you read a phrase, verse, or short paragraph of Scripture, ask yourself:

Personalize	Apply
What Truths does this passage teach?	Do I Affirm them?
What Commands does the Lord give?	Do I Obey them?
What Examples does Scripture present?	Do I Heed them?

This TA-CO, EH? approach not only invigorates your experience each time you read a passage of Scripture but it can also change your life!

Truths to Affirm

Remarkably, you and I can read page after page of the Bible without ever stopping to ask, *Do I really believe this? And this? And that?* Yet if we don't wholeheartedly affirm the Bible's truths, we can easily lose our way in this crazy, confusing, mixed-up world of half-truths, misconceptions, and outright lies.

It's important to read God's Word, make no mistake. But it's even more important for us to actively say yes to Scripture's rich and trustworthy declarations about God, creation, the Fall, the ancient world, God's chosen people, and God's love for the whole world; about Jesus's life, ministry, teaching, miracles, betrayal, death, burial, and resurrection; and about the church's miraculous birth, expansion, teachings, and blessed hope.

How important is this?

In answering that question, here is one person's story:

> During a profound time of crisis a decade ago, I suddenly stopped reading the Bible, after reading it daily since I was a teenager. I couldn't even pray. After several shattering back-to-back trials, I had wrongly concluded that God's own hand was crushing me.
>
> Days went by. Weeks. Finally, in desperation, I opened my Bible again. I knew I couldn't immediately read page after page, as had been my custom. So I simply read one verse, then asked myself, *Do I believe this?*
>
> Thankfully, my answer was yes. Not a *huge* yes, but a yes nevertheless. That gave me the courage to read another verse. And another. Within three days, God restored my faith in a remarkable way. I'll never be the same.
>
> Today, I delight in opening God's Word and affirming what he

says. And when crises come—and they always will—I'm more confident than ever that the Lord hasn't changed.

So how does it work to affirm truths from Scripture? Let's consider a few examples from the opening pages of Genesis and 1 John.

In Genesis 1:27, God's Word tells us, "So God created man in his own image; / in the image of God he created him; / male and female he created them" (NIV). In response to this verse, we can readily affirm, "I believe every person is created in the image of God." You and I also can affirm, "I believe I am created in the image of God." The key is to silently ask, *Do I really believe this?* If I do, I begin to gain a clearer picture of God and of myself.

In 1 John 1:9 we read, "If we confess our sins, He [God] is faithful and just to forgive us our sins and to cleanse us from all unrighteousness." We all know this. So what? In response you and I can affirm, "I believe God truly forgives me when I confess my sins." The key is to affirm this in prayer to the Lord himself . . . and to honestly tell him if we have any struggles or doubts.

It isn't enough to mentally assent the truths of Scripture. To apply them to our lives, we need to actively and wholeheartedly *affirm* them.

Commands to Obey

Incredibly, you and I can listen to Scripture, nod our heads, stand up, walk out the door, and never once stop to wonder, *What would Jesus have me do in this situation?* Yet if we don't wholeheartedly obey the Lord's commands, we'll quickly go astray, risk our lives in mad pursuit of the tempting and trivial, get terribly hurt in the process, and then have the audacity to point the finger at others—even God.

No wonder Scripture urges us "to say 'No' to ungodliness and worldly passions, and to live self-controlled, upright and godly lives in this present age, while we wait for the blessed hope—the glorious appearing of our great God and Savior, Jesus Christ" (Titus 2:12–13 NIV).

So how does it work to obey commands from Scripture? Let's consider a few examples from Exodus and 2 Peter.

In Exodus 20:12 (also in Lev. 19:3; Deut. 5:16; Matt. 15:4; Mark 7:10; Luke 18:20; Eph. 6:2) the Lord commands us, "Honor your father and your mother." The question isn't what you and I think of our parents. The question is, can we honestly say, "I honor my parents in obedience to the Lord's command"? Sometimes the answer is no. If that's the case, the point isn't to heap guilt upon ourselves. God simply asks us to be honest with him and invites us to claim his promises for wisdom and strength.

In 2 Peter 3:14 we're told, "And so, dear friends, while you are waiting for these things to happen [the new heavens and new earth], make every effort to live a pure and blameless life. And be at peace with God" (NLT). Our response shouldn't be to read past this verse and pretend we're already perfect. Instead, we should decide to conform our lives to Scripture so you and I can honestly say, "I am now making every effort to live a pure and blameless life and to be at peace with God." To do that, we first need to come clean with God, then start obeying this particular command.

It isn't enough to notice the commands in the Bible. To apply them to our lives, we need to gladly and consistently *obey* them.

Examples to Heed

It's not enough to know the great Sunday school stories about Noah and Sarah, Joshua and Deborah, Ruth and Absalom, Elijah and Esther, Daniel and Mary, Nicodemus and Cornelius, John Mark and Timothy. True, the biblical narratives are intriguing. But what lessons can we learn from each character's faith and failings, victories and vices?

Experience truly is the best teacher—especially the experiences of others who have gone before us. So every time we read from God's Word, we should seek to import lessons from the lives of both biblical scoundrels (1 Cor. 10:1–13) and heroes of the faith (Heb. 11:4–40).

So how does it work to heed examples from Scripture? Let's consider a couple of examples from Leviticus and 1 Peter.

In Leviticus 8:4 we read, "So Moses did as the LORD commanded him. And the congregation was gathered together at the door of the tabernacle of meeting." You and I can keep reading. Or we can stop, note Moses's positive example, and then affirm, "I too choose to do what the Lord commands."

In 1 Peter 2:21 the apostle Peter spells out the example we're to heed when he writes, "For to this you were called [suffering for doing right, not for doing wrong], because Christ also suffered for us, leaving us an example, that you should follow His steps." He's calling for an immediate response. Will you and

I say, "I follow Jesus Christ's example and am willing to suffer for doing right"?

It isn't enough to ponder the examples in Scripture. To apply them to our lives, we need to willingly and readily *heed* them.

{ A Second Look at . . . Today's Second Question: }
Does Scripture Apply to All of Life? If So, How?

Scripture speaks to every fiber of our beings. It speaks to your looks and health, to my attitudes and actions, to your relationships with family and friends, to my use of time and money, to your employment and career options, to my educational and athletic pursuits, to your beliefs and convictions about God and the Bible.

Scripture also speaks to your interests in literature and postmodern art, to my love of extreme sports and alternative music, to your hobbies and habits, to my enjoyment of rhythm and dance, to your Christian commitment and love for the Lord.

In other words, Scripture speaks to *all of life*!

That's why it's crucial to read God's Word with a clear sense of *who you are*. How well do you understand your strengths and weaknesses, your current situation, your relationships with others, your relationship with God? Actively bring that understanding to the table when you read the Bible.

That's why it's also so important to *meditate on Scripture*. It's not enough just to read the words on the page. You and I need to wash our minds with God's Word. Meditation can involve

- reflecting on the meaning of key words in a Bible phrase, verse, or paragraph;
- memorizing a verse, paragraph, or longer section of God's Word; and
- rewriting a Scripture passage in your own words.

Because Scripture speaks to all of life, we also need to *prayerfully talk with God* about what he says in Scripture about each area of our lives.

The average person in the Western world today has well over a dozen spheres of life. Remarkably, Scripture speaks to every area! It's no wonder. Using the three TA-CO, EH? questions, you can find thousands of relevant truths, commands, and examples from Genesis through Revelation.

Imagine what God could do in and through you if you read the Bible and *responded* as God desired.

In Joshua 1, Psalm 1, Psalm 119, 2 Peter 1, and other Scriptures, God promises that he will *prosper* those who delight in his Word, take it to heart, and apply its truths.

Why hold back?

Why not take God at his Word?

If you haven't read the Bible cover to cover, there's no excuse—this book is your guide for taking that incredible journey.

If you have read through the Bible, don't stop! Keep reading. We've provided several reading guides you can use. Feel free to photocopy them. Give an extra one to a friend who's willing to read with you.

Whether it's in your favorite coffee shop, church, or home, meet with at least one friend weekly while you're reading through the Bible. Swap stories and insights. Encourage each other. Celebrate when you finish! Then start again.

Never forget . . .

The Lord wants to prosper *every* area of your life!

How?

Through his Word.

Read it! Embrace it! Live it!

Our prayer for you today: "By his power . . . may [God] fulfill every good purpose of yours and every act prompted by your faith" (2 Thess. 1:11 NIV).

Let God's Word prompt your faith in wonderful ways in the days ahead!

(61 days)

Want to read highlights from every book of the Bible? It doesn't take long! The advantages of this approach include simplicity, comprehensiveness, and brevity.

As you read, ask the Lord to help you understand, personalize, and apply his Word. Then be sure to thank God for what he's going to do in each area of your life.

Day	Today's Scripture Reading
❑ Day 1:	Genesis 1–3, 12, 15, 22
❑ Day 2:	Exodus 1–5
❑ Day 3:	Exodus 12–14, 20
❑ Day 4:	Leviticus 1, 10, 16, 25
❑ Day 5:	Numbers 3–4, 6, 11–14
❑ Day 6:	Deuteronomy 5–8, 28–31, 34
❑ Day 7:	Joshua 1–6 , 23–24
❑ Day 8:	Judges 1–4, 13–16
❑ Day 9:	Ruth 1–4
❑ Day 10:	1 Samuel 7–10, 12
❑ Day 11:	1 Samuel 15–20, 28, 31
❑ Day 12:	2 Samuel 5–8, 11–13, 15, 18
❑ Day 13:	1 Kings 3, 6–12
❑ Day 14:	1 Kings 17–19, 21
❑ Day 15:	2 Kings 1–2, 6–7, 11–12
❑ Day 16:	2 Kings 17–23
❑ Day 17:	1 Chronicles 15–17, 21–22, 28–29
❑ Day 18:	2 Chronicles 5–10, 14–16
❑ Day 19:	2 Chronicles 24–26, 29–35
❑ Day 20:	Ezra 3, 6–7
❑ Day 21:	Nehemiah 1–2, 4, 6

❏ Day 22:   Esther 1–4
❏ Day 23:   Job 1–3, 38–42
❏ Day 24:   Psalms 1, 8, 19, 23
❏ Day 25:   Psalms 51, 100, 103, 139
❏ Day 26:   Proverbs 1–3
❏ Day 27:   Ecclesiastes 1–5, 12; Song of Songs 1–2
❏ Day 28:   Isaiah 1–2, 6, 40, 52–55
❏ Day 29:   Jeremiah 1–5; Lamentations 3
❏ Day 30:   Ezekiel 1–3, 18, 33
❏ Day 31:   Daniel 1–2, 4–6
❏ Day 32:   Hosea 1–4; Joel 2
❏ Day 33:   Amos 3, Obadiah; Jonah 1
❏ Day 34:   Micah 1–2; Nahum 1
❏ Day 35:   Habakkuk 1; Zephaniah 3; Haggai
❏ Day 36:   Zechariah 1–2; Malachi 1
❏ Day 37:   Matthew 1–2, 5–7
❏ Day 38:   Matthew 17, 26–28
❏ Day 39:   Mark 1–4, 10, 15–16
❏ Day 40:   Luke 1–2, 4–6
❏ Day 41:   Luke 8–10, 22–24
❏ Day 42:   John 1, 3–4
❏ Day 43:   John 13–17, 19–21
❏ Day 44:   Acts 1–4
❏ Day 45:   Acts 8–10, 12–15
❏ Day 46:   Romans 5–8, 12
❏ Day 47:   1 Corinthians 1–2, 13
❏ Day 48:   2 Corinthians 4–5, 8–9
❏ Day 49:   Galatians 5–6
❏ Day 50:   Ephesians 4–6
❏ Day 51:   Philippians 2, 4
❏ Day 52:   Colossians 1, 4
❏ Day 53:   1 Thessalonians 2, 4; 2 Thessalonians 3
❏ Day 54:   1 Timothy 1, 3
❏ Day 55:   2 Timothy 3–4
❏ Day 56:   Titus 2; Philemon
❏ Day 57:   Hebrews 10–13
❏ Day 58:   James 1–3
❏ Day 59:   1 Peter 1, 5; 2 Peter 1
❏ Day 60:   1 John 1–2; 2 John; 3 John
❏ Day 61:   Jude; Revelation 19–22

If you have completed this two-month Bible reading plan, congratulations! You can use the *How to Read Your Bible* biographical or comprehensive
plan to read Scripture again.

Remember, God delights to prosper those who take him at his Word.

So keep reading!

(121 days)

Want to read Bible highlights from Adam to Zechariah? It's easy! The advantages of this approach include ease in seeing the story of the Bible and becoming acquainted with the entire *Who's Who of the Bible.*

As you read, be sure to thank God for what he's going to do in and through you during the months ahead!

	Day	Key Figure	Today's Scripture Reading
❏	Day 1:	Adam	Genesis 1:26–2:17
❏	Day 2:	Eve	Genesis 2:18–3:24
❏	Day 3:	Abel	Genesis 4:1–18
❏	Day 4:	Enoch	Genesis 5:18–24
❏	Day 5:	Noah	Genesis 6:1–9:17
❏	Day 6:	Abraham	Genesis 15, 17, 22; Romans 4:1–5, 9–25
❏	Day 7:	Sarah	Genesis 16:1–15; 18:1–15; 21:1–7
❏	Day 8:	Isaac	Genesis 24, 26
❏	Day 9:	Esau	Genesis 25:27–34
❏	Day 10:	Rebekah	Genesis 27
❏	Day 11:	Jacob	Genesis 31–32
❏	Day 12:	Joseph	Genesis 39, 41, 43, 45
❏	Day 13:	Moses's parents	Exodus 1:1–2:10
❏	Day 14:	Moses	Exodus 5:1–6:13; 14:5–31
❏	Day 15:	Miriam	Exodus 15:1–21
❏	Day 16:	Aaron	Exodus 32
❏	Day 17:	Rahab	Joshua 2, 6
❏	Day 18:	Caleb	Joshua 14:6–15:19
❏	Day 19:	Joshua	Joshua 23–24
❏	Day 20:	Deborah	Judges 4–5

❏	Day 21:	Gideon	Judges 6–8
❏	Day 22:	Jephthah	Judges 11:1–12:7
❏	Day 23:	Samson	Judges 13–16
❏	Day 24:	Ruth	Ruth 1–4
❏	Day 25:	Hannah	1 Samuel 1:1–2:21
❏	Day 26:	Eli	1 Samuel 2:27–4:22
❏	Day 27:	Samuel	1 Samuel 7:3–8:22; 12:1–25
❏	Day 28:	Jonathan	1 Samuel 14, 20
❏	Day 29:	Saul	1 Samuel 18–19
❏	Day 30:	Abigail	1 Samuel 25
❏	Day 31:	Amnon	2 Samuel 13
❏	Day 32:	Absalom	2 Samuel 15, 17–18
❏	Day 33:	Rehoboam	1 Kings 12:1–20; 14:21–31
❏	Day 34:	Jeroboam	1 Kings 11:26–40; 12:25–14:20
❏	Day 35:	Ahab	1 Kings 16:29–34; 20:1–21:29
❏	Day 36:	Elijah	1 Kings 17:1–19:18
❏	Day 37:	Elisha	2 Kings 2, 4, 6
❏	Day 38:	Gehazi	2 Kings 5
❏	Day 39:	Josiah	2 Kings 23
❏	Day 40:	Jabez	1 Chronicles 4:9–10
❏	Day 41:	Asa	2 Chronicles 14–16
❏	Day 42:	Jehoshaphat	2 Chronicles 17–20
❏	Day 43:	Uzziah	2 Chronicles 26
❏	Day 44:	Manasseh	2 Chronicles 33:1–20
❏	Day 45:	Hilkiah	2 Chronicles 34:14–33
❏	Day 46:	Ezra	Ezra 7–9
❏	Day 47:	Nehemiah	Nehemiah 1–2
❏	Day 48:	Esther	Esther 2:1–23; 4:1–5:8; 7:1–8:8
❏	Day 49:	Mordecai	Esther 3:1–15; 5:9–6:14; 10:1–3
❏	Day 50:	Job	Job 1–2
❏	Day 51:	Eliphaz, Bildad, and Zophar	Job 4–7
❏	Day 52:	Elihu	Job 32–37
❏	Day 53:	David	Psalms 3–8, 32; Romans 4:6–8
❏	Day 54:	Asaph	Psalms 73–77
❏	Day 55:	Phinehas	Psalms 106; Joshua 22:10–34
❏	Day 56:	Solomon	Proverbs 2–4
❏	Day 57:	Isaiah	Isaiah 6, 40, 53
❏	Day 58:	Hezekiah	Isaiah 36–37
❏	Day 59:	Jeremiah	Jeremiah 1, 18, 32

❑	Day 99:	The Samaritan Woman	John 4:1–42
❑	Day 100:	The Adulterous Woman	John 8:1–11
❑	Day 101:	Lazarus	John 11:1–12:36
❑	Day 102:	Pilate	John 18:28–19:16
❑	Day 103:	Thomas	John 20:1–29
❑	Day 104:	Ananias and Sapphira	Acts 4:32–5:11
❑	Day 105:	Stephen	Acts 6–7
❑	Day 106:	Philip	Acts 8:4–12, 26–40
❑	Day 107:	Simon the Sorcerer	Acts 8:9–25
❑	Day 108:	Ananias	Acts 9:1–18
❑	Day 109:	Cornelius	Acts 10:1–11:18
❑	Day 110:	Barnabas	Acts 11:19–30; 13:1–14:28
❑	Day 111:	John Mark	Acts 13:1–13
❑	Day 112:	Priscilla and Aquila	Acts 18
❑	Day 113:	Agrippa	Acts 25–26
❑	Day 114:	Paul	Galatians 1–2; Acts 22
❑	Day 115:	Epaphroditus	Philippians 1–2
❑	Day 116:	Timothy	1 Timothy 3–4
❑	Day 117:	Luke	2 Timothy 3:10–4:22
❑	Day 118:	Titus	Titus 1–3
❑	Day 119:	Philemon	Philemon
❑	Day 120:	James	James 1–2
❑	Day 121:	John	1 John 1–2; Revelation 1

If you have completed this four-month Bible reading plan, congratulations! You can now use the comprehensive or survey plan to read Scripture again.

Remember, God delights to prosper those who take him at his Word. So keep reading!

(365 days)

Ready for the incredible privilege and adventure of reading the Bible through cover to cover? We hope so! It takes only about fifteen minutes a day. Enjoy!

As you read, ask the Lord to help you see the redemptive story of the Bible. It's the heartbeat of every book from Genesis to Revelation.

	Day	Today's Scripture Reading			
❑	Day 1:	Genesis 1–3	❑	Day 24:	Exodus 22–24
❑	Day 2:	Genesis 4–6	❑	Day 25:	Exodus 25–27
❑	Day 3:	Genesis 7–9	❑	Day 26:	Exodus 28–30
❑	Day 4:	Genesis 10–12	❑	Day 27:	Exodus 31–33
❑	Day 5:	Genesis 13–15	❑	Day 28:	Exodus 34–36
❑	Day 6:	Genesis 16–18	❑	Day 29:	Exodus 37–40
❑	Day 7:	Genesis 19–21	❑	Day 30:	Leviticus 1–3
❑	Day 8:	Genesis 22–24	❑	Day 31:	Leviticus 4–6
❑	Day 9:	Genesis 25–27	❑	Day 32:	Leviticus 7–9
❑	Day 10:	Genesis 28–30	❑	Day 33:	Leviticus 10–12
❑	Day 11:	Genesis 31–33	❑	Day 34:	Leviticus 13–15
❑	Day 12:	Genesis 34–36	❑	Day 35:	Leviticus 16–18
❑	Day 13:	Genesis 37–39	❑	Day 36:	Leviticus 19–21
❑	Day 14:	Genesis 40–42	❑	Day 37:	Leviticus 22–24
❑	Day 15:	Genesis 43–46	❑	Day 38:	Leviticus 25–27
❑	Day 16:	Genesis 47–50	❑	Day 39:	Numbers 1–3
❑	Day 17:	Exodus 1–3	❑	Day 40:	Numbers 4–6
❑	Day 18:	Exodus 4–6	❑	Day 41:	Numbers 7–9
❑	Day 19:	Exodus 7–9	❑	Day 42:	Numbers 10–12
❑	Day 20:	Exodus 10–12	❑	Day 43:	Numbers 13–15
❑	Day 21:	Exodus 13–15	❑	Day 44:	Numbers 16–18
❑	Day 22:	Exodus 16–18	❑	Day 45:	Numbers 19–21
❑	Day 23:	Exodus 19–21	❑	Day 46:	Numbers 22–24
			❑	Day 47:	Numbers 25–27
			❑	Day 48:	Numbers 28–30

❑	Day 49:	Numbers 31–33	❑	Day 89:	2 Samuel 4–6
❑	Day 50:	Numbers 34–36	❑	Day 90:	2 Samuel 7–9
❑	Day 51:	Deuteronomy 1–3	❑	Day 91:	2 Samuel 10–12
❑	Day 52:	Deuteronomy 4–6	❑	Day 92:	2 Samuel 13–15
❑	Day 53:	Deuteronomy 7–9	❑	Day 93:	2 Samuel 16–18
❑	Day 54:	Deuteronomy 10–12	❑	Day 94:	2 Samuel 19–21
❑	Day 55:	Deuteronomy 13–15	❑	Day 95:	2 Samuel 22–24
❑	Day 56:	Deuteronomy 16–18	❑	Day 96:	1 Kings 1–3
❑	Day 57:	Deuteronomy 19–21	❑	Day 97:	1 Kings 4–6
❑	Day 58:	Deuteronomy 22–24	❑	Day 98:	1 Kings 7–9
❑	Day 59:	Deuteronomy 25–27	❑	Day 99:	1 Kings 10–12
❑	Day 60:	Deuteronomy 28–30	❑	Day 100:	1 Kings 13–15
❑	Day 61:	Deuteronomy 31–34	❑	Day 101:	1 Kings 16–18
❑	Day 62:	Joshua 1–3	❑	Day 102:	1 Kings 19–22
❑	Day 63:	Joshua 4–6	❑	Day 103:	2 Kings 1–3
❑	Day 64:	Joshua 7–9	❑	Day 104:	2 Kings 4–6
❑	Day 65:	Joshua 10–12	❑	Day 105:	2 Kings 7–9
❑	Day 66:	Joshua 13–15	❑	Day 106:	2 Kings 10–12
❑	Day 67:	Joshua 16–18	❑	Day 107:	2 Kings 13–15
❑	Day 68:	Joshua 19–21	❑	Day 108:	2 Kings 16–18
❑	Day 69:	Joshua 22–24	❑	Day 109:	2 Kings 19–21
❑	Day 70:	Judges 1–3	❑	Day 110:	2 Kings 22–25
❑	Day 71:	Judges 4–6	❑	Day 111:	1 Chronicles 1–6
❑	Day 72:	Judges 7–9	❑	Day 112:	1 Chronicles 7–9
❑	Day 73:	Judges 10–12	❑	Day 113:	1 Chronicles 10–12
❑	Day 74:	Judges 13–15	❑	Day 114:	1 Chronicles 13–15
❑	Day 75:	Judges 16–18	❑	Day 115:	1 Chronicles 16–18
❑	Day 76:	Judges 19–21	❑	Day 116:	1 Chronicles 19–21
❑	Day 77:	Ruth 1–4	❑	Day 117:	1 Chronicles 22–25
❑	Day 78:	1 Samuel 1–3	❑	Day 118:	1 Chronicles 26–29
❑	Day 79:	1 Samuel 4–6	❑	Day 119:	2 Chronicles 1–3
❑	Day 80:	1 Samuel 7–9	❑	Day 120:	2 Chronicles 4–6
❑	Day 81:	1 Samuel 10–12	❑	Day 121:	2 Chronicles 7–9
❑	Day 82:	1 Samuel 13–15	❑	Day 122:	2 Chronicles 10–12
❑	Day 83:	1 Samuel 16–18	❑	Day 123:	2 Chronicles 13–15
❑	Day 84:	1 Samuel 19–21	❑	Day 124:	2 Chronicles 16–18
❑	Day 85:	1 Samuel 22–24	❑	Day 125:	2 Chronicles 19–21
❑	Day 86:	1 Samuel 25–27	❑	Day 126:	2 Chronicles 22–24
❑	Day 87:	1 Samuel 28–31	❑	Day 127:	2 Chronicles 25–27
❑	Day 88:	2 Samuel 1–3	❑	Day 128:	2 Chronicles 28–30

❑	Day 129:	2 Chronicles 31–33	❑	Day 169:	Psalms 71–75
❑	Day 130:	2 Chronicles 34–36	❑	Day 170:	Psalms 76–80
❑	Day 131:	Ezra 1–3	❑	Day 171:	Psalms 81–85
❑	Day 132:	Ezra 4–6	❑	Day 172:	Psalms 86–90
❑	Day 133:	Ezra 7–10	❑	Day 173:	Psalms 91–95
❑	Day 134:	Nehemiah 1–3	❑	Day 174:	Psalms 96–100
❑	Day 135:	Nehemiah 4–6	❑	Day 175:	Psalms 101–105
❑	Day 136:	Nehemiah 7–9	❑	Day 176:	Psalms 106–110
❑	Day 137:	Nehemiah 10–13	❑	Day 177:	Psalms 111–115
❑	Day 138:	Esther 1–3	❑	Day 178:	Psalms 116–120
❑	Day 139:	Esther 4–6	❑	Day 179:	Psalms 121–125
❑	Day 140:	Esther 7–10	❑	Day 180:	Psalms 126–130
❑	Day 141:	Job 1–3	❑	Day 181:	Psalms 131–135
❑	Day 142:	Job 4–6	❑	Day 182:	Psalms 136–140
❑	Day 143:	Job 7–9	❑	Day 183:	Psalms 141–145
❑	Day 144:	Job 10–12	❑	Day 184:	Psalms 146–150
❑	Day 145:	Job 13–15	❑	Day 185:	Proverbs 1–3
❑	Day 146:	Job 16–18	❑	Day 186:	Proverbs 4–6
❑	Day 147:	Job 19–21	❑	Day 187:	Proverbs 7–9
❑	Day 148:	Job 22–24	❑	Day 188:	Proverbs 10–12
❑	Day 149:	Job 25–27	❑	Day 189:	Proverbs 13–15
❑	Day 150:	Job 28–30	❑	Day 190:	Proverbs 16–18
❑	Day 151:	Job 31–33	❑	Day 191:	Proverbs 19–21
❑	Day 152:	Job 34–36	❑	Day 192:	Proverbs 22–24
❑	Day 153:	Job 37–39	❑	Day 193:	Proverbs 25–27
❑	Day 154:	Job 40–42	❑	Day 194:	Proverbs 28–31
❑	Day 155:	Psalms 1–5	❑	Day 195:	Ecclesiastes 1–3
❑	Day 156:	Psalms 6–10	❑	Day 196:	Ecclesiastes 4–6
❑	Day 157:	Psalms 11–15	❑	Day 197:	Ecclesiastes 7–9
❑	Day 158:	Psalms 16–20	❑	Day 198:	Ecclesiastes 10–12
❑	Day 159:	Psalms 21–25	❑	Day 199:	Song of Songs 1–4
❑	Day 160:	Psalms 26–30	❑	Day 200:	Song of Songs 5–8
❑	Day 161:	Psalms 31–35	❑	Day 201:	Isaiah 1–3
❑	Day 162:	Psalms 36–40	❑	Day 202:	Isaiah 4–6
❑	Day 163:	Psalms 41–45	❑	Day 203:	Isaiah 7–9
❑	Day 164:	Psalms 46–50	❑	Day 204:	Isaiah 10–12
❑	Day 165:	Psalms 51–55	❑	Day 205:	Isaiah 13–15
❑	Day 166:	Psalms 56–60	❑	Day 206:	Isaiah 16–18
❑	Day 167:	Psalms 61–65	❑	Day 207:	Isaiah 19–21
❑	Day 168:	Psalms 66–70	❑	Day 208:	Isaiah 22–24

❑	Day 209:	Isaiah 25–27	❑ Day 248: Ezekiel 19–21
❑	Day 210:	Isaiah 28–30	❑ Day 249: Ezekiel 22–24
❑	Day 211:	Isaiah 31–33	❑ Day 250: Ezekiel 25–27
❑	Day 212:	Isaiah 34–36	❑ Day 251: Ezekiel 28–30
❑	Day 213:	Isaiah 37–39	❑ Day 252: Ezekiel 31–33
❑	Day 214:	Isaiah 40–42	❑ Day 253: Ezekiel 34–36
❑	Day 215:	Isaiah 43–45	❑ Day 254: Ezekiel 37–40
❑	Day 216:	Isaiah 46–48	❑ Day 255: Ezekiel 41–44
❑	Day 217:	Isaiah 49–51	❑ Day 256: Ezekiel 45–48
❑	Day 218:	Isaiah 52–54	❑ Day 257: Daniel 1–3
❑	Day 219:	Isaiah 55–57	❑ Day 258: Daniel 4–6
❑	Day 220:	Isaiah 58–60	❑ Day 259: Daniel 7–9
❑	Day 221:	Isaiah 61–63	❑ Day 260: Daniel 10–12
❑	Day 222:	Isaiah 64–66	❑ Day 261: Hosea 1–3
❑	Day 223:	Jeremiah 1–3	❑ Day 262: Hosea 4–6
❑	Day 224:	Jeremiah 4–6	❑ Day 263: Hosea 7–10
❑	Day 225:	Jeremiah 7–9	❑ Day 264: Hosea 11–14
❑	Day 226:	Jeremiah 10–12	❑ Day 265: Joel 1–3
❑	Day 227:	Jeremiah 13–15	❑ Day 266: Amos 1–3
❑	Day 228:	Jeremiah 16–18	❑ Day 267: Amos 4–6
❑	Day 229:	Jeremiah 19–21	❑ Day 268: Amos 7–9
❑	Day 230:	Jeremiah 22–24	❑ Day 269: Obadiah
❑	Day 231:	Jeremiah 25–27	❑ Day 270: Jonah 1–4
❑	Day 232:	Jeremiah 28–30	❑ Day 271: Micah 1–3
❑	Day 233:	Jeremiah 31–33	❑ Day 272: Micah 4–7
❑	Day 234:	Jeremiah 34–36	❑ Day 273: Nahum 1–3
❑	Day 235:	Jeremiah 37–39	❑ Day 274: Habakkuk 1–3
❑	Day 236:	Jeremiah 40–42	❑ Day 275: Zephaniah 1–3
❑	Day 237:	Jeremiah 43–45	❑ Day 276: Haggai 1–2
❑	Day 238:	Jeremiah 46–48	❑ Day 277: Zechariah 1–3
❑	Day 239:	Jeremiah 49–52	❑ Day 278: Zechariah 4–6
❑	Day 240:	Lamentations 1–3	❑ Day 279: Zechariah 7–10
❑	Day 241:	Lamentations 4–5	❑ Day 280: Zechariah 11–14
❑	Day 242:	Ezekiel 1–3	❑ Day 281: Malachi 1–2
❑	Day 243:	Ezekiel 4–6	❑ Day 282: Malachi 3–4
❑	Day 244:	Ezekiel 7–9	❑ Day 283: Matthew 1–3
❑	Day 245:	Ezekiel 10–12	❑ Day 284: Matthew 4–6
❑	Day 246:	Ezekiel 13–15	❑ Day 285: Matthew 7–9
❑	Day 247:	Ezekiel 16–18	❑ Day 286: Matthew 10–12

❏	Day 287:	Matthew 13–15
❏	Day 288:	Matthew 16–18
❏	Day 289:	Matthew 19–21
❏	Day 290:	Matthew 22–24
❏	Day 291:	Matthew 25–28
❏	Day 292:	Mark 1–3
❏	Day 293:	Mark 4–6
❏	Day 294:	Mark 7–9
❏	Day 295:	Mark 10–12
❏	Day 296:	Mark 13–16
❏	Day 297:	Luke 1–3
❏	Day 298:	Luke 4–6
❏	Day 299:	Luke 7–9
❏	Day 300:	Luke 10–12
❏	Day 301:	Luke 13–15
❏	Day 302:	Luke 16–18
❏	Day 303:	Luke 19–21
❏	Day 304:	Luke 22–24
❏	Day 305:	John 1–3
❏	Day 306:	John 4–6
❏	Day 307:	John 7–9
❏	Day 308:	John 10–12
❏	Day 309:	John 13–15
❏	Day 310:	John 16–18
❏	Day 311:	John 19–21
❏	Day 312:	Acts 1–3
❏	Day 313:	Acts 4–6
❏	Day 314:	Acts 7–9
❏	Day 315:	Acts 10–12
❏	Day 316:	Acts 13–15
❏	Day 317:	Acts 16–18
❏	Day 318:	Acts 19–21
❏	Day 319:	Acts 22–24
❏	Day 320:	Acts 25–28
❏	Day 321:	Romans 1–3
❏	Day 322:	Romans 4–6
❏	Day 323:	Romans 7–9
❏	Day 324:	Romans 10–12
❏	Day 325:	Romans 13–16
❏	Day 326:	1 Corinthians 1–3
❏	Day 327:	1 Corinthians 4–6
❏	Day 328:	1 Corinthians 7–9
❏	Day 329:	1 Corinthians 10–12
❏	Day 330:	1 Corinthians 13–16
❏	Day 331:	2 Corinthians 1–3
❏	Day 332:	2 Corinthians 4–6
❏	Day 333:	2 Corinthians 7–9
❏	Day 334:	2 Corinthians 10–13
❏	Day 335:	Galatians 1–3
❏	Day 336:	Galatians 4–6
❏	Day 337:	Ephesians 1–3
❏	Day 338:	Ephesians 4–6
❏	Day 339:	Philippians 1–4
❏	Day 340:	Colossians 1–4
❏	Day 341:	1 Thessalonians 1–5
❏	Day 342:	2 Thessalonians 1–3
❏	Day 343:	1 Timothy 1–3
❏	Day 344:	1 Timothy 4–6
❏	Day 345:	2 Timothy 1–4
❏	Day 346:	Titus 1–3
❏	Day 347:	Philemon
❏	Day 348:	Hebrews 1–3
❏	Day 349:	Hebrews 4–6
❏	Day 350:	Hebrews 7–9
❏	Day 351:	Hebrews 10–13
❏	Day 352:	James 1–3
❏	Day 353:	James 4–5
❏	Day 354:	1 Peter 1–5
❏	Day 355:	2 Peter 1–3
❏	Day 356:	1 John 1–3
❏	Day 357:	1 John 4–5
❏	Day 358:	2 and 3 John, Jude
❏	Day 359:	Revelation 1–3
❏	Day 360:	Revelation 4–6
❏	Day 361:	Revelation 7–9
❏	Day 362:	Revelation 10–12
❏	Day 363:	Revelation 13–15
❏	Day 364:	Revelation 16–18
❏	Day 365:	Revelation 19–22

If you have completed this twelve-month Bible reading plan, congratulations! You may want to use the *How to Read Your Bible* biographical or survey plan to read Scripture again.

Remember, God delights to prosper those who take him at his Word.

So keep reading!

(Calendar Year)

Ready for the incredible privilege and adventure of reading the Bible through cover to cover? We hope so! It takes only about fifteen minutes a day. Enjoy!

As you read, ask the Lord to help you see the redemptive story of the Bible. It's the heartbeat of every book from Genesis to Revelation.

Day	Today's Scripture Reading		Day	Today's Scripture Reading
❏ Jan. 1:	Genesis 1–3	❏	Jan. 23:	Exodus 19–21
❏ Jan. 2:	Genesis 4–6	❏	Jan. 24:	Exodus 22–24
❏ Jan. 3:	Genesis 7–9	❏	Jan. 25:	Exodus 25–27
❏ Jan. 4:	Genesis 10–12	❏	Jan. 26:	Exodus 28–30
❏ Jan. 5:	Genesis 13–15	❏	Jan. 27:	Exodus 31–33
❏ Jan. 6:	Genesis 16–18	❏	Jan. 28:	Exodus 34–36
❏ Jan. 7:	Genesis 19–21	❏	Jan. 29:	Exodus 37–40
❏ Jan. 8:	Genesis 22–24	❏	Jan. 30:	Leviticus 1–3
❏ Jan. 9:	Genesis 25–27	❏	Jan. 31:	Leviticus 4–6
❏ Jan. 10:	Genesis 28–30	❏	Feb. 1:	Leviticus 7–9
❏ Jan. 11:	Genesis 31–33	❏	Feb. 2:	Leviticus 10–12
❏ Jan. 12:	Genesis 34–36	❏	Feb. 3:	Leviticus 13–15
❏ Jan. 13:	Genesis 37–39	❏	Feb. 4:	Leviticus 16–18
❏ Jan. 14:	Genesis 40–42	❏	Feb. 5:	Leviticus 19–21
❏ Jan. 15:	Genesis 43–46	❏	Feb. 6:	Leviticus 22–24
❏ Jan. 16:	Genesis 47–50	❏	Feb. 7:	Leviticus 25–27
❏ Jan. 17:	Exodus 1–3	❏	Feb. 8:	Numbers 1–3
❏ Jan. 18:	Exodus 4–6	❏	Feb. 9:	Numbers 4–6
❏ Jan. 19:	Exodus 7–9	❏	Feb. 10:	Numbers 7–9
❏ Jan. 20:	Exodus 10–12	❏	Feb. 11:	Numbers 10–12
❏ Jan. 21:	Exodus 13–15	❏	Feb. 12:	Numbers 13–15
❏ Jan. 22:	Exodus 16–18	❏	Feb. 13:	Numbers 16–18
		❏	Feb. 14:	Numbers 19–21
		❏	Feb. 15:	Numbers 22–24

❏	Feb. 16:	Numbers 25–27	❏	Mar. 28:	1 Samuel 28–31
❏	Feb. 17:	Numbers 28–30	❏	Mar. 29:	2 Samuel 1–3
❏	Feb. 18:	Numbers 31–33	❏	Mar. 30:	2 Samuel 4–6
❏	Feb. 19:	Numbers 34–36	❏	Mar. 31:	2 Samuel 7–9
❏	Feb. 20:	Deuteronomy 1–3	❏	Apr. 1:	2 Samuel 10–12
❏	Feb. 21:	Deuteronomy 4–6	❏	Apr. 2:	2 Samuel 13–15
❏	Feb. 22:	Deuteronomy 7–9	❏	Apr. 3:	2 Samuel 16–18
❏	Feb. 23:	Deuteronomy 10–12	❏	Apr. 4:	2 Samuel 19–21
❏	Feb. 24:	Deuteronomy 13–15	❏	Apr. 5:	2 Samuel 22–24
❏	Feb. 25:	Deuteronomy 16–18	❏	Apr. 6:	1 Kings 1–3
❏	Feb. 26:	Deuteronomy 19–21	❏	Apr. 7:	1 Kings 4–6
❏	Feb. 27:	Deuteronomy 22–24	❏	Apr. 8:	1 Kings 7–9
❏	Feb. 28:	Deuteronomy 25–27	❏	Apr. 9:	1 Kings 10–12
❏	Mar. 1:	Deuteronomy 28–30	❏	Apr. 10:	1 Kings 13–15
❏	Mar. 2:	Deuteronomy 31–34	❏	Apr. 11:	1 Kings 16–18
❏	Mar. 3:	Joshua 1–3	❏	Apr. 12:	1 Kings 19–22
❏	Mar. 4:	Joshua 4–6	❏	Apr. 13:	2 Kings 1–3
❏	Mar. 5:	Joshua 7–9	❏	Apr. 14:	2 Kings 4–6
❏	Mar. 6:	Joshua 10–12	❏	Apr. 15:	2 Kings 7–9
❏	Mar. 7:	Joshua 13–15	❏	Apr. 16:	2 Kings 10–12
❏	Mar. 8:	Joshua 16–18	❏	Apr. 17:	2 Kings 13–15
❏	Mar. 9:	Joshua 19–21	❏	Apr. 18:	2 Kings 16–18
❏	Mar. 10:	Joshua 22–24	❏	Apr. 19:	2 Kings 19–21
❏	Mar. 11:	Judges 1–3	❏	Apr. 20:	2 Kings 22–25
❏	Mar. 12:	Judges 4–6	❏	Apr. 21:	1 Chronicles 1–6
❏	Mar. 13:	Judges 7–9	❏	Apr. 22:	1 Chronicles 7–9
❏	Mar. 14:	Judges 10–12	❏	Apr. 23:	1 Chronicles 10–12
❏	Mar. 15:	Judges 13–15	❏	Apr. 24:	1 Chronicles 13–15
❏	Mar. 16:	Judges 16–18	❏	Apr. 25:	1 Chronicles 16–18
❏	Mar. 17:	Judges 19–21	❏	Apr. 26:	1 Chronicles 19–21
❏	Mar. 18:	Ruth 1–4	❏	Apr. 27:	1 Chronicles 22–25
❏	Mar. 19:	1 Samuel 1–3	❏	Apr. 28:	1 Chronicles 26–29
❏	Mar. 20:	1 Samuel 4–6	❏	Apr. 29:	2 Chronicles 1–3
❏	Mar. 21:	1 Samuel 7–9	❏	Apr. 30:	2 Chronicles 4–6
❏	Mar. 22:	1 Samuel 10–12	❏	May 1:	2 Chronicles 7–9
❏	Mar. 23:	1 Samuel 13–15	❏	May 2:	2 Chronicles 10–12
❏	Mar. 24:	1 Samuel 16–18	❏	May 3:	2 Chronicles 13–15
❏	Mar. 25:	1 Samuel 19–21	❏	May 4:	2 Chronicles 16–18
❏	Mar. 26:	1 Samuel 22–24	❏	May 5:	2 Chronicles 19–21
❏	Mar. 27:	1 Samuel 25–27	❏	May 6:	2 Chronicles 22–24

❏	May 7:	2 Chronicles 25–27	❏	June 16:	Psalms 61–65
❏	May 8:	2 Chronicles 28–30	❏	June 17:	Psalms 66–70
❏	May 9:	2 Chronicles 31–33	❏	June 18:	Psalms 71–75
❏	May 10:	2 Chronicles 34–36	❏	June 19:	Psalms 76–80
❏	May 11:	Ezra 1–3	❏	June 20:	Psalms 81–85
❏	May 12:	Ezra 4–6	❏	June 21:	Psalms 86–90
❏	May 13:	Ezra 7–10	❏	June 22:	Psalms 91–95
❏	May 14:	Nehemiah 1–3	❏	June 23:	Psalms 96–100
❏	May 15:	Nehemiah 4–6	❏	June 24:	Psalms 101–105
❏	May 16:	Nehemiah 7–9	❏	June 25:	Psalms 106–110
❏	May 17:	Nehemiah 10–13	❏	June 26:	Psalms 111–115
❏	May 18:	Esther 1–3	❏	June 27:	Psalms 116–120
❏	May 19:	Esther 4–6	❏	June 28:	Psalms 121–125
❏	May 20:	Esther 7–10	❏	June 29:	Psalms 126–130
❏	May 21:	Job 1–3	❏	June 30:	Psalms 131–135
❏	May 22:	Job 4–6	❏	July 1:	Psalms 136–140
❏	May 23:	Job 7–9	❏	July 2:	Psalms 141–145
❏	May 24:	Job 10–12	❏	July 3:	Psalms 146–150
❏	May 25:	Job 13–15	❏	July 4:	Proverbs 1–3
❏	May 26:	Job 16–18	❏	July 5:	Proverbs 4–6
❏	May 27:	Job 19–21	❏	July 6:	Proverbs 7–9
❏	May 28:	Job 22–24	❏	July 7:	Proverbs 10–12
❏	May 29:	Job 25–27	❏	July 8:	Proverbs 13–15
❏	May 30:	Job 28–30	❏	July 9:	Proverbs 16–18
❏	May 31:	Job 31–33	❏	July 10:	Proverbs 19–21
❏	June 1:	Job 34–36	❏	July 11:	Proverbs 22–24
❏	June 2:	Job 37–39	❏	July 12:	Proverbs 25–27
❏	June 3:	Job 40–42	❏	July 13:	Proverbs 28–31
❏	June 4:	Psalms 1–5	❏	July 14:	Ecclesiastes 1–3
❏	June 5:	Psalms 6–10	❏	July 15:	Ecclesiastes 4–6
❏	June 6:	Psalms 11–15	❏	July 16:	Ecclesiastes 7–9
❏	June 7:	Psalms 16–20	❏	July 17:	Ecclesiastes 10–12
❏	June 8:	Psalms 21–25	❏	July 18:	Song of Songs 1–4
❏	June 9:	Psalms 26–30	❏	July 19:	Song of Songs 5–8
❏	June 10:	Psalms 31–35	❏	July 20:	Isaiah 1–3
❏	June 11:	Psalms 36–40	❏	July 21:	Isaiah 4–6
❏	June 12:	Psalms 41–45	❏	July 22:	Isaiah 7–9
❏	June 13:	Psalms 46–50	❏	July 23:	Isaiah 10–12
❏	June 14:	Psalms 51–55	❏	July 24:	Isaiah 13–15
❏	June 15:	Psalms 56–60	❏	July 25:	Isaiah 16–18

❑	July 26:	Isaiah 19–21	
❑	July 27:	Isaiah 22–24	
❑	July 28:	Isaiah 25–27	
❑	July 29:	Isaiah 28–30	
❑	July 30:	Isaiah 31–33	
❑	July 31:	Isaiah 34–36	
❑	Aug. 1:	Isaiah 37–39	
❑	Aug. 2:	Isaiah 40–42	
❑	Aug. 3:	Isaiah 43–45	
❑	Aug. 4:	Isaiah 46–48	
❑	Aug. 5:	Isaiah 49–51	
❑	Aug. 6:	Isaiah 52–54	
❑	Aug. 7:	Isaiah 55–57	
❑	Aug. 8:	Isaiah 58–60	
❑	Aug. 9:	Isaiah 61–63	
❑	Aug. 10:	Isaiah 64–66	
❑	Aug. 11:	Jeremiah 1–3	
❑	Aug. 12:	Jeremiah 4–6	
❑	Aug. 13:	Jeremiah 7–9	
❑	Aug. 14:	Jeremiah 10–12	
❑	Aug. 15:	Jeremiah 13–15	
❑	Aug. 16:	Jeremiah 16–18	
❑	Aug. 17:	Jeremiah 19–21	
❑	Aug. 18:	Jeremiah 22–24	
❑	Aug. 19:	Jeremiah 25–27	
❑	Aug. 20:	Jeremiah 28–30	
❑	Aug. 21:	Jeremiah 31–33	
❑	Aug. 22:	Jeremiah 34–36	
❑	Aug. 23:	Jeremiah 37–39	
❑	Aug. 24:	Jeremiah 40–42	
❑	Aug. 25:	Jeremiah 43–45	
❑	Aug. 26:	Jeremiah 46–48	
❑	Aug. 27:	Jeremiah 49–52	
❑	Aug. 28:	Lamentations 1–3	
❑	Aug. 29:	Lamentations 4–5	
❑	Aug. 30:	Ezekiel 1–3	
❑	Aug. 31:	Ezekiel 4–6	
❑	Sept. 1:	Ezekiel 7–9	
❑	Sept. 2:	Ezekiel 10–12	
❑	Sept. 3:	Ezekiel 13–15	
❑	Sept. 4:	Ezekiel 16–18	
❑	Sept. 5:	Ezekiel 19–21	
❑	Sept. 6:	Ezekiel 22–24	
❑	Sept. 7:	Ezekiel 25–27	
❑	Sept. 8:	Ezekiel 28–30	
❑	Sept. 9:	Ezekiel 31–33	
❑	Sept. 10:	Ezekiel 34–36	
❑	Sept. 11:	Ezekiel 37–40	
❑	Sept. 12:	Ezekiel 41–44	
❑	Sept. 13:	Ezekiel 45–48	
❑	Sept. 14:	Daniel 1–3	
❑	Sept. 15:	Daniel 4–6	
❑	Sept. 16:	Daniel 7–9	
❑	Sept. 17:	Daniel 10–12	
❑	Sept. 18:	Hosea 1–3	
❑	Sept. 19:	Hosea 4–6	
❑	Sept. 20:	Hosea 7–10	
❑	Sept. 21:	Hosea 11–14	
❑	Sept. 22:	Joel 1–3	
❑	Sept. 23:	Amos 1–3	
❑	Sept. 24:	Amos 4–6	
❑	Sept. 25:	Amos 7–9	
❑	Sept. 26:	Obadiah	
❑	Sept. 27:	Jonah 1–4	
❑	Sept. 28:	Micah 1–3	
❑	Sept. 29:	Micah 4–7	
❑	Sept. 30:	Nahum 1–3	
❑	Oct. 1:	Habakkuk 1–3	
❑	Oct. 2:	Zephaniah 1–3	
❑	Oct. 3:	Haggai 1–2	
❑	Oct. 4:	Zechariah 1–3	
❑	Oct. 5:	Zechariah 4–6	
❑	Oct. 6:	Zechariah 7–10	
❑	Oct. 7:	Zechariah 11–14	
❑	Oct. 8:	Malachi 1–2	
❑	Oct. 9:	Malachi 3–4	
❑	Oct. 10:	Matthew 1–3	
❑	Oct. 11:	Matthew 4–6	
❑	Oct. 12:	Matthew 7–9	
❑	Oct. 13:	Matthew 10–12	

❏	Oct. 14:	Matthew 13–15	❏	Nov. 23:	1 Corinthians 4–6
❏	Oct. 15:	Matthew 16–18	❏	Nov. 24:	1 Corinthians 7–9
❏	Oct. 16:	Matthew 19–21	❏	Nov. 25:	1 Corinthians 10–12
❏	Oct. 17:	Matthew 22–24	❏	Nov. 26:	1 Corinthians 13–16
❏	Oct. 18:	Matthew 25–28	❏	Nov. 27:	2 Corinthians 1–3
❏	Oct. 19:	Mark 1–3	❏	Nov. 28:	2 Corinthians 4–6
❏	Oct. 20:	Mark 4–6	❏	Nov. 29:	2 Corinthians 7–9
❏	Oct. 21:	Mark 7–9	❏	Nov. 30:	2 Corinthians 10–13
❏	Oct. 22:	Mark 10–12	❏	Dec. 1:	Galatians 1–3
❏	Oct. 23:	Mark 13–16	❏	Dec. 2:	Galatians 4–6
❏	Oct. 24:	Luke 1–3	❏	Dec. 3:	Ephesians 1–3
❏	Oct. 25:	Luke 4–6	❏	Dec. 4:	Ephesians 4–6
❏	Oct. 26:	Luke 7–9	❏	Dec. 5:	Philippians 1–4
❏	Oct. 27:	Luke 10–12	❏	Dec. 6:	Colossians 1–4
❏	Oct. 28:	Luke 13–15	❏	Dec. 7:	1 Thessalonians 1–5
❏	Oct. 29:	Luke 16–18	❏	Dec. 8:	2 Thessalonians 1–3
❏	Oct. 30:	Luke 19–21	❏	Dec. 9:	1 Timothy 1–3
❏	Oct. 31:	Luke 22–24	❏	Dec. 10:	1 Timothy 4–6
❏	Nov. 1:	John 1–3	❏	Dec. 11:	2 Timothy 1–4
❏	Nov. 2:	John 4–6	❏	Dec. 12:	Titus 1–3
❏	Nov. 3:	John 7–9	❏	Dec. 13:	Philemon
❏	Nov. 4:	John 10–12	❏	Dec. 14:	Hebrews 1–3
❏	Nov. 5:	John 13–15	❏	Dec. 15:	Hebrews 4–6
❏	Nov. 6:	John 16–18	❏	Dec. 16:	Hebrews 7–9
❏	Nov. 7:	John 19–21	❏	Dec. 17:	Hebrews 10–13
❏	Nov. 8:	Acts 1–3	❏	Dec. 18:	James 1–3
❏	Nov. 9:	Acts 4–6	❏	Dec. 19:	James 4–5
❏	Nov. 10:	Acts 7–9	❏	Dec. 20:	1 Peter 1–5
❏	Nov. 11:	Acts 10–12	❏	Dec. 21:	2 Peter 1–3
❏	Nov. 12:	Acts 13–15	❏	Dec. 22:	1 John 1–3
❏	Nov. 13:	Acts 16–18	❏	Dec. 23:	1 John 4–5
❏	Nov. 14:	Acts 19–21	❏	Dec. 24:	2 and 3 John, Jude
❏	Nov. 15:	Acts 22–24	❏	Dec. 25:	Revelation 1–3
❏	Nov. 16:	Acts 25–28	❏	Dec. 26:	Revelation 4–6
❏	Nov. 17:	Romans 1–3	❏	Dec. 27:	Revelation 7–9
❏	Nov. 18:	Romans 4–6	❏	Dec. 28:	Revelation 10–12
❏	Nov. 19:	Romans 7–9	❏	Dec. 29:	Revelation 13–15
❏	Nov. 20:	Romans 10–12	❏	Dec. 30:	Revelation 16–18
❏	Nov. 21:	Romans 13–16	❏	Dec. 31:	Revelation 19–22
❏	Nov. 22:	1 Corinthians 1–3			

If you have completed this twelve-month Bible reading plan, congratulations! You may want to use the *How to Read Your Bible* biographical or survey plan to read Scripture again.

Remember, God delights to prosper those who take him at his Word.

So keep reading!

LEADER'S GUIDE

The best way to read the Bible is with a friend or small group of friends cheering you on!

To get started, here are seven things to discuss.

1. Discuss whom you want in your group. You may want to keep your group small—just you and a close friend. Or you may want to invite others to join you.

2. Discuss when you want to meet. You may want to meet weekly for an hour. You may need a little more time if your group is larger.

3. Discuss where you want to meet. Ideally, select a location that's comfortable for everyone. That might be a quiet restaurant, favorite coffee shop, conference room, or someone's living room.

4. Discuss how you want to read the Bible. This book offers two-month, four-month, and twelve-month plans. You may want to select a shorter reading plan the first time.

5. Discuss your level of commitment to each other. Your relationship with each other is more important than finishing a reading plan on time. Still, the group benefits if everyone keeps up with his or her reading.

6. Discuss the focus of your meetings. You'll probably want to discuss some of the things you've read in the Bible that week. You might discuss overall impressions or talk about something God taught you. Also, you might read key verses you've underlined or ask one of the questions you've written down.

7. Discuss how you'll finish your reading plan. It's always good to have an end date in mind. While you're at it, be sure to choose how you want to celebrate!

If someone in your small group hasn't read this book yet, encourage that person to read it right away! That way, everyone will be on the same page.

If your group would prefer to integrate its reading, here are three recommended schedules.

1. *Survey Bible Reading Plan* (see pages 217–19).

Week	Book Chapters	Scripture Readings
1	1, 5	Genesis–Joshua
2	2, 6	Judges–1 Kings
3	3	2 Kings–Nehemiah
4	7	Ezra–Isaiah
5	8	Jeremiah–Haggai
6	4, 9	Zechariah–John
7	10–11	John–Galatians
8	12	Ephesians–Philemon
9	13	Hebrews–Revelation

2. *Biographical Bible Reading Plan* (see pages 221–24).

Week	Book Chapters	Scripture Readings
1	1	Genesis
2	5	Genesis–Exodus
3	6	Exodus–Judges
4	2	Judges–1 Samuel
5	3	1 Samuel–1 Kings
6	4	1 Kings–2 Chronicles
7	7	2 Chronicles–Esther
8	8	Job–Proverbs
9	10	Isaiah–Daniel
10	9	Daniel–Matthew
11	11	Matthew–Mark
12	12	Mark–Luke
13	13	Luke
14		Luke–John
15		John–Acts
16		Acts
17		Acts–Philemon
18		James–Revelation

3. *Comprehensive Bible Reading Plan* (see pages 225–30 and 231–36)

Month	Book Chapters	Scripture Readings
1	1–2	Genesis–Leviticus
2	5	Leviticus–Deuteronomy
3	6	Deuteronomy–2 Samuel
4	3	2 Samuel–2 Chronicles
5	7	2 Chronicles–Job
6	4	Job–Psalms
7	8	Psalms–Isaiah
8	10	Isaiah–Ezekiel
9	11	Ezekiel–Nahum
10	9	Habakkuk–Luke
11	12	John–2 Corinthians
12	13	2 Corinthians–Revelation

Use whatever schedule works best for your small group. That may mean modifying one of the schedules we've listed above or creating something new.

If you do create a new schedule, we'd love to receive a copy via e-mail. Just send it to us at yourbible@earthlink.net. Who knows? We may ask for permission to include your schedule in an updated edition of this book or distribute it at our seminars. If we do, we'll be sure to credit you and send you a $50 honorarium.

All God's best as your small group reads God's Word these next few months. We trust it will be a life-changing experience!

If you're teaching a Bible class, great! We hope this book will be a great help to your class and to you!

If your class will be meeting for the next year or longer, we recommend that you ask everyone to read the entire Bible cover to cover using the 365-day comprehensive reading plan (see pages 225–30).

Month	Book Chapters	Scripture Readings
1	1–2	Genesis–Leviticus
2	5	Leviticus–Deuteronomy
3	6	Deuteronomy–2 Samuel
4	3	2 Samuel–2 Chronicles
5	7	2 Chronicles–Job
6	4	Job–Psalms
7	8	Psalms–Isaiah
8	10	Isaiah–Ezekiel
9	11	Ezekiel–Nahum
10	9	Habakkuk–Luke
11	12	John–2 Corinthians
12	13	2 Corinthians–Revelation

If your class will be meeting during the school year, we recommend that you ask everyone to read Genesis through Revelation twice using the survey and biographical Bible reading plans (see pages 217–19 and 221–24), then focus on one New Testament book for the last two months. We recommend planning a celebration at the end of each unit!

Month	Book Chapters	Scripture Readings

Survey Bible Reading Plan

1	1, 5	Genesis–Daniel
2	2–3	Hosea–Revelation

Biographical Bible Reading Plan

3	6	Genesis–1 Samuel
4	7, 8	2 Samuel–Jeremiah
5	9	Ezekiel–Luke
6	4	Luke–Revelation

Focus on a New Testament Book

7	10, 11	Read one book weekly
8	12, 13	Read one book weekly

During the last two months, we suggest asking your class to focus on Ephesians, Philippians, 1 or 2 Timothy, Titus, James, or one of the other shorter New Testament letters. Ask class members to read that one New Testament letter weekly—at a deliberately slower pace than they have read the previous six months.

During these final two months, you'll probably want to ask your class to actively use the principles outlined in chapters 10–13. This is best done by asking them to focus on a small section of Scripture, often twelve verses or less. The excitement in your class will grow as class members improve their ability to observe, understand, personalize, and apply God's Word to their lives.

If you create specific assignment sheets or other teaching resources, we'd love to receive copies via e-mail. You can send them to us at yourbible@earthlink.net. Who knows? We may ask for permission to include your teaching resources in an updated edition of this book. If we do, we'll be sure to credit you and send you a $50 to $250 honorarium.

All God's best as your class reads God's Word these next few months. We trust it will be a life-changing experience!

[Acknowledgments]

It's been a joy to work together as a couple to write this book, but we want to gratefully acknowledge the Lord and the *many* individuals who also have been a part of our team. Our heartfelt thanks go to each one!

The Author and Finisher of our faith, Jesus Christ. Thank you for ministering to us all of these years through the gift of your Word. May we always say, "Speak, [Lord,] for your servant is listening" (1 Sam. 3:10 NIV).

The late Dr. Lowell C. Wendt, who served as senior pastor of Alderwood Manor Community Church for many years. Dr. Wendt preached the Word of God dynamically and set us on a lifelong path of loving and learning God's Word.

The late Dr. John G. Mitchell, who founded Multnomah Bible College. We'll never forget his winsome smile and Scottish brogue, which still rings in our ears: "Don't you folks ever read your Bibles?" We're glad to say we still do!

Our many professors at Multnomah Bible College years ago, the professors at Multnomah Bible College and Biblical Seminary in more recent years, and the professors and students at Corban College (formerly Western Baptist College), where David has served as an adjunct professor.

Luis Palau. Your friendship, support, mentoring, and prayers have blessed us immeasurably. We thank God for the privilege of serving together for twenty years.

Steve Grissom, Scott Dawson, Dan Owens, Dr. Don Brake, Mike Silva, Tim Beals, Jose Zayas, Focus on the Family, Christian Book Summaries, Billy Graham Evangelistic Association, American Bible Society, and the many others who helped launch Sanford Communications, Inc. This book comes out of our vision to create life-changing books and Bible-related products.

Our family, church, and many friends who prayed for us and our endeavors writing this book. Don't stop praying! Your prayers will continue to make a difference every time this book encourages someone to read the Bible cover to cover.

The many individuals who encouraged and helped us along the way. You critiqued our proposal and sample chapters, championed the idea for this book, insisted that we had to write it, kept asking how the book was coming along, critiqued the rest of our chapters, and cheered when we submitted the finished manuscript.

Elizabeth Honeycutt and Elizabeth Jones, editors extraordinaire at Sanford Communications, Inc., who pulled together so many details to make this book complete. In addition, our thanks to Elizabeth Honeycutt and Beyth Hogue for helping manage and coordinate SCI, and to Shawna Sanford, Rebekah Clark, and Amanda Bird.

Shawna and Jonathan. You have been an encouragement in more ways than you'll ever know. Thanks so much for the phone calls and visits, Shawna, and for the spring-break trip to New England, Jonathan.

Roy and Venetta Sanford, David's parents. Every visit to your home in the country is a retreat of sorts! We have many fond memories of Grandpa and Grandma Johnson reading their Bibles. Thank you so much for caring for them during their final years here on earth. We can't wait to attend the reunion they're planning in heaven.

Chuck and Chris Hord, Renée's parents. What an incredible privilege to know you believe in us and are praying for us every day. Without your loving care of our two youngest children, Benjamin and Annalise, our writing retreats would not have happened. And without those retreats, this book would not have happened!

Queta Chapas. You're a gift from God! Thank you again so much for watching Annalise every Wednesday.

Dennis and Thea Weczorek. Your lakeside home on Anderson Island was the perfect setting for our last major writing retreat. Thank you for sharing it with us.

Greg Daniel, Kate Etue, Mary Hollingsworth, and the rest of the team at W Publishing Group. You've been great! Your vision for this book has meant the world to us.

52418358R00142

Made in the USA
San Bernardino, CA
20 August 2017